Citizenship and Governance
in the European Union

Citizenship and Governance in the European Union

Edited by

Richard Bellamy and Alex Warleigh

CONTINUUM
London and New York

To Amy and Louise, who gave me rather a lot of freedom of movement in pursuit of European citizenship. (Richard Bellamy)

For my parents, who taught me all about citizenship. For Samantha, who had to practise that teaching first. And for Gráinne, struggling to refashion citizenship for a direct action, 'no logo' world. (Alex Warleigh)

Continuum
The Tower Building, 11 York Road, London SE1 7NX
370 Lexington Avenue, New York, NY 10017–6503

First published 2001

British Library Cataloguing-in-Publication Data
A catalogue record for this book is available from the British Library.

ISBN 0–8264–5348–1 (hardback)
0–8264–5347–3 (paperback)

Typeset by YHT Ltd, London
Printed and bound in Great Britain by Creative Print and Design
Wales, Ebbw Vale

Contents

———

Contents

Part III: External Aspects of European Citizenship

Acknowledgements

The editors gratefully acknowledge the generous financial support of the Leverhulme Trust (Grant F/239/AA) and the European Commission (Thematic Socio-Economic Research, Framework 4: Contract SOE2-CT97-3056).

About the Contributors

Richard Bellamy is Professor of Politics and International Relations at the University of Reading. His many publications include *Liberalism and Pluralism: Towards a Politics of Compromise* (Routledge, 1999), *Rethinking Liberalism* (Continuum, 2000), and (as editor with Dario Castiglione) *Constitutionalism in Transformation: Theoretical and European Perspectives* (Blackwell, 1996). He has directed both a Leverhulme and an EC/TSER research programme on European Citizenship and is currently involved in an ESRC-funded project on civic inclusion in Pan-European society.

Mita Castle-Kanerova is an independent consultant and East-Central European expert, having been Senior Lecturer at the University of North London until 1997. She has been an advisor to the EU on its PHARE programme and has also acted as referee for research proposals for the ESRC. She has also been Honorary Professor at Charles University in Prague since 1991. Mita is now working as a project worker for the International Organization for Migration in Prague. Her publications include 'Social Policy in Czechoslovakia', in B. Deacon *et al.* (eds), *The New Eastern Europe* (Sage, 1992), 'Social Insurance in the Czech Republic', in J. Clasen (ed.), *Social Policy in Europe* (Polity Press, 1999), and (as editor) *High Hopes: Young Voices of Eastern Europe* (Virago, 1992).

Tony Downes is Professor of Law and Pro-Vice-Chancellor at the University of Reading. He is an expert in both EU competition law and European constitutionalism, focusing on EC rights and their assertion in national contexts. His many publications include *Legal Control of Mergers in the European Community* (Blackstone Press, 1992), 'Trawling for a Remedy: State Liability Under Community Law' (*Legal Studies*), 'After Maastricht' (*Reading University Law Review*), and (as co-author) 'Making Sense of Rights: Community Rights in EC Law' (*European Law Review*).

Philip Giddings is Senior Lecturer in Politics at the University of Reading and convenor of the Study of Parliament Group's research on Westminster and Europe. He is also co-convenor of the PSA's Law and Politics Group, and has given evidence to the House of Commons Select Committee on the Parliamentary Commissioner for Administration (1992/3). His publications include *The Citizens and the Public Agencies* (Justice, 1976), (as co-editor) *The Ombudsman: Present Practice and Future Prospects* (The Edwin Mellen Press, 1995) (with Roy Gregory, Victor Moore and Jane Pearson) and (as joint-editor) *Westminster and Europe: The Impact of the European Union on the Westminster Parliament* (Macmillan, 1996 (with G. Drewry)) and *Righting Wrongs: The Ombudsman in Six Continents* (with Roy Gregory, see below).

Roy Gregory is Emeritus Professor of Politics at the University of Reading, a member of the Centre for Ombudsman and Governance Studies, and an Academic Visitor at the London School of Economics. He is the author of numerous works on the UK and overseas Ombudsman systems, and is joint editor (with Philip Giddings) of *Righting Wrongs: The Ombudsman in Six Continents* (International Institute of Administrative Sciences, 1999).

R. J. Barry Jones is Professor of International Relations at the University of Reading. He is general editor of the *Routledge Encyclopaedia of International Political Economy* and co-editor of Cassell's new series of *Studies in International Relations*. He is also a member of the International Board of the Review of International Political Economy and Co-Director of the Centre for the Study of Global Change and Governance at the University of Reading. His publications include 'The Economic Agenda', in G. Wyn Rees (ed.), *International Politics in Europe: The New Agenda* (Routledge, 1993), *Globalisation and Interdependence in the International Political Economy: Rhetoric and Reality* (Pinter, 1995), *The Worlds of Political Economy: Alternative Approaches to the Study of Contemporary Political Economy* (Pinter, 1998) (as editor with a major personal contribution), and *The World Turned Upside Down? Globalization and the Future of the State* (Manchester University Press, 2000).

Bill Jordan is Professor of Social Policy at the Universities of Exeter and Huddersfield and Reader in Social Policy at the University of North London. He is the author of 18 books on citizenship, poverty and social exclusion, social policy and social work, including most recently *Social Work and the Third Way: Tough Love as Social Policy* (Sage, 2000).

Theodora Kostakopoulou is Lecturer in the School of Law at the University of Manchester. Her research interests lie in the intersection of political theory and EU law, and she is the author of *Citizenship, Identity and*

Immigration: Between Past and Future (Manchester University Press, 2001).

Stelios Stavridis holds the Jean Monnet Chair in European Political Studies at the University of Reading. He is also currently (2000–2001) a Jean Monnet Fellow at the Robert Schuman Centre of the European University Institute. His publications include (as co-author with D. Chryssochoou, M. Tsinisizelis, S. Stavridis and K. Infantis) *Theory and Reform in the European Union* (Manchester University Press, 1999), and (as co-editor with personal contributions) *The Foreign Policies of the EU's Mediterranean States and Applicant Countries in the 1990s* (with S. Stavridis, T. Couloumbis, T. Veremis and N. Waites (Macmillan, 1999)), *New Challenges to the European Union: Policies and Policy Making* (with S. Stavridis, E. Mossialos, R. Morgan and H. Machin (Dartmouth, 1997)), and *Domestic Sources of Foreign Policy: West European Reactions to the Falklands Conflict* (with S. Stravridis and C. Hill (Berg, 1996)).

Carl F. Stychin is Professor of Law and Social Theory at the University of Reading. His publications include *A Nation by Rights: National Cultures, Sexual Identity Politics and the Discourse of Rights* (Temple University Press, 1998), *Law's Desire: Sexuality and the Limits of Justice* (Routledge, 1995), (as co-editor with Didi Herman) *Sexuality in the Legal Arena* (Athlone, 2000) and *Legal Inversions: Lesbians, Gay Men, and the Politics of Law* (Temple University Press, 1995). His current research explores the dynamics of sexual citizenship in a European arena.

Colleen Thouez is Senior Programme Officer at the inter-agency Internal Migration Policy (IMP) based in Geneva. She has also worked as a legal consultant to the United Nations High Commissioner for Refugees (UNHCR) Europe Bureau, and has lectured in international relations, European politics and US foreign policy at the Fletcher School, Tufts and McGill Universities. She has published widely in the field of international relations and migration, and is currently pursuing research on migration-related prerequisites to EU accession, funded by the International Research and Exchanges Board.

Alex Warleigh is Lecturer in European Studies at the University of Reading. His publications include articles in leading journals such as the *Journal of European Public Policy*, *West European Politics*, the *Journal of European Integration* and *Millennium*, as well as (as author) *The Committee of the Regions: Institutionalising Multi-level Governance?* (Kogan Page, 1999) and (as editor) *Institutions of the European Union* (Routledge, 2001). He is currently working on both civil society formation in the enlarged EU as part of the ESRC's *One Europe or Several?* project and flexible integration in the EU.

Part I

Citizenship of the European Union

Introduction: The Puzzle of EU Citizenship

RICHARD BELLAMY AND ALEX WARLEIGH

I. THE PARADOXES AND CONTEXTS OF EU CITIZENSHIP

Like the Union itself, the new status of EU citizenship arouses mixed reactions by offering too little for some and too much for others. Its introduction at Maastricht had a clear normative purpose: to make the EU more legitimate and its benefits more tangible to the populations of the member states. However, the conferment of this status has gone largely unnoticed by the mass of ordinary EU citizens. It remains firmly tied to national citizenship, thereby excluding EU residents who do not possess member-state nationality, such as Turkish workers in Germany, and does little to enhance the political accountability of the EU to ordinary people. By and large it simply codifies those rights member-state nationals already possess as a result of European law and policy. Indeed, the scope and character of the equality conferred by EU citizenship is more akin to that of the subjects of a common ruler than of citizens capable of being both rulers and ruled in turn.

These limitations disappoint not only those who look for the EU's transformation into some form of federal polity (Mancini, 1998) but also those who see the EU as breaking the mould of the nation-state and who desire the creation of a new type of postnational global citizenship tied to human rights rather than national sovereignty (Habermas, 1992; Linklater, 1998: Ch. 6). Meanwhile, the very creation of the new status appears excessive to others who view the Union as an essentially intergovernmental association, justified only to the extent it serves and is limited by the interests of its member states (Aron, 1974; Gustavsson, 1998). From this perspective, citizenship is properly exercised solely within sovereign states in order to control the governments that negotiate the treaties on their electorates' behalf. To introduce a European citizenship threatens to undermine rather than reinforce the legitimacy of the current arrangements by creating a European state few member-state nationals desire or require.

The existence of EU citizenship presents a puzzle, therefore. Though the EU has many polity-like features, it is not a state. Yet no other international organization has citizens of its own, even if at present individuals can only attain EU citizenship through meeting the various nationality requirements of one of the member states. Nor is there any other example of international governance where ordinary people can claim a direct, if mediated, relationship with the new international structures – even if these relations are far more passive and legal, and rather less active and political, than within most democratic states. Numerous questions arise, therefore. Why has this status developed and is it properly designated as citizenship? Are the hopes and fears of its supporters and detractors warranted? Does it herald the advent of a new Euro-state? Does it show the EU to be the first step towards a global system of governance, in which ties to the state are replaced by a new kind of postnational citizenship centred on human rights rather than place or community? Or is it merely empty and even obfuscatory rhetoric? At best, a sop to those who might desire a shift in these directions; at worst a device for legitimizing the current unaccountable and unrepresentative decision-making processes?

The contributors to this volume share some of the ambivalences and worries expressed in their different ways by Europhiles and Europhobes alike, without necessarily regarding European citizenship as either as empty or as paradoxical as it often appears. The reason lies in the ways the EU both complements and interacts with the activities of the member states, making the possession of dual or even multiple citizenships of different kinds both necessary and coherent. To a degree, all the characterizations outlined above are misconceived, failing to see the symbiotic relationship between Union and member-state citizenship arising from the dual character of the Union itself as at once supranational and intergovernmental.

To dissolve certain of the paradoxes surrounding European citizenship, we need to place it within the triple context of the changing concepts and practices of national citizenship, the variegated nature of the EU, and the notorious democratic and legitimacy deficit which afflicts not only the EU but increasingly the member states as well. With regard to the first context, it has become commonplace to note that nation-states are now challenged by the related processes of globalization and social differentiation (Archibugi, Held and Köhler, 1998; Held, McGrew, Goldblatt and Perraton, 1999). The one involves greater interconnectedness at an international level, the other leads to enhanced heterogeneity at regional and local levels. These forces have constrained both the functional efficacy of states to frame independent economic, social and defence policies, and their ability to draw on or forge a national identity capable of sustaining an allegiance to either the public good or the collective institutions and decisions that define and uphold it. Global market pressures have led to a reduction in the size and scope of the public sector, particularly in the economic sphere where the state has increasingly taken on a regulatory rather than a planning role (Majone, 1990, 1996). Moreover, in both economic and security matters, states have become more involved in, and subject to, international bodies and agreements, with a concomitant loss of power. Certain sub-state minority nations and regions have argued in consequence that they can be as viable as the larger political units to which they currently belong, and have demanded greater autonomy and even independence. Likewise, immigrant groups look for recognition of their ethnic identities in special rights and group representation. Meanwhile, a more diffuse and fragmented set of attachments that are both sub-national and transnational in character have developed amongst people generally. The ties of family, work, ideology, religion and sport, for example, increasingly operate either below or beyond the nation-state, competing with and diluting any sense of a purely national identity. Relatedly, as scholars of comparative politics have long observed, there has also been a steady, if partial, trend away from class-based to issue-based and identity politics linked to the development of new social movements and the growing importance of political activity within civil society (Budge and Newton, 1997: 177–93). Finally, the growth of private agencies performing public functions and the importance of international agreements in regulating domestic affairs have served to exacerbate the tendency for executives to break free from parliamentary controls (Andersen and Burns, 1996).

Commentators divide over how far these changes have gone (for an overview, see Holden, 2000). Most accept that though the functional and affective capacities of the state have been significantly weakened, states retain considerable power and national parliaments remain the single most important locus of political activity. Nevertheless, there has been a horizontal dispersal of sovereign power as government by states has been supplemented and partially displaced by multiple levels and kinds of governance that operate not only beyond and below but also across them (Rosenau and Czempiel, 1992). These developments partially reflect and have begun to promote alterations in the character of national citizenship. Three related factors are especially noteworthy. First, the state appears to offer fewer rewards for loyalty and belonging than in the past, thereby at least potentially reducing the cost to the individual of modifying, displacing and supplementing national citizenship. Second, as noted above, citizens are increasingly motivated by sectoral, identity and issue-based concerns. Individuals view their political engagement less, or not solely, as a general commitment to a particular political party and system, and more as a concern with various causes and issues. As a result, people become members of a range of new alliances, some of a sub-national and others increasingly of a transnational nature. According to the policy or concern, people line up with different groups and focus their attention on different loci of power. In consequence, they participate in a number of overlapping structures of governance, from neighbourhoods and municipalities up to supranational bodies such as the EU, and belong to a multiplicity of demoi. Finally, both these features are further reinforced by the shifts towards executive government, on the one hand, and privatized governance, on the other. These encourage citizens to become active in new spheres and in novel ways, since orthodox methods of seeking redress are no longer adequate (Tully, 1999). In many cases, elected sub-national or national representatives simply cannot provide the solutions citizens seek because in both practice and law they no longer possess the requisite powers. Thus, environmentalists, for example, pursue their cause not simply at national and local level within orthodox parties or a specifically Green Party, but also – and arguably more effectively – via a whole gamut of environmental groupings, from Greenpeace to the Royal Society for the Protection of Birds, and in numerous fora, from shareholders' meetings to the UN and gatherings of the G7 or the IMF. Moreover, they adopt a variety of forms of participation, from letter-writing campaigns, through the use of professional lobbyists, to demonstrations and direct action. In sum, there has been a certain fragmentation of both the sites and practices of national citizenship.

The second context, the EU, is in large part a manifestation of these developments (Axtmann, 1998). The earliest theorists of Community integration, the neo-functionalists, believed the ever greater interconnectedness of the economy meant that pressures for integration in certain areas would gradually 'spill over' into others, with the removal of direct barriers to trade, such as tariffs, leading to the tackling of indirect constraints through measures such as the harmonization of banking, trade marks and ultimately the single currency. They also assumed that as regulative power passed to Community institutions, there would be a build-up of political pressure for further integration as relevant interest groups sought direct access to where the action now lay (e.g. Haas, 1958: 16; George, 1996: 38). Nonetheless, liberal intergovernmentalists have rightly observed that most EU measures have remained closely tied to and limited by the furtherance of member-state interests – a response to their need for cooperation in global conditions (Moravcsik, 1993: 485). On this account, the demand for integration arises from domestic preference formation as channelled through national political systems, with support for the EU closely related to its perceived benefits for furthering domestic interests

(Moravcsik, 1993: 480–1). There is certainly plenty of evidence for this last position – not least the Luxembourg Accords and successive Eurobarometer polls in which support for Europe is treated as a mere function of its promotion of national goals. However, if neo-functionalists have over-emphasized the degree of 'spill-over' from the economic to the political, it is also true that many interest groups have increasingly concentrated their attention on directly influencing the EU's ever-growing regulatory power. Thus Greenwood estimates there are 688 formally organized EU-level interest groups, whilst the Commission estimates up to 3000 sets of actors are involved in lobbying it, ranging from individual firms to Euro-federations from given sectors (Greenwood, 1997: 57–9). Meanwhile, EU institutions, such as the European Parliament (EP) and the European Court of Justice (ECJ), have taken on a life of their own with a legitimacy and dynamic that is to some degree autonomous from the member states (Wincott, 1995; Craig, 1999: 11–12; Smith, 1999).

A middle way between these two accounts is developing, therefore. As a number of commentators have noted, within the EU 'authority and policy-making are shared across multiple levels of government – subnational, national and supranational' (Marks, Hooghe and Blank, 1996: 341–2). Though national arenas remain crucial for the formation of state preferences, sub-national actors are not 'nested exclusively within them'. State executives may be prime players in the integration process, but states 'no longer provide the sole interface between supranational and sub-national arenas, and they share, rather than monopolize, control over many activities that take place in their respective territories' (Marks, Hooghe and Blank, 1996: 346–7). Like neo-functionalist analysts, proponents of the multi-level governance thesis note how the development of European rules, standards and institutions shape not only policy outcomes but also policy-making behaviours, establishing the bases for interaction and points of influence for a nascent transnational society (Stone Sweet and Sandholtz, 1997: 305–7).

Thus, the EU is a variegated and experimental polity, partially autonomous from, but still heavily dependent on, its component member states. It is vital, if obvious, to appreciate that the Union is an unfinished system, subject to internal differentiation, almost certainly shy of its ultimate condition, whatever that may be, with member governments locked in a long process of slow reform. Moreover, the way in which the EU actually works – its governance – is evolving, and shifts along a spectrum between intergovernmentalism and supranationalism in a highly complex manner. There is no single *modus operandi* in the EU, unless its need to generate policy through compromise, both between the member governments in Council and also between the Council and the other institutions, is taken as a generally valid baseline. Instead, different policy areas function in different ways – the balance of power between the member governments and the EU institutions changes according to the policy in question, and also over time. For example, in environment policy, the EP has extensive powers over legislation since the codecision procedure applies. In matters of the putative Common Foreign and Security Policy, both the EP and the Commission are relatively powerless in formal terms, although as evinced by the Amsterdam Treaty this institutional pattern is somewhat subject to revision.

This betwixt-and-between character of the EU arises from the various forces making for the partial fragmentation of national citizenship described above, with Union citizenship a symbol of that development. From a purely intergovernmental perspective, Union citizenship appears something of a misnomer. If the member states are totally in control of the integration and policy process, with integration driven by domestic concerns, then what use is there for anything like 'European' citizenship? At the same time, political 'spill-over' – especially in the sense of creating an affective attachment to the EU for its own sake – is clearly patchier and weaker than neo-functionalist accounts might lead one to expect. The EU passport, flag and anthem are largely empty symbols. Union citizenship in part reflects this mixed and limited situation. Grounded in nationality, it is to some extent no more than the reciprocal recognition of those rights required for member-state citizens freely to move and trade with each other. But the provisions also reflect, and to a limited degree encourage, a direct relationship between citizens and the Union. In this respect, Union citizenship represents one layer of the multiple citizenships and demoi to which people increasingly belong. The nature of this multiplicity needs careful handling, however (Weiler, 1999: 344–8). The Treaty of Amsterdam declares in deference to intergovernmental worries that Union citizenship 'shall complement and not replace national citizenship' (TEU Article 17.1 (ex Article 8) as amended at Amsterdam). This statement makes it appear a discrete and detachable addition to, with no effect upon, national citizenship. Clearly this is not the case. Nor is it true that, as postnationalists fondly imagine, national citizenships are neatly incorporated within an over-arching European citizenship grounded in a common legacy of liberal democratic values. As the numerous clashes between the ECJ and member-state constitutional courts reveal, there is considerable argument over how these values should be interpreted and their bearing on European law (De Witte, 1991). Rather, as we noted, Union citizenship reflects the fragmentation of national citizenship and not only supplements but replaces, interacts and occasionally competes and conflicts with it. As such, it reflects the multi-level character of governance within Europe more generally.

If this fact largely unravels the paradoxical-seeming nature of European citizenship, it does not excuse all its shortcomings. The final context, the democratic deficit, comes in here. Integration has never been about democracy in any direct way (although the search for institutionalized peace and economic prosperity were of course vital to the re-establishment of democracy in Western Europe after World War Two). It has been an élite-led process which has been largely unexplained and certainly under-advocated to the average citizen. It has also been heavily opportunistic, resulting in the acquisition at EU level of a set of policy competences which appear hardly to match public perceptions of what the EU, or indeed any international governance system, should undertake (Blondel, Svensson and Sinott, 1998). It is ironic, if retrospectively unsurprising, that the creation of the formal status of EU citizenship at Maastricht should have occurred just as the crisis of the 'democratic deficit' erupted. The national referenda on the Treaty were often problematic: the Danes initially rejected the Treaty, and were persuaded to accept it only after being granted several exemptions from EU policy and being reassured about subsidiarity; the French voted for the Treaty by the smallest of margins. Yet it is unclear if the formal provisions of European citizenship provide even a minimally adequate response to this situation.

Definitions of the EU's democratic deficit abound, but the standard view is helpfully summarized by Dimitris Chryssochoou (1998) as a mixture of the institutional inadequacies of the EU when judged by standard liberal democratic criteria of accountability and responsiveness, and the absence of a substantial feeling of solidarity/community between the different peoples of the member states. Indeed, the second shortcoming partly explains the first, for without a clear sense of a European demos it is difficult to adequately institutionalize government either by or for the European people. However, there are two problems with conceptualizing EU democracy in these standard liberal democratic terms.

First, there is a tendency to concentrate on the EU's democratic shortcomings whilst assuming the arrangements of the member states to be infinitely better. As we noted above, this is far from being the case. Indeed, the EU's deficit both mirrors and reinforces many of the deficiencies of democracy at the national level – not least by increasing the range of executive discretion, enhancing bureaucratic and economic pressures to rationalize and harmonize products and procedures regardless of cultural difference or the popular will, encouraging the tendency to marketize greater areas of public life, and making decision-making ever more obscure and subject to the influence of powerful partial and private interests – not least in the increasingly important comitology process. As Fritz Scharpf (1999) has noted, the EU's essential rationale lies in increasing the international competitiveness of the member states through 'negative integration' or the removal of barriers to the free movements of goods, services, capital and persons. The EU lacks the capacity for 'positive integration' needed to solve market failures in areas such as employment and welfare through intervention. Conflicts of ideology and interest between the member states and the lack of a European demos make it unlikely that it will acquire this ability, which requires above all powers to raise tax, redistribute income and implement policies. Meanwhile, the success of its 'negative integration' of European markets is undercutting the ability of member states to act positively in many areas. For example, measures such as subsidies to declining regions or industries and various macro-economic employment-generating strategies are prohibited because they inhibit free competition. Yet removing the EU will not miraculously improve the accountability and effectiveness of national governance. Globalization and social differentiation will continue to challenge the democracy of member states. The EU does at least provide a framework for tackling these difficulties. The challenge is to find ways whereby the Union could modify its commitment to market integration in a manner that might help rather than inhibit the capacity of the member states to tackle social and economic problems – say, by controlling not just unfair state aids but also regulatory and tax concessions that promote an excessive race to the bottom.

The second problem with the standard view comes in here. Democratic legitimacy within the EU cannot be obtained by modelling its institutions on those of the nation-state. The very global economic and social forces that have promoted European integration have undermined liberal democracy at the nation-state level without creating appropriate conditions for its establishment within a supranational European polity (Bellamy and Castiglione, 2000a). Those who regard the strengthening of the EP as key to resolving the deficit make this mistake. The democratic deficit, in the narrow sense of the relative absence of any influence by ordinary citizens over European decision-makers and the policies they enact in their name, is tied in with what might be called the federal and constitutional deficits (Castiglione, 1995). The federal deficit derives from the absence of any clear demarcation of the respective competences of European and national political institutions. The constitutional deficit stems from the lack of any systematic normative and popular legitimization of European political institutions and the absence of any constituent European people who might be appealed to in order to provide it. Making the EP into a European legislature begs the important questions of who can decide what, where, when and how (Bellamy and Castiglione, 2000a). Yet these issues are crucial to the acceptability and appropriateness of any solution to the EU's democratic weaknesses. If the EU is a multi-level polity containing multiple demoi, then a central political institution based on the principle of majority rule is likely to exacerbate rather than ameliorate the situation (Bellamy and Warleigh, 1998; Bellamy and Castiglione, 2000b). It will lack popular support whilst remaining inefficient as a system of control (Weiler, 1993).

Both these problems are highlighted by the prospect of enlargement. On the one hand, meeting the criteria for 'negative integration' is having a devastating, if in certain respects necessary, impact on the employment and welfare regimes of many of the aspirant states. On the other hand, the entry of countries ranging from Poland and the Czech Republic to micro-states like Malta and culturally Islamic Turkey will dramatically enhance the diversity of the EU. As a result, the potential for clashes between different political cultures and national economic interests is likely to rise. The flexibility that increasingly characterizes the EU with its various opt-outs and multiple tracks and speeds in such areas as monetary union is likely to increase. Such differentiation can be beneficial in preserving the positive capacities of the member states. However, it can also lead to inequities that are likely to favour the developed and bigger states at the expense of the smaller and less developed. Resolving the democracy deficit within the EU requires quite complex decision-making procedures, therefore, that balance national and supranational concerns in ways that may vary between policy areas. The result will be to multiply the sites and practices of citizenship in ways that appear paradoxical within a nation-state context, but are well suited to the new context of governance of which the EU forms a part (for some creative proposals in this regard, see Schmitter, 2000).

Regrettably, the will for institutional reform remains weak. Moreover, the role of European citizenship within any reformed democratic process is likely to be addressed last of all. Yet the continued development of the EU combined with the erosion of national citizenship mean the need for creative thinking about European citizenship and democracy remain as urgent as ever. This volume provides an interim report on progress thus far and examines the prospects for, and possible contours of, future developments.

II. AIMS AND ARGUMENT OF THE BOOK

The central aim of this volume is hence to map and analyse the evolution of EU citizenship, both in its own formal right (as Articles 17–22 of the Treaty) and as the mixture of policies and institutional practices which give EU citizenship its expression and real-world meaning. In order to achieve this aim, we have selected a team of scholars who are able to draw on expertise in social and political theory, comparative government, international relations, public administration, law and sociology. Taken together, this mix of foci allows us to develop a holistic understanding of the current condition of EU citizenship, which of necessity requires attention to several different issues. The general conclusion arising from this study is that, like the Union itself, EU citizenship is a novel mixture of nation-state-based and innovative supranational and transnational practices, subject to a variegated pattern of evolution according to policy area. Perhaps unsurprisingly, the findings suggest an uneven process of development. Because of the more advanced nature of the *acquis communautaire* in the first, 'community', pillar, which covers mainly economic cooperation, and where European law is binding and European institutions enjoy their full powers, market-related issues of citizenship have received the greatest attention. Issues related to pillars II and III, dealing respectively with 'Common Foreign and Security Policy' (CFSP) and 'Police and Judicial Cooperation in Criminal Matters', where intergovernmental decision-making prevails, trail somewhat in their wake. Even within the first pillar, however, significant problems remain. Institutional practices related to citizenship, for example, remain inadequate (see Giddings and Gregory, this volume). Moreover, the continuing weakness of Union competence in areas such as social policy means the attempt to make EU citizenship more meaningful by presenting it as part of a bundle of policies has been only partially successful. In the second and third pillars, similar but starker problems are evident. Although the prospects are by no means entirely bleak, the continued limits to Union policy in areas such as diplomatic protection have frustrated attempts to develop Union citizenship beyond the formal requirements of the Treaty.

Consequently, the contributions to this volume produce a wealth of evidence to support the hypothesis that a market-based citizenship has proved insufficient as a means of generating support for, and loyalty to, the EU. So far, Union citizenship has failed to provide the mechanism for a significant attachment between either the publics of the member states or the Union and the various national demoi. Unable to 'bribe' its way into the hearts of citizens through the provision of public welfare (thanks to its small budget, the rise of the regulatory state as a means of governance, and the ideological resistance by certain national governments to any further integration of redistributive policies on the grounds of national sovereignty), the EU has also largely failed to capitalize on the opportunity to provide citizens with an alternative means of effecting political change. To date, EU citizenship has not been sufficiently devoted to the encouragement of political engagement with the Union and its decision-making. The failure adequately to open, advertise and facilitate access to new political opportunity structures has left the EU with an important dilemma: the need to create a public sphere in the absence of a familiar institutional structure and in the face of the persistent problem of the 'democratic deficit'. As a result, the principal message of this book is that for EU citizenship to be meaningful, it must be reinvented as an instrument of political engagement: a tool for the expression of opinions and the resolution of problems rather than simply a batch of entitlements. Indeed, certain findings of the chapters by Warleigh, Bellamy, Giddings and Gregory, Stychin, and Kostakopoulou suggest that there are tentative moves in this direction.

III. STRUCTURE AND CONTENTS OF THE BOOK

We have divided the book into three parts. Part I, 'Citizenship of the European Union', provides the analytical context of the volume. The relevant institutional and normative issues are explored in order to set out the content, scope and evolution to date of Union citizenship. The theoretical framework of the book is also laid out, in order to guide the reading of the subsequent chapters. Part II, 'Internal Aspects of EU Citizenship', deals with institutional and policy issues related to the 'domestic politics' of the EU – its public policies and regimes in the first (Community) pillar. Part III, 'External Aspects of EU Citizenship', treats issues pertaining to the second and third pillars of EU competence, respectively the 'Common Foreign and Security Policy' (CFSP) and 'Police and Judicial Cooperation in Criminal Matters' (formerly known under the rather more user-friendly term 'Justice and Home Affairs').

Part I opens with Alex Warleigh's empirical assessment of the development of Union citizenship in Chapter 2. Drawing lessons from the institutional development of the EU itself, Alex Warleigh demonstrates that Union citizenship must be considered a matter of institutional practices and structures, as well as the formal entitlements provided by the Treaty. He also argues that by working as 'purposeful opportunists', interested parties including EU institutions but also member governments and individual citizens may yet facilitate the evolution of Union citizenship beyond its currently rather limited circumstances. In Chapter 3, Richard Bellamy complements this empirically focused chapter with a normative analysis. He argues that European citizenship will not provide the EU with the legitimacy it plainly needs so long as it is conceptualized in passive terms as a mere catalogue of the entitlements acquired through an élite-driven integration process. Drawing on the social movement literature and the civic republican tradition, he shows how citizenship performs an important constitutive role in making and sustaining a democratic polity. The challenge is to find the appropriate structures for citizens to play their part in shaping the Union.

Part II explores these institutional and policy issues further. In chapter 4, Philip Giddings and Roy Gregory examine the contribution made by the EU Ombudsman to the development of both Union citizenship – to which it is explicitly tied in the Treaty – and 'good governance' in the EU. They provide a solid historical and conceptual description of the Union Ombudsman's office, and analyse its performance to date. Giddings and Gregory maintain that the Ombudsman has managed to make a limited, but definite, mark on the EU, helping install good administrative practice and boost transparency – two essential features of good governance which the EU must develop in order to facilitate citizens' engagement with European integration.

A similarly complex but nuanced view emerges from Tony Downes's examination of the role of both EU law and the European Court of Justice (ECJ) in the making of Union citizenship in Chapter 5. Downes argues that it is mistaken to lay too much emphasis on the idea of 'market citizenship', since it is difficult to erect clear barriers between economic rights and those which might be considered of broader and even 'constitutional' signifi- cance. Looking at the jurisprudence of the ECJ, Downes argues that the ECJ has often made rulings which collectively approach the creation of a European legal identity for individuals and take the scope of economic rights further than may originally have been intended. However, as Downes reminds us, the ECJ is able to use as a legal basis only the provisions of the Treaty. Regardless of whether the ECJ is 'activist' or not, and of how far this is democratically acceptable, there are limits to what kind of citizenship can be constructed out of the narrow bases provided by the Treaty.

A broadening of the Treaty is much more likely from actors who lie outside the constraints of the EU institutional framework. In Chapter 6, Carl Stychin provides a case study of how struggles by citizens for recognition can lead to the *acquis* being employed to extend Union citizenship and in turn reconstitute the EU itself. Stychin focuses on how the legal struggles of lesbians and gay men have created the potential for a trans-national public sphere. He notes that this possibility turns not on the construction of the sort of common European political identity proposed by top-down approaches, but through actors discovering the various 'affinities' that exist between them notwithstanding their diverse back- grounds and different points of departure. This bottom-up approach makes it possible to forge a common European space whilst preserving differences held to be important by individuals because difference *per se* is not problematized. A more agonic model of active Union citizenship is thereby revealed to offer a mechanism for creating an EU premised on diversity rather than uniformity.

Though occasionally considered as distinct, struggles for recognition and for redistribution are intimately related (Tully, 2000). Calls for the former usually entail an element of the latter and *vice versa*. Thus far, however, substantive social redistribution has lagged considerably behind formal legal recognition at the EU level. Part II thus closes with an analysis of the shortcomings of EU social citizenship. In Chapter 7 Mita Castle-Kanerova and Bill Jordan argue that it has been truncated both by its links to the idea of the market (echoing the conclusions of Downes) and by the models of social change which appear to be gaining the upper hand in the EU as a result of the so-called 'Third Way'. Focusing on gender policy relating to equality of income and opportunity, Castle-Kanerova and Jordan's rather bleak conclusion is that enlargement may well provide an opportunity for leaders to escape the solidaristic traditions of both Western and Central/ Eastern Europe in the rush to create flexible labour markets.

Part III opens in similarly cautious vein. Barry Jones argues in Chapter 8 that for all its successes, the EU has so far failed to replace its member states as the principal focus of affective loyalty or as the main provider of valued collective goods and services. In consequence, EU citizenship remains trapped in a no-win situation, for without these structures and powers it is unable to prove its value as an instrument for achieving policy goals. Thus, citizenship of the Union symbolizes rather than alters the EU's legitimacy crisis, and is unable to justify either the accretion or the use of new decision-making powers in major areas of policy by the EU. Analysis of the second pillar provides further grounds for scepticism. Chapter 9 probes the agreement made in the Treaty on European Union giving EU citizens the right to diplomatic representation by other member states in third countries without representation from their member state of origin. Stelios Stavridis and Colleen Thouez argue that member governments continue to hold the key to such protection, since it is awarded not because of an independent 'European' right but as an exercise in reducing transaction costs. The rights to diplomatic protection are limited and will need to be re-examined in the context of enlargement. The absence of a European demos is felt particularly acutely in this respect. Seen from the Stavridis–Thouez perspective, EU action to increase the security of the (EU) citizen either internally or vis-à-vis the rest of the world remains a second order priority for EU leaders. Moreover, differences between national publics on the issue of what EU foreign and security policies should comprise remain too great to allow the essential parameters of a common European policy to evolve through citizen-led pressures.

However, the final chapter lends the volume a more sanguine

conclusion. Investigating the development of EU immigration law – a classic focus of citizenship studies, since it illustrates where boundary lines are drawn in terms of inclusion/exclusion from the polity – Theodora Kostakopoulou charts a complex trajectory of policy regime development. Initially opposed to the development of a European citizenship based primarily on cosmopolitan principles of human rights on the grounds that it would make a tough immigration policy more difficult to establish, member governments appear to be revising their positions. Although member governments are not (yet?) seeking to promote normative reform of the EU as such, and are certainly not on the verge of creating a fully inclusive Europolity, they may be using the Charter of Fundamental Rights (still under negotiation at the time of writing) as a means of continuing a recent trend towards clarifying and improving the rights of third-country nationals in the EU. Such individuals may still be given a status inferior to that enjoyed by member-state nationals, but it is likely that there will be progress from the very low level of rights afforded third-country nationals in the EU in previous periods of integration. Nevertheless, this limitation reveals the problems of top-down approaches and the consistent failure of the member states to conceive citizenship in active and participatory, as opposed to passive, terms.

Taken together, the chapters of this volume indicate that much remains to be done in order to develop EU citizenship to the point at which it can either make a significant contribution to the eradication of the institutional aspects of the 'democratic deficit', or act as a catalyst for powerful bottom-up pressures for reform. And yet citizenship of the Union is more than symbolically important. It comprises rights and practices which distinguish the EU from any other international organization. If, as is likely, popular concern about the democratic deficit of the EU persists and gets ever more explicitly related to concerns about democracy at the national levels, member governments may well have to inject Union citizenship with greater salience. However, the result is unlikely to be the creation of the super-state Eurosceptics fear, even if it heralds a weakening or, more properly, a reconfiguration of the nation-state. EU citizenship may be only a potential instrument of change at present, but our analysis suggests that sooner, or more likely somewhat later, that potential will have to be realized.

REFERENCES

Andersen, S. and Burns, T. (1996) 'The European Union and the Erosion of Parliamentary Democracy: A Study of Post-parliamentary Governance', in S. Andersen and K. Eliassen (eds), *The European Union: How Democratic Is It?* (London: Sage).

Archibugi, D., Held, D. and Köhler, M. (eds) (1998) *Re-imagining Political Community: Studies in Cosmopolitan Democracy* (Cambridge: Polity).

Aron, R. (1974) 'Is Multinational Citizenship Possible?', *Social Research* 41: 4, pp. 638–56.

Axtmann, R. (ed.) (1998) *Globalization and Europe: Theoretical and Empirical Investigation* (London: Pinter).

Bellamy, R. and Castiglione, D. (2000a) 'Democracy, Sovereignty and the Constitution of the European Union: The Republican Alternative to Liberalism', in Z. Bankowski and A. Scott (eds), *The European Union and its Order* (Oxford: Blackwell) pp. 170–90.

Bellamy, R. and Castiglione, D. (2000b) 'The Uses of Democracy: Reflections on the EU's Democratic Deficit', in E. O. Eriksen and J. E. Fossum (eds), *Democracy in the European Union – Integration through Deliberation?* (London: Routledge) pp. 65–84.

Bellamy, R and Warleigh, A. (1998) 'From an Ethics of Integration to an Ethics of Participation: Citizenship and the Future of the European Union', *Millennium* 27: 3, pp. 447–70.

Blondel, J., Svensson, S. and Sinott, R. (1998) *People and Parliament in the European Union: Participation, Democracy and Legitimacy* (Oxford: Clarendon).

Budge, I. and K. Newton (*et al.*) (1997) *The Politics of the New Europe – Atlantic to Urals* (Harlow, Essex: Longman).

Castiglione, D. (1995) 'Contracts and Constitutions', in R. Bellamy, V. Bufacchi and D. Castiglione (eds), *Democracy and Constitutional Culture in the Union of Europe* (London: Lothian Foundation Press) pp. 59–79.

Chryssochoou, D. (1998) *Democracy in the European Union* (London: Tauris).

Craig, P. (1999) 'The Nature of Community: Integration, Democracy and Legitimacy', in P. Craig and Grainne de Burca (eds), *The Evolution of EU Law* (Oxford: Oxford University Press) pp. 1–54.

De Witte, B. (1991) 'Droit communautaire et valeurs constitutionelles nationales', *Droits* 14, pp. 87–96.

George, S. (1996) *Politics and Policy in the European Union*, 3rd edn (Oxford: Oxford University Press).

Greenwood, J. (1997) *Representing Interests in the European Union* (London: Macmillan).

Gustavsson, S. (1998) 'Defending the Democratic Deficit', in A. Weale and M. Nentwich, *Political Theory and the European Union: Legitimacy, Constitutional Choice and Citizenship* (London: Routledge) pp. 63–79.

Haas, E. (1958) *The Uniting of Europe: Political, Social and Economic Forces 1950–1957* (Stanford: Stanford University Press).

Habermas, J. (1992) 'Citizenship and National Identity: Some Reflections on the Future of Europe', *Praxis International* 12, pp. 1–19.

Held, D., McGrew, A., Goldblatt, D. and Perraton, J. (1999) *Global Transformations: Politics, Economics and Culture* (Cambridge: Polity Press).

Holden, B. (ed.) (2000) *Global Democracy: Key Debates* (London: Routledge).

Linklater, A. (1998) *The Transformation of Political Community: Ethical Foundation of the Post-Westphalian Era* (Cambridge: Polity).

Majone, G. (ed.) (1990) *Deregulation or Re-Regulation: Regulatory Reform in Europe and the United States* (London: Pinter).

Majone, G. (1996) *Regulating Europe* (London: Routledge).

Mancini, G. F. (1998) 'Europe: The Case for Statehood', *European Law Journal* 4, pp. 29–42.

Marks, G., Hooghe L. and Blank, K. (1996) 'European Integration from the 1980s: State-Centric v. Multi-level Governance', *Journal of Common Market Studies* 34, pp. 341–78.

Moravcsik, A. (1993) 'Preferences and Power in the European Community: A Liberal Intergovernmentalist Approach', *Journal of Common Market Studies* 31, pp. 473–524.

Rosenau, J. N. and Czempiel, E. O. (eds) (1992) *Governance without Government: Order and Change in World Politics* (Cambridge: Cambridge University Press).

Scharpf, F. (1999) *Governing in Europe: Effective and Democratic?* (Oxford: Oxford University Press).

Schmitter, P. C. (2000) *How to Democratize the European Union ... And Why Bother?* (Maryland: Rowman and Littlefield Publishers, Inc.).

Smith, J. (1999) *Europe's Elected Parliament* (Sheffield: Sheffield Academic Press).

Stone Sweet, A. and Sandholtz, W. (1997) 'European Integration and Supranational Governance', *Journal of European Public Policy* 4, pp. 297–317.

Tully, J. (1999) 'The Agonic Freedom of Citizens', *Economy and Society* 28: 2, pp. 161–82.

Tully, J. (2000) 'Struggles over Recognition and Distribution', *Constellations* 7: 3.

Weiler, J. H. H. (1993) 'Parliamentary Democracy in Europe 1992: Tentative Questions and Answers', in D. Greenberg, S. N. Katz, M. B. Oliveiro and S. C. Wheatly (eds), *Constitutionalism and Democracy: Transitions in the Contemporary World* (Oxford and New York: Oxford University Press) pp. 249–63.

Weiler, J. H. H. (1999) *The Constitution of Europe: 'Do the New Clothes Have an Emperor?' and Other Essays on European Integration* (Cambridge: Cambridge University Press).

Wincott, D. (1995) 'Institutional Interaction and European Integration: Towards an Everyday Critique of Liberal Intergovernmentalism', *Journal of Common Market Studies* 33, pp. 597–609.

2

Purposeful Opportunists? EU Institutions and the Struggle over European Citizenship

ALEX WARLEIGH

I. INTRODUCTION

At the turn of the century, 'European' citizenship[1] has still to reach maturity. There is even admissible doubt as to whether EU citizenship as such really exists. Magnette (1999) points out that except for a brief period around the time of the Maastricht Treaty (TEU), governments and other actors have preferred to speak of a 'Europe of citizens' – a much vaguer term which can cover a multitude of sins – than EU citizenship proper. The latter has implied too much state-building for many to stomach. Instead, member governments have promoted the former in order to make the Union more popular. Other EU institutions – notably the European Parliament (EP) and the European Commission – have attempted to use citizenship as a means of self-advancement. This has even met with some success: after all, refusing to accept a proposal for consumer protection couched in the language of the citizen can be made to represent voting against motherhood and *tarte aux pommes* (Magnette, 1999). In recent years, citizenship construction has switched from the elaboration of supposedly identity-generating symbols to the supply of further means of practical popular engagement with Union policy-making (Wiener, 1998). However, both take-up rates and the actual influence of those citizens and citizens' groups who rise to the challenge are often relatively low (Warleigh, 2000). Moreover, such opportunities are not extensive. Much remains to be done to encourage popular agency and breathe life into EU citizenship. This is a key battleground in the struggle over European integration. Consequently, the role of the Union institutions – the bodies which conceive, contest and co-author all EU policy – in the citizenship construction process is a crucial issue.

It is part of the 'new conventional wisdom' in EU studies (Church, 2000) that institutions 'matter', that at the very least they can 'serve as an intervening variable between the power and preferences of EC member governments ... and subsequent choices about both institutional change and policy-making' (Pollack, 1996: 430). In the 'new institutionalism', attention is paid to the role of institutional factors in the resolution of political struggles (Bulmer, 1993), to the influence that organization and structure exert on shaping actors' decisions and behaviour. Rules, routines and codes shape perceptions of what is possible or acceptable; actors do not simply make rational cost-benefit calculations but also consider duties, obligations, (institutional) cultures, and structural factors when deciding a course of action (March and Olsen, 1984). Over time, engagement with the integration process shapes even member governments as the law of path dependency and the unintended consequences of previous decisions restrain their scope for action and make exit an increasingly costly option (Pierson, 1996). Institutions – including member governments and their collective supranational organs, the EU and the European Councils – are not neutral, but participate in overlapping 'governance régimes' (Bulmer, 1998) which make policy as an ongoing process of contestation, alliance-building and 'partnership'. Moreover, no EU institution is monolithic. Sub-cultures and intra-institutional rivalries make for complex alliance structures and an entertainingly plural set of attitudes to any given issue in a particular institution.

Building on Cram (1997: 181), I maintain that each Union body can be a *purposeful opportunist*, that is an organization which 'has a notion of its overall objectives and aims but is quite flexible as to the means of achieving them'. Strategy and opportunism fuse to produce an uneven development of policy, which is shaped not entirely by clear rationale but by creativity and the exploitation of opportunity. In the quixotic EU arena, both goals and their selected means of delivery are likely to evolve, and to some extent it is inevitable that opportunity will dictate the ability to succeed in realizing any given goal. Moreover, failure to develop the requisite entrepreneurial skills[2] can lead to (temporary) policy stagnation, since opportunity spaces will be filled or created by more able actors even when the climate is favourable to the desired change. Goals may thus take considerable time and sustained effort to be realized, as with the Commission's attempt to shift the Union towards a Europe of the Regions (Tömmel, 1998). As in the same case, the eventual outcome of the strategy may not be entirely in keeping with the original plan. Moreover, certain goals may never be met since the right opportunity may never be present; nothing is inevitable in European integration. Nonetheless, if goals are sufficiently important for reasons of either self-advancement or polity-building, they will remain on the relevant institution's wish-list, and be reactivated when an opportunity can be found or constructed.

In this chapter I argue that the evolution of European citizenship can be usefully understood in this light.[3] Union citizenship is about more than the

Treaty. It resides in secondary legislation as much as summit-agreed documents, in a 'practice' of citizenship[4] as much as formal entitlements and duties.[5] It is part of the institutional struggle over the development of the EU itself. Amongst the new institutions and bodies created by the TEU were some tasked with helping develop democracy by increasing transparency and bringing the Union 'closer to the citizen' (the Ombudsman; the Committee of the Regions; the fully institutionalized Court of Auditors). The Amsterdam Treaty (ToA) indicated that, formally at least, significant further progress was not yet feasible. The Charter of Fundamental Rights, under negotiation at the time of writing, appears likely to be similarly cautious. Nonetheless, deepening citizenship remains a wish of certain member governments and other EU actors. There are also signs that nongovernmental organizations (NGOs) and even individuals are entering the fray in order to develop EU citizenship further, thereby enlarging the number of concerned 'purposeful opportunists'.

The structure of the chapter is as follows. In the next section, I ask why formal EU citizenship was created, arguing that it had a double rationale – a utilitarian justification, centred on making a success of the single market, coupled with a more normative *telos* of helping reduce the notorious democratic deficit. This dualism at the heart of EU citizenship helps explain its uneven development, since there is no clear agreement about its proper scope or purpose. In the following section, I seek to define Eurocitizenship as more than the contents of Articles 17–22. It also comprises rights, practices and entitlements contained in, and provoked by, secondary legislation. In the next section, I trace the evolution of citizenship's expression in primary law from Maastricht to Amsterdam and analyse its 'freezing' in terms of primary legislation, maintaining that this should not be equated with total inertia. Although the Treaties give advocates of a strong formal citizenship at the EU level scant grounds for optimism, a more indirect approach to building 'European' citizenship may yet bear fruit; furthermore, even at the formal level citizenship remains on the agenda. Finally, in the last section, I argue that in the aftermath of Amsterdam, EU citizenship has successfully become more than a matter of 'history-making decisions' (Peterson, 1995) taken at intergovernmental conferences (IGCs), and is slowly evolving as part of the *experienced acquis* – thanks in large part to institutional sponsorship and opportunism.

II. WHY FORMALIZE EUROPEAN CITIZENSHIP?

Why did citizenship (as opposed to citizens' rights) figure in the TEU? The question is important since its answer provides a clue to help understand the future scope for development of this status. I argue here that two main concerns were prevalent: making a success of the single market, and bridging the democratic deficit.

The early stages of European integration gave no role to the citizen, since popular involvement with the integration process was less important than élite mobilization and, if possible, securing the active support of interest groups. Success would be judged by efficiency, and support, so far as it was needed, generated by rational popular appreciation of the role the then EEC was playing in maximizing the general welfare (Bellamy and Warleigh, 1998). Relaunching the integration process in the 1980s required a change of policy; it was impossible to envisage successful economic regeneration without a single market (SEM), and this in turn necessitated a shift in the way the individual and the Union interacted. Integration could continue in *bricolage* fashion, but, in deepening, it would have to be complemented by some form of popular identification and a means of demonstrating European 'added value' after years of virtual, if often exaggerated, neglect. Thus, Everson (1995) maintains that economic integration provides the ultimate rationale for EU citizenship. As with so much in the Union, its justification lies in the Single European Act (1986). Making the SEM work required increased freedom of movement of labour, itself necessitating for migrants a greater degree of access to welfare in a host member state of which they were not nationals. Citizenship provided a degree of stability (being a traditional means of linking individual to state/ governance structure) without necessitating a more thoroughgoing federal settlement. The more reluctant members of the Council could accept it in this light, considering it part of the limited acceptance of EU redistributive (cohesion) policy in the context of an internal market of winners and losers (Everson and Preuss, 1995).

However, another rationale was also at play, and the tension between these two remains unresolved. Many EU actors (including governments, especially the Danish and Spanish) sought to make a direct link between the Union and the individual as part of the *democratization* process (Closa, 1992; Marias, 1994a). Taschner (1993) cites a long history of Commission activism in the attempt to forge Union citizenship, democratization being considered part of the path to polityhood. In this attempt, the role of the European Court of Justice (ECJ) was crucial. By ruling that the Rome Treaty was different from international law and that member governments could not prevent the EC/U creating rights for their citizens directly rather than through the member states, it facilitated the growth of citizenship rights and carved out a legal space for formal citizenship (Marias, 1994a). Whether or not such judgements were deliberately teleological, they clearly created possibilities which were then taken up by other entrepreneurial actors. The European Parliament (EP) too had called for the creation of EU citizenship, seeing institutional advantage in democratization.[6] Instead of creating a federal system, and even whilst producing formal structures which are clearly incomplete, the member states provided at Maastricht a means partially to rectify the democratic deficit, just as popular disquiet about it began in earnest.

It is possible to read Union citizenship in both ways. The provisions of the Treaty are both instrumental and normative, both the offspring of calculations about system need and part of the still incomplete process of democratization. Whilst altering the relationship between the individual and the integration process, EU citizenship also provided part of the means for that process to succeed *and* served to detract attention from the other (democratic) failings of the Union (D'Oliveira, 1994). Citizenship reached the Treaty because it served a useful purpose for the minimalists and gave hope (as well as potential means) to the maximalists. It reflected long-term strategy on the part of certain actors, and the particular needs of others at a specific, important historical juncture. Like the Union itself, then, EU citizenship is hybrid and with evolutive potential.

III. DEFINING EUROPEAN CITIZENSHIP

Reading the Treaty

Perhaps unsurprisingly, there is thus much debate about whether EU citizenship is 'thick' or 'thin', in other words how substantive it is. This debate in turn has two foci: readings of the formal Treaty provisions (which themselves offer different positions), and accounts which give primacy to a broader conception of citizenship (citizens' rights/protection) – *acquis*.[7] I argue that a frank admission of the formal limits of Union citizenship does not preclude support for the second position. Understanding not just formal entitlements but how they are used in conjunction with other legislation generates a far more accurate view of the real value of EU citizenship, which although less than revolutionary is far from a dead letter. Table 2.1 sets out the main areas of the debate, which are explored below.

The Treaty provisions on citizenship are certainly ambiguous. As the key to the full extent of Union citizenship is nationality of a member state,[8] citizens do not 'belong' to the Union (Neunreither, 1995). Union citizenship confers limited new rights on its holders. These centre on increased freedom of movement, the right to stand and vote in local and EP elections of member states in which one is resident but of which one is not a national, the right to petition the newly created Ombudsman as well as the EP, and the right to diplomatic protection by another member state in third countries where one's 'own' state is not represented. Are member-state

Table 2.1 The Treaty – thin or thick citizenship?

Thin	Thick
EU citizenship entails no voting rights in national elections, thereby keeping it at the fringes of real political involvement.	EU citizenship is situated in the main body of the Treaty, not the preamble, and is thus justiciable.
'Market citizenship' is the predominant characteristic – EU citizenship is all about making freedom of movement possible.	EU citizenship affords the holder voting rights for local and EP elections – even formally, it is more than simply economic.
Member-state nationality remains the key, since you need this to access the whole range of EU citizenship rights – and member governments control very tightly whom they will allow to have nationality.	EU citizenship also grants the holder a right to diplomatic protection by another member government in a third country without representation from one's 'home' state. This blurs the distinction between nationality and citizenship.
'European' citizenship applies only to the first pillar – the intergovernmentalism of pillars II and III precludes the extension of citizenship to the whole range of EU competence.	EU citizenship has caused the changing of national constitutions, a step not undertaken lightly. It also removes the absolute right of each member state to control access to its public welfare provisions.
Articles 17–22 fail to add anything significant to the citizenship provisions which already existed in the Treaty.	The partial codification in the Treaty makes EU citizenship more visible.
The Treaty provisions are not implemented, making EU citizenship worthless in reality.	Member governments can be forced to comply.

nationals citizens of the Union or just of the Community? O'Leary (1996) argues that the latter is the case given the predominantly intergovernmental nature of the second and third pillars,[9] a point which carries some salience even after the ToA brought adaptations to the pillar structure. This would deny citizens access to rights and protection in some of the most sovereignty-threatening areas of EU activity. Nonetheless, given the links between the first and third pillars and the potential to cultivate spill-over from one to the other, it is possible to conceive of citizenship applying across the full range of EU activity (Springer, 1996).

Does the Treaty confer political rights? Everson and Preuss (1995) find an acknowledgement in the TEU that political community construction requires more than economic rights, and Gamberale (1995) argues that the right to joint diplomatic protection blurs the distinction between citizenship and nationality (which is usually interpreted as citizenship's external face). On the other hand, Martiniello (1994) maintains that the pivotal role played by the member states in determining who has the full complement of political rights means that the relationship between citizenship and nationality has at best been revised, not severed. Perhaps the greatest subject of debate is in the area of the classic function of citizenship: exclusion. Everson and Preuss (1995) provide an optimistic analysis, pointing to the right of all residents to petition the Ombudsman as proof that the Treaty confers at least some rights on all individuals, to be enjoyed regardless of nationality. These can be significant, for they allow the citizen to act against the Community institutions, as well as their 'own' member state and its counterparts in matters of EC law.[10] However, this in turn creates a mixed signal for member-state nationals: what is the affective (and thus identity-generating) value of a supposedly 'European' citizenship, parts of which are accessible to all (O'Keeffe, 1994)?

Does EU citizenship simply award rights to individuals or do they thereby come closer to the heart of power? Laffan (1996) holds that citizens are not engaged with directly by the Treaty; the latter does nothing to alter the fact that popular involvement with the Union remains largely tied to voting every five years for MEPs and one's role as a consumer. Everson (1995) concurs, pointing out that the market logic of citizenship – ensuring at least some freedom of movement of labour – remains apparent after Maastricht, which she sees as granting a legal but at best anaemic socio-economic content to membership of the Union. The power of member states to filter citizenship policy means that mutual reciprocity of rights, rather than a bill of rights at even EC level, has been the order of the day (Hyland *et al.*, 1995). The probable limits of the Charter of Fundamental Rights confirm this reading. Further, as O'Leary (1996) points out, what now constitutes Articles 17–22 does nothing to guarantee that member states will protect citizens' fundamental rights. It is interesting that these commitments – the Charter, but also the declarations in the ToA – are kept away from the provisions on citizenship. The Ombudsman (see Giddings and Gregory, this volume) cannot investigate national authorities *qua* national authorities, even for maladministration of EC law (O'Keeffe, 1994); there is no procedure to ensure that member governments coordinate voting rights or diplomatic protection provisions within the EC/U framework, leaving open the possibility that multilateral agreements will be used instead (Closa, 1992).

Moreover, it is not clear whether citizenship rights can be invoked against one's 'own' member state – Neuwahl (1998) finds no evidence of this, but O'Leary (1996) argues that freedom of movement law – the nucleus of EU citizenship – has been used against 'home' member states, for example to oblige them to recognize qualifications gained in other member states. Weiler (1996) points out a significant problem, namely the difficulty of operationalizing citizenship on the ground. His survey uncovered no evidence that any of the provisions of the then Article 8 had been fully implemented by any of the member states. At the time of writing, some member states are still being taken to task by the Commission for failure to implement EU citizenship provisions either at all or correctly – Belgium,

Germany and Greece are cases in point. The limits of Community (Union?) competence must also be those of formal citizenship of the Union. Member-state nationals may thus have acquired a limited extra citizenship which is beyond their scope to enforce, particularly given the fact that the ECJ is scarcely accessible to individuals (Duff, 1997). Nonetheless this is not the whole story. Marias (1994b) points out that since even Articles 17–22 form part of the main text of the Treaty (rather than the preamble) they have a legal significance which is enhanced by the consideration that it brings additional rights to the citizens.

Other writers have signalled that it is at least true to say that citizenship clips the wings of the member governments. For instance, Guild (1996) argues that the nationality/citizenship distinction is blurred in a Union which is increasingly recognized as an autonomous external actor by third countries (e.g. by the World Trade Organization, or by the European Court of Human Rights (ECHR), which has noted the ECJ's semi-constitutiona-lization of the Rome Treaty). Moreover, the constitutions of some member states have been altered to allow the ratification of the Treaty; in the French case, this has boosted the powers of the national Assembly (Corbett, 1994) as well as those of the citizen. As Leibfried and Pierson (1996) point out, EU citizenship goes to the heart of national sovereignty over the welfare state, since member governments no longer have the right to decide on whether certain non-nationals are entitled to receive social security benefits. Electoral rights vis-à-vis the EP are given great significance by La Torre (1995), since the EP can now justifiably be seen as the seat of deputies sent to Brussels and Strasbourg by a cross-border electorate. There is thus a partial shift towards political citizenship from its economic variant (Neunreither, 1995), which has been hailed as the culmination of assiduous, long-term activity by the Commission (Taschner, 1993).

Thus, although there is no uniform view, it is clear that most commentators identify significant gaps in the formal content of EU citizenship, which is obviously on the thin side. This formal poverty, however, must be set alongside the way in which citizenship is used, as well as the full set of citizenship provisions in EU legislation.

Living the *acquis*

As claimed by Wiener (1996), EU citizenship is not uniform but 'fragmented': it is composed of different functions, which in turn require varying degrees of popular mobilization to be meaningful. The right to move freely within the SEM, for example, requires less of a sense of solidarity than a common (political) identity, but may of course help to generate it. Moreover, Union citizens have rights and legal protection which stem from secondary legislation as well as the Treaty, as consumers, human beings and inhabitants of the single market zone. Thus, interpreting the Treaty, either maximally or minimally, can only reveal part of the picture. The increasing range of EU powers in, *inter alia*, consumer protection, public health, and environmental and social policies, gives citizens entitlements and protections which they would otherwise lack. Sbragia (1996), for instance, notes that in several member states environment policy is almost entirely of EU origin. Although there are dangers inherent in considering citizenship as merely a set of rights and entitlements – issues of identification and mobilization are essential in making active citizenship, and, as argued below, seeking to prioritize 'people issues' does not necessarily make for substantive citizenship – it is also true that much of what makes EU citizenship worth having is scattered throughout the *acquis* rather than encapsulated in Articles 17–22. Furthermore, citizenship of the Union is now perforce part of member-state nationals' lived experience. The latter will inevitably shape existing politico-legal provisions and public reaction to them (Shaw, 1998); group engagement with EU policy-making is growing and can be seen by both participants and decision-makers as effective (Warleigh, 2000). Citizenship may be expanded by other policies just as the ECJ engineered its initial incarnation in freedom of movement and equal treatment rulings (Shaw, 1997a). Moreover, even the Treaty specifically allows for the expansion, but not the (formal) reduction of Union citizenship (Article 22). As a result, Union citizenship is an evolving experience, or 'practice' (Wiener, 1998).

IV. THE FORMAL PATH OF CITIZENSHIP: FROM MAASTRICHT TO AMSTERDAM

To summarize the chapter so far: I have argued that EU citizenship was created for two reasons: the facilitation of the single market and the Council's need to be seen to rectify the democratic deficit. This dual rationale has given EU citizenship a schizophrenic nature, itself complicated by the interinstitutional struggles over its development as an undeclared facet of the 'state-building' process. As a 'lived experience' based on political engagement and the wider set of entitlements generated by the wider *acquis*, citizenship of the Union is beginning to take root. In this context it is necessary to return to an analysis of primary law, since this sets the formal parameters of EU citizenship and creates the arena into which may enter 'purposeful opportunists'. How far were the member governments prepared to upgrade EU citizenship at the first IGC after Maastricht? How many 'purposeful opportunists' sought to force their hands?

At first sight, the signs are not encouraging. The sole change made by the ToA to the formal citizenship provisions was to renumber the articles containing them, thus effectively reaffirming EU citizenship's second-order importance compared with its national equivalents. Indeed, given the apparent change in the Danish position (Magnette, 1998a) after the lost referendum on Maastricht (itself largely due to worries about citizenship), it is possible to argue that, formally speaking, citizenship has reached its high water mark. One of the EU's most 'progressive' member states is either unwilling or unable to withhold its veto, and, in the face of member-government opposition or lack of interest, other actors have switched their focus to battles they can win (Magnette, 1998a). Moreover, analysis reveals that during the 1996 IGC, institutional reform was not justified by the member states with reference to bringing Europe closer to the citizen, but with regard to enlargement (Melchior, 1999). Purposeful opportunism – the search for institutional gain and expansion – could thus be the nemesis as well as the creator of Union citizenship.

It remains possible, however, that a more favourable moment may arise or be engineered.[11] Looking behind the scenes of the IGC negotiation, we see actors in the Union institutions, member governments and the Reflection Group who wanted to go further on citizenship than provided for in the eventual Treaty outcome. The ToA is a holding document in which almost all the major considerations of reform and policy are postponed. Launching – and qualifying for – the single currency stalked the IGC like the ghost of Deepening Future. Deepening Present was helpless in the face of massive political change in France, Britain and Germany towards the end of the IGC process (Devuyst, 1998). The post-Maastricht legitimacy crisis proved that Deepening Past was highly controversial. Heads of state/government thus chose expediency over radicalism, failing to follow the recommendations of the very Reflection Group composed largely of their own ministers (ECAS, 1997).

Amsterdam instead marked a return from citizenship proper to 'people issues' – those supposed to resonate with the concerns of the various national publics, such as freedom of movement, the environment, and health (Duff, 1997).[12] The Schengen Accords were communitarized, facilitating freedom of movement. Issues such as the environment, public health and job creation were given a higher profile and, in some cases, further 'European' competence was conceded. Freedom of information was somewhat increased, as was transparency, and the expansion of EP powers of codecision into many areas of 'citizen interest', such as freedom of movement, was far more than symbolic although unanimity often remains in the Council. There is a new European Voluntary Service, although it is weaker than the initially envisaged peace corps. The shift of visa, immigration and asylum policy from the third to the first pillar was significant, as was the admittedly rhetorical commitment to making the Union an area of 'freedom, security and justice'. Some 'people issues', such as the new Treaty Article 13 on anti-discrimination, were rescued from rejection by an *ad hoc* coalition of member governments, Commission officials, MEPs and nongovernmental organizations (NGOs) (Shaw, 1997b). Despite the Treaty's ambiguity and lack of ambition, the NGO community counts itself reasonably pleased with the IGC outcome, citing as significant gains the incorporation of the Social Chapter into the Treaty, the expansion of codecision to all areas of social policy previously subject to the cooperation procedure, and the provision of a new legal basis for anti-poverty action (ECAS, 1997).

Nonetheless it is true that such a shift from justiciable Treaty provisions to secondary legislation often ultimately decided by member governments does little to reinforce even the utilitarian appeal and worth of Union citizenship (Magnette, 1998a). No attempt was made to resolve the tension between market-making and democracy in the elaboration of Union citizenship; consequently, the Treaty remains problematic. However, examining documents produced by the Reflection Group and the main EU institutions involved indicates that this was not inevitable. Purposeful opportunists sought, to some degree, to advance the cause of EU citizenship during the 1996 IGC. The less than radical Treaty outcome indicates a lost battle rather than an abandoned struggle. This becomes clear through an analysis of the IGC agendas of the key actors.

The Reflection Group[13]

Assembled to prepare the negotiations of the actual IGC, the Reflection Group was composed of national government representatives as well as, in far smaller numbers, those of the EP and Commission. It made 'The Citizen and the Union' the second section of its four-part 'annotated agenda' for the IGC. This document emphasized that citizens' concerns should be the primary reference point for institutional reform, developing a dual strategy for bringing the citizen to the centre of EU affairs: first, giving centrality to fundamental rights and clarifying the rights and duties of EU citizens and third-country nationals; second, increasing EU competence in matters of concern to the citizen, e.g. employment. The majority of its members felt that the Union should have legal personality and adhere to the ECHR (Reflection Group on the 1996 IGC, 1995). Subsidiarity was presented as a problem, in that no unanimity could be reached that the EC/U rather than the member states should have a Bill of Rights. Nonetheless, the majority of members of the group considered that 'citizenship of the Union [is] an essential aspect of making the Treaty acceptable to public opinion'

(Reflection Group, 1995, p. 47) and should therefore be developed. Explicit advice was given that citizenship rights should be deepened, and existing rights (e.g. freedom of movement) realized. A 'sizeable majority' of the group was in favour of creating a peace corps (p. 47). Other issues such as transparency and boosting EU powers in environment policy were recommended as priority areas for the IGC (pp. 53–4). Despite the existence of minority objections, the overall view of the Reflection Group was thus favourable to the expansion of both citizenship and Union competence in 'people issues'.

The European Commission

The Commission also afforded top priority to building a 'People's Europe' in the Opinion it submitted to the IGC (CEC, 1997a). Linking Union citizenship to the elusive 'European Social Model', it considered that the primary objectives of the IGC were to guarantee fundamental rights; increase solidarity; secure freedom of movement and establishment; and improve the intelligibility of Union decision-making structures (CEC, 1997a, p. 21). It supported an increase in the Union's commitment to human rights and anti-discrimination measures, as well as the expansion of social policy. Citizens should be granted a right to a healthy environment (p. 23), and the third pillar should be comprehensively communitarized. Member governments should move towards a 'common strategy for employment' (p. 23). National parliaments should become more actively involved with scrutiny of EU decision-making, and both the Treaty and the decision-making procedures should be simplified. The Commission thus also favoured primary and secondary legislative improvements to Union citizenship, despite an emphasis on the latter.[14]

The EP

The EP, perhaps unsurprisingly, set great store by an 'improved definition of European citizenship and enhanced respect for human rights' (EP, 1997a, p. 43). In fact, it stated that this is the 'key priority' for the Union's future. The Union must extend the scope of EC/U rights, strengthen its position on fundamental rights, enhance its provisions on non-discrimination and consolidate all citizenship provisions in one, high-profile part of the Treaty. Access to the ECJ for all individuals alleging violation of their fundamental rights by EU bodies must be guaranteed (EP, 1997b). The Union must accede to the ECHR. More attention must be paid to the cultural dimension of integration, and solidarity/exchange programmes increased. The second EP key priority was improving internal security (anti-crime activity and judicial/police cooperation). The third was an expansion of EU social, environmental and employment policies. Economic and social cohesion should be a 'fundamental goal of the Union' (EP, 1997a, p. 43). Transparency and simplification of the Treaties were advocated, as was an increase in the EP's own powers. Citizens' political rights should be improved by the long-awaited creation of a single electoral system for voting in EP elections, and also by aiding the formation of truly European political parties. Representatives of the citizen – MPs and MEPs – should be more involved with the IGC process. The third pillar must be communitarized. The EP thus made some far-reaching, if self-advancing, proposals for the development of EU citizenship, with a fairly equal balance between the Treaty, secondary legislation and governance-style matters.

The European Council

The initial stance of the Council was relatively fluid (Italian Presidency, 1997). Respect for fundamental rights and freedoms was acknowledged as the bedrock of Union membership. There was agreement that the provision for further development of EU citizenship (Maastricht Article 8e) should be retained. However, a majority of Council members (i.e. heads of state/ government) were already opposed to radical changes such as individual access to the ECJ, and matters such as the non-discrimination clause or Union adherence to the ECHR were not capable of early decision. Difficulties in developing a list of citizens' rights would result, thanks to the existence of different national traditions and perspectives. Discussion about extension of EU rights centred on the likely economic costs. The importance of improving transparency was accepted, but there was no agreement to make it a legal obligation or to extend transparency to the whole EU as opposed to the first pillar. Access to information was treated similarly. There was agreement on a partial shift of competences from pillar III to pillar I, but none on the adoption of a single procedure for elections to the EP. This position was slightly modified during the negotiation process, but under the Irish Presidency (Irish Presidency, 1997), agreement was reached to keep citizenship matters separate from the new area of 'freedom, security and justice'. Presidency documents clearly treat the two as separate categories. Citizenship matters were to be treated through the mechanism of meeting citizens' presumed concerns, such as employment and environment policy, subsidiarity and transparency, a stance which subsequently remained unchanged (Dutch Presidency, 1998). The European Council thus developed a gradually hardening stance towards citizenship; as negotiations continued and ambitions reduced, no national government policy entrepreneur emerged to champion the cause of citizenship proper, and the result was Treaty commitment further to Europeanize certain people issues, as detailed above.

Summary

The treatment of citizenship at Amsterdam was thus deceptively complex. All involved parties made proposals which would have added to its development, both formally and more broadly construed. Of course, it is possible to argue that when this became clear, member governments simply drew a line in the sand: witness the difference between the Treaty and the recommendations of the Reflection Group. However, as demonstrated by Bauböck *et al.* (1999: 14–16), the IGC negotiations revealed seven major elements of an attempt by all the institutions to flesh out the rhetoric about bringing Europe 'closer to the citizen', of which developing 'citizenship' was only one.[15] Support for the several elements varied across institutions – for instance, the EP and Commission gave greater priority to transparency than the member states. Further, and importantly, member governments concentrated on social cohesion at the national level, whereas the EP and Commission emphasized community-building at the EU level (Bauböck *et al.*, 1999). Nonetheless a certain commonality of agendas was discernible, and it is clear that at least some of the actors involved with the IGC (and thus at least some of those with an agenda-setting capacity) remained committed to Union citizenship's further development.

Be that as it may, it is equally clear that such a process will not be either easy or automatic. *Agenda 2000*, the document produced by the Commission to guide reform after the shortcomings of the ToA, fails to mention Union citizenship in its first volume, 'For a Stronger and Wider Union'. Social cohesion and inclusion are, however, addressed, but no concrete proposals for their improvement are made. Citizenship is not mentioned as one of the political criteria for evaluation of applicant countries' suitability to join the Union, but 'how democracy works in practice' within their borders is (CEC, 1997b, p. 42). Volume II makes no analysis of the impact of enlargement on EU citizenship *per se*. Instead, there is sectoral analysis of impact by policy area. Citizenship is thus conceived as an amalgam of 'people policies' rather than a codified batch of rights and duties or as a process of actual engagement by individuals with Union governance. As a result, the traditional EU manner of approaching a difficult issue – crablike – is once again employed.

V. AFTER AMSTERDAM: THE CONTINUING STRUGGLE OVER EUROPEAN CITIZENSHIP

After Amsterdam there thus remain significant impediments to the further evolution of EU citizenship. Paul Magnette (1999) argues forcefully that the potential of EU citizenship is so great that most member governments are determined to truncate it. Since they consider citizenship and democracy in statist terms, member governments are very wary of allowing citizenship great leaps forward; in their zero-sum view, EU citizenship's gain must be their loss.[16] It is thus no surprise that certain of the ToA's few reforms may serve to limit the development of even citizen rights, let alone formal citizenship. For instance, by obliging proposals for consumer policy to show their links with the SEM, member governments may be ready to use the subsidiarity argument as a means of blocking opportunism (ECAS, 1997). In the absence of significant further democratization of the Union, it remains valid to question whether EU citizenship can help bridge the democratic deficit or whether the latter will severely constrain its evolution. Present indications about the Charter of Fundamental Rights imply that the latter must be a possibility. The forthcoming enlargement of the Union will pose significant challenges to EU citizenship, given the diversity in political culture of the likely new member states from the former Soviet bloc and culturally Islamic Turkey.

Nonetheless institutional and individual practice since the ToA lends some credibility to a more sanguine outlook. To list a few examples: the Commission has taken Belgium to the ECJ for non-transposition of local election rights for EU citizens other than Belgian nationals (Corbett, 1998); the EP has supported the Ombudsman in his call for more powers (*European Voice*, 15–21/4/99); the Ombudsman has been successful in improving public access to Council documentation, even in the third pillar (*European Voice*, 28/1/99–3/2/99); and the new committee structure of the EP places citizens' rights alongside civil liberties rather than legal affairs, thereby increasing coherence and enhancing the likely expertise pool in Rue Wiertz. Moreover, against its current trend, the ECJ's ruling in *Martinez Sala* (1996) appears to imply that a large part of national sovereignty in welfare matters is now under the scope of EC law since priority must be given to ensuring non-discrimination for all EU citizens (Fries and Shaw, 1998). In addition, reforms to the IGC process itself – Amsterdam was the first Treaty to result from negotiations in which the Commission and the EP were involved, and around which NGOs mobilized in great numbers – mean that 'EU constitutional negotiations provide an arena for informal actors to shape outcomes' (Closa, 1998: 390). In future, member states' collective grip on the outcome of IGCs will be ever so slightly less secure. Moreover, the method chosen to draw up the EU Fundamental Charter on Human Rights is at least interesting; national and European parliamentarians worked together with Commission and Council representatives as well as NGOs and even (on the sidelines) actors from the applicant countries. It is possible that such an inclusive approach may set a precedent for a new style of deliberative culture, albeit at an élite level, although certainly this cannot be assumed as a given.

In terms of 'people policies', certain institutional actors' judgements remain positive. Transparency matters have been prioritized by the recent UK and Finnish presidencies. MEPs consider that they have a responsibility to develop EU citizenship, in the first instance by consumerizing the SEM, but also by seeking to represent citizens' interests as a matter of routine.[17] Commission officials remain aware of the importance of developing 'European' citizenship, and are favourable to this.[18] President Prodi has made many speeches along these lines. Council officials can be similarly well-disposed.[19] The Economic and Social Committee is seeking to convert itself into a forum for civil society rather than predominantly for the social partners (*European Voice*, 22–28/10/98).[20] Consultants have noticed an increasing ability to use citizen rights as lobbying arguments, and expect this development to deepen over the coming years as the EU makes greater inroads into areas like consumer policy.[21]

Of course, none of this amounts to, or is a substitute for, formal reform of the Treaty. It merely serves to indicate that pressure for reform continues, and that reliance upon secondary legislation to make changes may not be the only possible means of change – even if it is likely to be the primary one over the next few years. Shifts towards a more participatory culture, at least in terms of civil society/public and private sector local élites, have also sprung up thanks to the partnership principle in cohesion policy (Scott, 1998), and both NGOs and citizens' groups continue to mobilize. Indeed, as the Europolity develops, a multi-level form of citizenship practice is emerging, in which individuals and their nongovernmental representatives do play a role in shaping legislation (Warleigh, 2000). 'European' citizenship, created both to make the single market work and to help ease the democratic deficit, remains both schizophrenic in character and incomplete in primary (Treaty) and secondary (legislative-participatory) terms. Thanks to the agency of an increasing number of both institutional and nongovernmental purposeful opportunists, however, it is slowly evolving in ways which mean citizenship as an experienced practice may in some respects outpace citizenship as a Treaty entitlement. Citizenship is part of the political development of the EU. As such, it is likely to evolve in the classic Union fashion: gradually and elliptically, with gaps and inconsistencies, as opportunities, agents and sponsors can be found. In that fascinating struggle, 'European' citizenship will move beyond its formally frozen condition, but in a direction and to an extent that it would be foolhardy to predict.

NOTES

1. I refer to EU citizenship, Union citizenship etc. as synonyms for the sake of variety. 'European' citizenship is adorned on its first appearance with quotation marks to signal the fact it is not pan-continental in scope. Indeed, as EU enlargement negotiations with the former Soviet bloc countries on freedom of movement continue, it appears that EU citizenship may become a two-tier status.
2. These are summed up by Helen Wallace (1996: 28) as the ability to 'mobilize and manipulate policy-building resources in order to sustain policy change and policy replacement'.
3. I do not here attempt to develop 'purposeful opportunism' as a theory of EU decision-making; I merely suggest that it constitutes a useful lens through which to develop an understanding of the development of EU citizenship. Scope for useful study of the term remains plentiful – for example, how 'opportunistic' can any actor be and remain purposeful? – but such enquiries are not appropriate here.
4. Wiener (1998: 7) defines citizenship practice as both 'political rights of participation and representation' and 'an identity-based link between citizen and polity/community', i.e. a phenomenon which is not simply formal and which builds, through participation, a sense of belonging. This is a useful concept for understanding EU citizenship because it focuses on its developmental and elusive character. It also stresses the role of engagement in building EU citizenship; Wiener recommends an active citizenship which will generate both a sense of loyalty and a sense of belonging to and in the new European space through a sense of 'ownership' and stakeholding.
5. Primary legislation consists in the Treaties, periodically reviewed by the member governments. Secondary legislation is that made on a daily basis by the Union institutions (Parliament, Commission, Council, and, via its rulings, the Court of Justice) in order to meet the goals set out in the Treaty. Such legislation is what actually comprises EU policy.
6. However, Magnette (1998b) argues that the EP had no clear view of Eurocitizenship, particularly on the issue of the rights of third-country nationals.
7. The following paragraphs draw on Warleigh (1998: 120–9).
8. The right to petition the EP and access to the Ombudsman are available to all legal persons in EU (member-state) territory.

9. The TEU separated the Union's remit into three 'pillars': pillar I, the European Community, comprises all matters included in the body of European legislation up to that point; pillar II is the Common Foreign and Security Policy (CFSP); pillar III was another new area, Justice and Home Affairs, now renamed Police and Judicial Cooperation in Criminal Matters by the Amsterdam Treaty. The purpose of the pillar structure was to expand the EU remit whilst retaining member-state control over the new policy areas – decision-making in pillars II and III is far more intergovernmental than in pillar I, in which the Commission, EP and ECJ play a very important role.

10. The view that citizenship rights can be invoked against one's 'own' member state is not universally agreed, however – see below.

11. I argue elsewhere that although 'democratic' reforms can be expected in the first decade of the new millennium, formally EU citizenship will probably remain much as it is. Reform will instead centre on institutional issues, such as the powers of the Ombudsman and Committee of the Regions, and on policy styles, which will be altered to allow further engagement with EU policy-making by citizens and citizens groups (Warleigh, 2001a, forthcoming).

12. It is worth noting here that member governments appear so far to have been almost totally incorrect in their assumptions of which policies will make the EU popular (Blondel *et al.*, 1998: 66–7).

13. I draw here on Reflection Group (1995).

14. Melchior (1999) writes that the Commission had a clear agenda for the IGC, seeking the full communitarization of pillars II and III, and stressing democratization and transparency rather than an expansion of EU competence *per se*.

15. The list is as follows: provision of a statement of common values and principles; securing access to public services and cultural practices; improving EU efficiency and effectiveness; developing popular EU policies; strengthening the rule of law; transparency; and European citizenship.

16. See Warleigh (2001a, forthcoming) for a more thorough exploration of this argument, with reference to flexible integration and non-liberal forms of democracy.

17. Interview with PES MEP, 27/1/99; interview with PES MEP, 18/2/99; interview with Green MEP, 26/1/99; interview with PPE MEP, 25/1/99.

18. Interview with Commission official, 20/1/99; interview with Commission official, 22/1/99; interview with Commission Director General (identity of DG withheld to preserve anonymity), 26/1/99.

19. Interview with Council General Secretariat official, 25/2/99.

20. See Warleigh (2001b, forthcoming) for a discussion of this issue.
21. Interview with professional consultants, 22/1/99.

CASES

Case C–85/96, *Martinez Sala v. Freistaat Bayern.*

REFERENCES

Bauböck, R., Cowen, M., Landsteiner, G., Melchior, J. and Shenton, B. (1999) 'Introduction', in R. Bauböck *et al., Zu Einer Europäischen Union der Bürger* (Vienna: Institute for Advanced Studies).

Bellamy, R. and Warleigh, A. (1998) 'From an Ethics of Integration to an Ethics of Participation: Citizenship and the Future of the European Union', *Millennium* 27: 3, pp. 447–70.

Blondel, J., Svensson, S. and Sinnot, R. (1998) *People and Parliament in the European Union: Participation, Democracy and Legitimacy* (Oxford: Clarendon).

Bulmer, S. (1993) 'The Governance of the EU: A New Institutionalist Approach', *Journal of Public Policy* 13: 4, pp. 351–80.

Bulmer, S. (1998) 'New Institutionalism and the Governance of the Single European Market', *Journal of European Public Policy* 5: 3, pp. 365–86.

CEC (1997a) 'Opinion to the 1996 IGC: Reinforcing Political Union and Preparing for Enlargement', reprinted in Italian Presidency (1997).

CEC (1997b) *Agenda 2000* (COM (97) 2000 final).

Church, C. (2000) 'Afterword', in A. Warleigh and D. Howarth (eds), *State of the Art: Theoretical Approaches to the EU In the Post-Amsterdam Era* (special issue of *Current Politics and Economics of Europe* 9: 2).

Closa, C. (1992) 'The Concept of Citizenship in the Treaty on European Union', *Common Market Law Review* 29, pp. 1139–69.

Closa, C. (1998) 'International Limits to National Claims in EU Constitutional Negotiations: The Spanish Government and The Asylum Right for EU Citizens', *International Negotiation* 3, pp. 389–411.

Corbett, R. (1994) 'Representing the People', in A. Duff *et al.* (eds), *Maastricht and Beyond: Building the Union* (London: Routledge).

Corbett, R. (1998) 'Governance and Institutions', in G. Edwards and G. Wiessala (eds), *The European Union 1997: Annual Review of Activities* (supplement to *Journal of Common Market Studies* 36: 3).

Cram, L. (1997) *Policy Making in the European Union – Conceptual Lenses and the Integration Process* (London: Routledge).

D'Oliveira, H. (1994) 'European Citizenship – Its Meaning, Its Potential', in R. Dehousse (ed.), *Europe After Maastricht: An Ever Closer Union?* (Munich: Beck).

Devuyst, Y. (1998) 'Treaty Reform in the European Union: The Amsterdam Process', *Journal of European Public Policy* 5: 4, pp. 615–31.

Duff, A. (1997) *The Treaty of Amsterdam* (London: Federal Trust/Sweet & Maxwell).

Dutch Presidency (1998) *Intergovernmental Conference on the Revision of the Treaties: Collected Texts* (Luxembourg: Office for Official Publications of the European Communities).

ECAS (1997) *The Treaty of Ambiguity* (Brussels: ECAS, Circular 23/97).

EP (1997a) 'Resolution Embodying (i) Parliament's Opinion on the Convening of the Intergovernmental Conference, and (ii) An Evaluation of the Work of the Reflection Group and a Definition of the Political Priorities of the European Parliament with a View to the Intergovernmental Conference' (in Italian Presidency (1997)).

EP (1997b) *EP Taskforce on the IGC Note to the President and Secretary General on the European Parliament's Priorities for the IGC and the New Amsterdam Treaty: Report and Initial Evaluation of Results* (DOC_EN\DV\332\332457).

Everson, M. (1995) 'The Legacy of the Market Citizen', in J. Shaw and G. More (eds), *New Legal Dynamics of European Union* (Oxford: Clarendon).

Everson, M. and Preuss, U. (1995) *Concepts, Foundation and Limits of European Citizenship* (Bremen; Zentrum fur Europäische Rechtspolitik).

Fries, S. and Shaw, J. (1998) 'Citizenship of the Union – First Steps in the Court of Justice', *European Public Law* 4, pp. 533–59.

Gamberale, C. (1995) 'National Identities and Citizenship in the European Union', *European Public Law* 1: 4, pp. 629–57.

Guild, E. (1996) 'The Legal Framework of Citizenship of the European Union', in D. Cesarini and M. Fulbrook (eds), *Citizenship, Migration and Nationality in Europe* (London: Routledge).

Hyland, N., Loftus, C. and Whelan, A. (1995) *Citizenship of the European Union* (Dublin: Institute for European Affairs).

Irish Presidency (1997) *Intergovernmental Conference on the Revision of the Treaties: Collected Texts* (Luxembourg: Office for Official Publications of the European Communities).

Italian Presidency (1997) 'Presidency Report to the European Council on the Progress of the Conference (First Phase of the IGC)' (in *Italian Presidency: Intergovernmental Conference on Revising the Treaties: Collected Texts* (Luxembourg: Office of Official Publications of the European Communities)).

La Torre, M. (1995) 'Citizenship – A European Wager', *Ratio Juris* 8: 1, pp. 113–23.

Laffan, B. (1996) 'The Politics of Identity and Political Order in Europe', *Journal of Common Market Studies* 34: 1, pp. 81–102.

Leibfried, S. and Pierson, P. (1996) 'Social Policy', in H. Wallace and W. Wallace (eds), *Policy-making in the European Union* (Oxford: Oxford University Press).

Magnette, P. (1998a) 'European Citizenship from Maastricht to Amsterdam – The Narrow Path of Legitimation', *Journal of European Integration* 21: 1, pp. 37–69.

Magnette, P. (1998b) 'Citoyenneté et Construction Européenne' (unpublished PhD dissertation, Université Libre de Bruxelles).

Magnette, P. (1999) *La Citoyenneté Européenne: Droits, Politiques, Institutions* (Brussels: Editions de l'Université de Bruxelles).

March, J. and Olsen, J. (1984) 'The New Institutionalism: Organizational Factors in Political Life', *American Political Science Review* 78, pp. 734–49.

Marias, E. (1994a) 'From Market Citizen to Union Citizen', in E. Marias (ed.), *European Citizenship* (Maastricht: European Institute of Public Administration).

Marias, E. (1994b) 'Le Droit de Pétition Devant le Parlement Européen', in E. Marias (ed.), *European Citizenship* (Maastricht: European Institute of Public Administration).

Martiniello, M. (1994) 'Citizenship of the European Union – A Critical View', in R. Bauböck (ed.), *From Aliens to Citizens: Redefining the Status of Immigrants in Europe* (Aldershot: Avebury).

Melchior, J. (1999) 'Bringing the Citizen Back In: The Case of the 1996 IGC', in R. Bauböck *et al.*, *Zu Einer Europäischen Union der Bürger* (Vienna: Institute for Advanced Studies).

Neunreither, K. (1995) 'Citizens and the Exercise of Power in the European Union – Towards a New Social Contract?', in A. Rosas and E. Antola (eds), *A Citizens' Europe: In Search of A New Order* (London: Sage).

Neuwahl, N. (1998) 'The Citizen of Amsterdam' (Paper to UACES Annual Conference, University of Leicester, 5–7 January 1998).

O'Keeffe, D. (1994) 'Union Citizenship', in D. O'Keeffe and P. Twomey (eds), *Legal Issues of the Maastricht Treaty* (London: Chancery).

O'Leary, S. (1996) *The Evolving Concept of Community Citizenship – From the Free Movement of Persons to Union Citizenship* (London: Kluwer).

Peterson, J. (1995) 'Decision Making in the EU: Towards a Framework for Analysis', *Journal of European Public Policy* 2: 1, pp. 69–93.

Pierson, P. (1996) 'The Path to European Integration: A Historical Institutionalist Analysis', *Comparative Political Studies* 29: 2, pp. 123–63.

Pollack, M. (1996) 'The New Institutionalism and EC Governance: The Promise and Limits of Institutional Analysis', *Governance* 9: 4, pp. 429–58.

Reflection Group on the 1996 IGC (1995) *Reflection Group Report and Other References for Documentary Purposes* (Brussels: General Secretariat of the Council of the European Union).

Sbragia, A. (1996) 'Environmental Policy', in H. Wallace and W. Wallace (eds), *Policy-making in the European Union* (Oxford: Oxford University Press).

Scott, J. (1998) 'Law, Legitimacy and EC Governance: Prospects for "Partnership"', *Journal of Common Market Studies* 36: 2, pp. 175–94.

Shaw, J. (1997a) 'The Many Pasts and Futures of Citizenship in the European Union', *European Law Review*, 22: 6, pp. 554–72.

Shaw, J. (1997b) 'European Union Citizenship – The IGC and Beyond', *European Public Law* 3: 3, pp. 413–39.

Shaw, J. (1998) 'The Interpretation of European Union Citizenship', *Modern Law Review* 61: 3, pp. 293–317.

Springer, B. (1996) *The European Union and Its Citizens – The Social Agenda* (London: Greenwood Press).

Taschner, H. (1993) 'The Rights of the European Citizen Under the Maastricht Treaty: Achievements and Open Questions', in J. Monar, W. Ungerer and W. Wessels (eds), *The Maastricht Treaty on European Union* (Brussels: European Interuniversity Press).

Tömmel, I. (1998) 'Transformation of Governance: The European Commission's Strategy for a "Europe of the Regions" ', *Regional and Federal Studies* 8: 2, pp. 52–80.

Wallace, H. (1996) 'Politics and Policy in the EU: The Challenge of Governance', in H. Wallace and W. Wallace (eds), *Policy-making in the European Union* (Oxford: Oxford University Press).

Warleigh, A. (1998) 'Frozen: Citizenship and European Unification', *Critical Review of International Social and Political Philosophy* 1: 4, pp. 113–51.

Warleigh, A. (2000) 'The Hustle: Citizenship Practice, NGOs and "Policy Coalitions" in the European Union – The Cases of Auto Oil, Drinking Water and Unit Pricing', *Journal of European Public Policy* 7: 2, pp. 229–43.

Warleigh, A. (2001a, forthcoming) 'Towards Network Democracy? The Potential of Flexible Integration', in M. Farrell, S. Fella and M. Newman (eds), *European Unity and Diversity: Challenges for the 21st Century* (London: Sage).

Warleigh, A. (2001b, forthcoming) 'The Economic and Social Committee', in A. Warleigh (ed.), *Institutions of the European Union* (London: Routledge).

Weiler, J. H. H. (1996) 'European Citizenship and Human Rights', in J. Winter (ed.), *Reforming the Treaty on European Union: The Legal Debate* (London: Kluwer).

Wiener, A. (1996) 'Rethinking Citizenship: The Quest for Place-oriented Participation in the EU', *Oxford International Review* 7, pp. 44–51.

Wiener, A. (1998) *'European' Citizenship Practice: Building Institutions of a Non-State* (Boulder, Colorado/Oxford: Westview Press).

3

The 'Right to Have Rights': Citizenship Practice and the Political Constitution of the EU

RICHARD BELLAMY

I. INTRODUCTION

EU citizenship is defined and frequently analysed in terms of the entitlements and potential obligations it bestows on beneficiaries of this status (e.g. Lyons, 1996; O'Leary, 1996). So conceived, citizenship becomes an epiphenomenon of how Europe is or might be constituted according to certain analytical typologies or ideal conceptions of capitalism, socialism and democracy. The main controversies surround its restriction to member-state nationals, its relationship to national citizenship, and the various packages of rights and duties that citizens have or might receive under differing visions of Europe as either a pure free market, a form of supranational social market democracy, a new kind of trans-national community and so on. The focus is on enumerating and either extending or limiting access and rights in order to classify or move Europe towards a given socio-economic and political model. Even those who characterize European citizenship as novel tend to see it in terms of the ways globalization, or a global theory of justice, have produced, or could produce, an additional layer of supranational rights and obligations or even herald a cosmopolitan political order (e.g. Soysal, 1994: 159; Linklater, 1998: Ch. 6).

EU citizenship was designed to bring the Union closer to ordinary people and provide it with the popular legitimacy the post-Maastricht debates confirmed it sorely lacked. However, citizenship consists of more than passive acceptance of a pre-constituted package of rights. As Joseph Weiler has pointedly remarked, 'you could create rights and afford judicial remedies to slaves' (Weiler, 1999: 336). What these accounts overlook is the independent role citizenship plays in the very constitution of a polity through citizens formulating, deliberating upon, and disputing different views of justice and rights. This alternative view conceives citizenship as 'the right to have rights' rather than as a given set of rights.[1] The need for such a conception has been masked by the increasingly juridified view of politics that typifies postwar understandings of constitutionalism. These accounts maintain legitimacy is secured through the principles under-pinning the polity satisfying certain universal norms of public reason and basic human interests (e.g. Rawls, 1993; Dworkin, 1995). Yet if these norms and interests underdetermine the available principles and their practical implications whilst being themselves matters of reasonable disagreement, then the associated criteria will be within rather than establishing the framework for politics. Such circumstances call for a more political conception of constitutionalism, whereby citizens negotiate the mutual acceptability of their collective arrangements (Bellamy, 1999; Waldron, 1999).

This chapter will argue the contested character of the EU renders such an active form of citizenship and a corresponding political approach to constitutionalism crucial to its legitimacy. My analysis and proposals draw on recent studies of citizenship practice and constitutionalism by a number of EU scholars (notably Curtin, 1997; Shaw, 1998, 1999; Wiener, 1998; Weiler, 1999) as well as related work on these general themes by normative political theorists such as James Tully (1995, 1999) and Herman van Gunsteren (1998), and certain political sociologists (Turner, 1990; Foweraker and Landman, 1997). However, I add to and occasionally depart from these accounts by positioning such constitutive citizenship activity within a distinctively neo-republican view of politics and a related analysis of the nature of citizenship struggles and their contribution to constitutional dialogues.[2] As the historical source of political constitu-tionalism (Bellamy, 1996), the republican approach treats the agonic politics of citizens as expressions and components of a condition of civic freedom (Pettit, 1999; Bellamy, 1999: Ch 5). As we shall see, to be free from domination, a self-governing society must embody norms of fairness and equality every bit as compelling as those desired by advocates of rights- and justice-based constitutional settlements. But these are both features and products of, rather than constraints upon, the political process.

I advance to this conclusion as follows. Section II explores the constitutive function of citizenship. Struggles for citizenship and between citizens are shown to entail redefinitions of the subjects, spheres, scopes and styles of politics that lead to a continuous reconstitution of the polity and hence of the rights of its citizens. Indeed, the EU partly manifests and promotes these very debates amongst and within the member states. Section III investigates the norms generated by these practical exercises of citizenship and their relationship to the standard packages of citizen rights. The latter are shown to require the former in order to resolve the conflicts between and within them. Meanwhile, the struggles over citizenship find their constitutional rationale within a neo-republican view of politics.

Section IV then suggests how this neo-republican approach might be applied to the EU. Its advantage lies in enabling the EU to retain its unique character as an evolving union of diverse parts without falling prey to the incoherences feared by those who advocate a more uniform system.

II. THE CONSTITUTIVE ROLE OF CITIZENSHIP

Historically, the processes of state-making, constitutionalism and the development of citizenship have gone hand in hand, reflecting not only external pressures, notably war, but also internal political struggles amongst citizens themselves. Most normative citizenship theorists and many legal and political scientists have discounted these factors. They have either seen them as a matter for historians and political sociologists or fallen back on an implicit teleology derived from a Whiggish reading of Marshall (1950), whereby an expanding set of citizenship rights forms part of the natural evolution of modern democratic societies. Their focus has been on various ideal models or typologies of just, democratic societies (e.g. Held, 1989: Ch. 7; Janoski, 1998). However, liberal democracies are far from converging on a single model, though many of their procedures and norms share certain affinities. At least part of this diversity is to be attributed to the various ways struggles between citizens have played out. Though these struggles have been geared towards securing justice for those involved, only a Panglossian optimist would regard them as moving towards a consensus on justice. Rather, they have been debates about justice – debates, to be sure, that might well assume that an objective and ideal account ultimately exists, but which arise because citizens disagree over what that account might be and have no common basis for determining whose version is right.

It is sometimes alleged that such disagreements result solely from the presence of injustice, the product of self-interest, ignorance or bad faith by one or more groups within the polity. Wittingly or unwittingly this is often the case. However, disagreement also arises because human beings value a variety of goods which different people prioritize and order in divergent and occasionally incompatible ways. This perspectival diversity stems not just from their different experiences, backgrounds and social positions, but also from the ways the sheer complexity of many political issues renders the relevance of different facts and considerations dependent upon rather than independent of the views of the discussants. Many contemporary rights- or justice-based constitutional theorists acknowledge the 'fact of pluralism' yet seek to circumvent it. Thus, John Rawls accepts the significance of what he calls 'the burdens of judgement' when seeking to adjudicate between different comprehensive conceptions of the good (Rawls, 1993: 56–7), but argues that they should lead to a consensus on common principles of political justice that limit what we may legitimately propose or impose on others in the name of our inevitably contentious beliefs (Rawls, 1993: 36–8). Unfortunately, for reasons explored more fully in the next section (see too Bellamy, 1999: Ch. 2), the right proves as controversial as various views of the good, as debates over abortion, affirmative action, the death penalty, taxation and welfare amply demonstrate.

If no collective agreement was ever necessary and we could each simply go our own way, such disagreements would be like academic quarrels about these same matters: challenging, provocative, diverting and occasionally frustrating but not an issue of life and death. However, what Rawls (1971: 126–30) (following Hume) calls the 'circumstances of justice' – namely, the conditions of moderate scarcity, limited altruism and unavoidable social coexistence – mean that some common rules are necessary. The benefits from collective action within a shared framework range from the security of the person and property to environmental protection and public health. The difficulty is that we disagree about the character of the framework, what should be pursued under it and even the best way to implement those policies we do agree to. Jeremy Waldron has coined the term 'the circumstances of politics' to describe the resulting condition of having to reach agreement in the face of such disagreements (Waldron, 1999: 102). The upshot of this predicament is that citizens search not for a just consensus but for a politics that shows equal respect for their different views in the ways common decisions get deliberated and decided. Waldron believes majoritarian voting satisfies this goal because of its procedural fairness (Waldron, 1999: 107–18). But he takes as given that all relevant views are adequately represented and that we can agree on forms of respect without invoking controversial views of justice. By contrast, I shall argue that disagreements about the nature of justice inevitably spill over into debates concerning who is recognized as respectworthy and how their beliefs are represented. Disagreement enters into the form of politics, therefore, producing an ongoing political constitutionalism whereby a polity is continually reconstituted more appropriately to recognize, respect and represent the opinions of its members. Herein lies the constitutive role of citizenship.

We can analyse this phenomenon via the ways political recognition, respect and representation get mediated through four intersecting dimensions of the polity: namely, the sphere, subjects, scope and styles of politics. The *sphere* of politics refers to where politics takes place. These borders involve not only the external frontiers of the polity but also its internal administrative divisions. These tend to be both territorially and functionally defined, with different functions usually mapping on to different territorial units and occasionally cutting across them. They are also frequently subdivided into more localized units that implement and inform central decisions. There are also demarcations between the political and non-political areas of life, as in attempts to distinguish a public from a private sphere. The *subjects* of politics concern the definitions of rulers and ruled, or who decides for and over whom. Even in a democracy, where the designated demos are potentially both governors and governed, the criteria for voting can be different to those for standing for election. Meanwhile, no polity identifies citizens simply with those physically present within a relevant sphere. Citizenship is standardly associated with certain capacities and commitments that only a subset of these will possess. The *scope* of politics has to do with its aims and the claims it makes upon people within its designated spheres. Different areas of political life may warrant a greater or lesser degree of intervention and be more or less demanding than others. A politics aimed at ensuring non-interference and forbearance will have a very different character and impact to one demanding positive action. Finally, the *styles* of politics relate to the ways politics is undertaken as a result of the various types of formal and informal consultation and influence that the political system allows. These may range from voting as determined by the electoral system, through membership of political parties, unions and various lobbying organizations, to consultative meetings, letter-writing campaigns, demonstrations, direct action and even – in extreme circumstances – terrorism and civil war.

These four dimensions of politics are clearly related, with the character of each influencing that of the others. Thus, the boundaries marking the sphere of politics will partly, though not entirely, determine its subjects, scope and styles by creating certain constituencies and designating which areas are political or not. Recognizing a region as a legitimate sphere of politics by granting it a degree of political autonomy may be tied implicitly or explicitly to recognition of a national minority as a subject of politics. Giving national minorities a degree of self-government, however, will also lead to acceptance that the claims of language or culture fall within the scope of politics, and that new styles of politics may be necessary to allow certain minority groups to participate according to their particular linguistic and cultural traditions. Similarly, if the scope of politics consists simply of upholding negative rights then its legitimate sphere, subjects and styles will differ from a view that includes positive rights. For example, it is more likely that the economy will be treated as a largely private sphere, employees not recognized as political subjects, and certain styles of consultation, such as workplace democracy, deemed inappropriate. When citizens struggle to be recognized as political subjects, therefore, they are not simply demanding access to a pre-constituted set of political rights, for that recognition will invariably have profound consequences for the other dimensions of politics and hence for the very constitution of the political. Moreover, struggles between citizens over any of the other dimensions, such as the appropriate scope of politics, will equally have constitutional consequences for how we conceive its sphere, subjects and styles.

Because political disagreements invariably turn on the definition of one or more of these dimensions, citizenship has performed a pivotal constitutive part in the transformation and re-formation of political communities across all four of these dimensions. In the nineteenth century, for example, nationalist movements played a significant role in defining the sphere of politics as the nation-state. Frequently tied to revolutionary and democratic movements, these struggles for national self-determination also served to make 'the people' the subject of politics and in the process altered both its scope and forms as well. Similarly, later struggles to extend the franchise to women and workers have not only expanded the subjects of politics but, as we noted above, inevitably changed its sphere, scope and styles as well. Though the United States constitution is sometimes treated as the archetypal rights-based document, establishing the republic on 'self-evident' just constitutional principles, its true foundations lie in 'we the people'. As Bruce Ackerman (1991) has shown, citizens have transformed it through successive waves of constitutional politics, from the extreme case of civil war, through the depression years that gave rise to the New Deal, to the civil rights movement of the 1960s. In all these cases, citizens have been struggling to construct a framework within which their concerns will be recognized and respected. Yet that has not been simply a matter of getting noticed under the established rules but, as we have seen, has inevitably meant challenging those rules as well.

Three features of these constitutive citizenship struggles need emphasizing. First, some commentators grant that such constitutional moments occasionally arise but like Ackerman regard them as exceptional, with 'normal' politics occurring within the framework set by the last constitutional struggle (Ackerman, 1991: 3–33). To some degree that is inevitably true. Revolutions are rare and even then attempts to start totally anew prove impossible. The constitutional ship is necessarily rebuilt at sea, with modifications in one area being realized through the established practices in another. Nevertheless, this is a more incremental and everyday process than Ackerman and others allow, with momentous transformations usually the cumulative result of a gradual alteration in public opinion produced by numerous small shifts within debates on a variety of particular issues.

Second, past struggles by workers, women and ethnic minorities (and occasionally majorities) are sometimes contrasted with current struggles over gender and multiculturalism (Fraser, 1997: Ch. 1). The former are typified as struggles for inclusion within the established framework – as demands that the cooperatively produced benefits and burdens of political community be shared more equitably. In sum, they are struggles for a fuller realization of justice. By contrast, the latter are characterized as struggles to be recognized as different and to enjoy an exclusive status. They seek a more diverse rather than a more equal society. Certain critics go so far as to villify them for promoting injustice by seeking to entrench the very inequities and hierarchies that past groups struggled to overturn. The foregoing analysis, however, suggests far greater continuity between the two (see too Tully, 2000). Like contemporary struggles, those of the past involved demands for recognition as well as distribution. They sought not only admission to, but also a reconstitution of, the political community and the forms of justice and equality it inscribes. Thus the enfranchisement of women brought with it an enlargement of the sphere of politics to include the domestic arena, a corresponding extension of the scope of politics to include issues such as sexual harassment and marital rape, and demands for new and less confrontational styles of politics. Like past struggles, those of the present are for a more inclusive and equitable society. However, once again these demands involve reconceptualizing how political goods are produced and distributed. As we saw, the struggles of workers and national minorities entail parallel transformations of the sphere, scope, subjects and styles of politics.

Third, and most importantly, it is impossible to say *a priori* what the 'best' conception of these dimensions and their relations to each other might be. Any criteria we might come up with will not only have to be tailored to varying and highly contingent circumstances in ways that are impossible to specify in advance, but also have to be subject to diverse judgements and interpretations by citizens themselves. Indeed, divergent priorities and values may lead groups to propose different criteria to each other. Meanwhile, as one group alters the ways they are recognized by others, that has knock-on effects both for the ways these others are recognized and how they recognize themselves. Thus, new struggles are spawned as identities, ideals and interests change in response to the new structures, producing in their turn further struggles for new forms of recognition. Consider, for example, how in recent times gains in certain domains by the feminist movement have given rise to 'post-feminist' discourses, on the one hand, and a reappraisal of masculine gender, on the other, fostering a further spate of political dialogue and change. The process of reconstituting the polity is a continuous one.

This section has endeavoured to show how the need to find agreement in circumstances of disagreement produces struggles over how different groups are recognized, respected and represented which are directly related to the ways the polity is constituted. Hence, citizens are not ready constituted by a pre-political or suprapolitical constitution: they seek to constitute themselves and thereby the very shape of politics itself. In the next section I shall describe how these struggles nevertheless involve certain citizenship practices that themselves serve as a form of political constitutionalism. Before doing so, though, we need to touch base and apply the argument so far to the EU.

Few would deny that all four political dimensions of the EU are matters of a greater or lesser degree of contestation. So far as its sphere is concerned, both its territorial extent and range of competences are at best uncertain and at worst matters of deep dispute. Similar doubts and discussions surround the designation of its subjects, both actual and potential. Though European citizenship is currently restricted to nationals of member states, for example, certain entitlements of the Union are enjoyed by resident third-country nationals and other 'legal persons' as well. The scope of the EU is likewise much debated, with some seeing it solely in terms of removing trade barriers whilst others extend this logic to a whole range of common financial, fiscal, welfare, security and other policies. Finally, discussion of the styles of EU politics ranges over such disparate issues as the introduction of qualified majority voting in the Council of Ministers and the establishment of European-wide political parties, to the direct election of the President of the Commission and the opening up of the comitology process to all through more freedom of information.

As we have seen, struggles over some aspect of any one of these domains has often unintended consequences for the others. Thus, a potent source of European integration has been the search by commercial interests for intergovernmental compliance and cooperation in certain policy areas, such as tariff harmonization, where economic interdependence renders such agreements beneficial. However, in the process they have created institutions that have served to alter the sphere, scope and styles of politics of the member states by changing both the context within which they and other subjects now operate, and the character of their domestic arrangements. The development of European citizenship offers a good case in point. Though orientated initially simply towards facilitating the free market of labour amongst member-state nationals, its various provisions provide a source of norms of a non-economic nature that, as Theodora Kostakopoulou and Carl Stychin respectively show in their chapters, can be exploited by other actors such as immigrants and gay and lesbian couples. In these cases, groups use the opportunity to create a supranational political subjectivity in order to circumvent and undercut state-centred definitions. In the process, they offer alternative reasons to mutual economic convenience for constraining certain nationally defined notions of the scope, subjects and styles as well as the sphere of politics.

Struggles within member states now invariably have a European aspect, be they over the recognition of certain subjects, such as regions, or the scope of politics, as arises in areas such as privatization and welfare reform. Moreover, the EU renders political struggles multilayered as well as multidimensional. Though within a polity there are multiple spheres of politics – from the domestic to the state, with individuals and groups possessing a somewhat different subjecthood in each and adopting a correspondingly different style and view of the scope of politics – these spheres are to some degree 'nested' within the larger constitutional order of the polity. Within the EU context, however, one has an interaction between the different constitutional orders of the member states and between each of these and that of the EU. The potential and actual conflicts between these different normative regimes are akin to those between different cultures and pose parallel challenges to those found in multicultural states.

These developments have rendered the constitutional implications of 'normal' politics particularly evident with regard to Europe. The EU now involves not only interest-group bargaining but also the negotiation of different normative perspectives, values and systems. Though analysts may disagree over how far the integration process results from the latter as opposed to the former factors, few (if any) dispute that a political and constitutional debate about the EU now exists within all of the member states. Given the predominant economic rationale of the EU, these debates admittedly centre on issues such as the nature of the economic benefits brought by the Union, whether the EU may be undermining some of these, and the possibility and acceptability of certain trade-offs between economic gains and various losses in other areas. Like most political disagreements, however, the actors' different normative positions lead them to diverge in their evaluation of the pay-offs and risks, and to hold contrasting views of what can and cannot be traded. Even if the motivations for integration remain primarily economic, therefore, the political principles invoked to legitimize them are not and they constrain what can and cannot be done in the name of economic interests alone. Put another way, the games of rational economic interest are overlaid with the language games of normative discourse.

Unlike interest pluralism, value pluralism is harder to conceptualize in ways that allow disputants to 'split the difference' or agree mutually beneficial trade-offs: their positions may be simply incommensurable (Bellamy, 1999: Ch. 4). In the absence of a common currency or agreed exchange rates, apples cannot be traded for pears without first discovering and negotiating links between the different ways the parties conceive them. When one cannot have both and no negotiation has occurred, then confrontation threatens. This experience has been all too common in multicultural and multinational states, such as Canada and Belgium, producing deep constitutional divides (Austin and O'Neill, 2000; Gagnon and Tully, 2001). As we have noted, the EU now shares certain features of such deeply divided societies. However, we have also remarked how these divisions are simply heightened versions of the normative conflicts that animate most political disagreements – the result of their reflecting general and systemic differences between whole forms of life rather than particular moral claims, goods or judgements. We remarked at the start of this section that a standard constitutional solution to the 'fact of pluralism' is to remove certain issues from the political agenda through agreement on the underlying rules of the political game. This approach consists of defining citizenship in terms of a certain agreed set of constitutional rights. The next section explores further the problems with this proposal and presents an alternative view of constitutionalism grounded in citizenship practice.

III. TWO MODELS OF CONSTITUTIONALISM, CITIZENSHIP AND RIGHTS

Constitutionalism can be divided into two broad families: the juridical and the political. Though they share certain elements and have been intertwined historically, they operate different and not entirely compatible logics – not least in the ways they conceptualize the relationship of citizenship to rights. Juridical conceptions of constitutionalism concentrate on the legal mechanisms for controlling the abuse of power and protecting individual rights. Their aim is to secure a just framework within which citizens and the government can legitimately act by constraining what may be matters of political dispute and decision. The constitution defines citizenship and regulates citizens' struggles. To a broad extent, therefore, this view assumes a consensus on the four dimensions of politics (Rawls, 1993 and Dworkin, 1995 both exemplify this position). By contrast, more political conceptions see constitutionalism as the various political practices through which citizens constitute their relations with each other. Instead of aiming at or assuming a just ordering of politics, this approach focuses on the ways citizens continually renegotiate the dimensions of politics in order mutually to determine the rules and institutional processes governing their collective life. This striving for reciprocal recognition guards against groups or individuals being subjected to another's will. A condition of civic freedom rather than a substantive conception of justice provides the primary rationale of politics, for freedom from oppression and domination are best secured through participation in framing the collective arrangements and public goods which provide the context for autonomous choice and development (for different versions of this view see Bellamy, 1999; Pettit, 1999; Sunstein, 1993; Tushnet, 1999; and Tully, 1999).

As noted, the juridical and political conceptions coexist within most constitutional democracies, the historical product of the roles played by the political languages of liberalism and republicanism respectively in the evolution of Western states. Thus, written constitutions standardly specify the components of the political system as well as containing provisions for the juridical protection of rights. If the second aspect prevails over the first, however, the political system will be designed in accord with the official understanding of justice and operate as an imperfect procedure for its realization, thereby justifying the occasional judicial overturning of purportedly unconstitutional political decisions. If the first aspect prevails, though, the legal system will play a more subordinate role. Since arbitrary rule is a prime source of domination, the court's protection of institutionalized rights and the formal properties of the rule of law will remain essential. But the definition of those rights and the guarantees of their fairness derive from the capacity of the political mechanisms and procedures to preserve civic freedom.

These two views of constitutionalism give rise to two different perspectives on citizenship, which I shall explore in turn. Juridical conceptions define citizenship by rights. Table 3.1 outlines three of the main models (for a fuller discussion see Bellamy, 2000: Ch.9). The libertarian and the social democrat models reflect two versions of liberalism and provide the main contemporary rights-based positions. The communitarian model is often aligned to the republican and contrasted to these. However, I shall argue it has more in common with them than the neo-republican account described below. I wish to focus on five features of these models, with the first two remarks directed at the rights-based conceptions alone, the last three at the communitarian as well.

First, the two rights-based conceptions offer not only contrasting but conflicting and incompatible views of rights. Certain accounts of citizenship rights assume one can simply add on new rights to come up with a maximal package that incorporates all legitimate points of view. However, this is not the case. Thus, libertarians claim that the taxation required to support the welfare and social policies desired by social democrats would necessarily conflict with their understanding of market freedoms and the system of property entitlements on which it rests (e.g. Barry, 1990). Social democrats necessarily accept that as true. Consequently, they offer an alternative account of coercion and interference that includes certain structural effects of a free market, such as the creation of discrete pockets of

Richard Bellamy

Table 3.1 Three models of citizenship

	Libertarian	*Social Democrat*	*Communitarian*
Legal Rights (liberties and immunities)	Formally equal negative liberties	Formally equal negative liberties though certain immunities for reasons of substantive equality and linked to social rights to defend their equal worth	Equal though often restricted to exclude other groups
Political Rights (powers)	Protective, limited	Protective and informative, limited	Stress on public service and participation
Social Rights (claims)	Few (mainly insurance and compensatory) or none	Broad range: including enabling and distributive as well as insurance and compensatory	Usually extensive
Civic Rights (powers)	Few (consumer) or none Strict divide between state/civil society, public/private	Workers and consumer Need for state to regulate and balance civil society	Usually workers and consumer (corporatism) State and civil society closely related
Duties	Of respect, with duties subordinate to rights	Of concern and respect, with duties being corollary of rights	Rights being a product of the general duty to uphold and pursue the values of the community

unemployment and the vulnerability of the poor and the uneducated to exploitative contracts (Plant, 1990). Libertarians, though, would deny the social democratic position is an improvement on theirs because it reinterprets aspects of the rights they favour as part of a fuller set of rights. In their view, there is no justification for the additional rights since the social democratic reinterpretation of coercion is mistaken (Barry, 1990).

Second, this problem cannot be circumvented by seeking a more minimalist set of negative liberty rights, such as the standard civil rights, as libertarians sometimes imagine (Barry, 1990; Nozick, 1974). Theoretically, upholding negative liberties imposes no costs on others and creates no clash between such rights. Rights to non-interference simply require we leave others alone. In practice, though, they need to be secured via a police force and the courts. The resulting costs can be as burdensome as welfare provision and may involve as many clashes with other negative rights. An official secrets policy, for example, usually has to be balanced against rights to freedom of expression and privacy. Meanwhile, different interpretative standpoints can lead to divergent views on when, if at all, interference takes place even amongst adherents of the negative position, leading to competing opinions on whether negative rights ever conflict. Such disputes surface when deciding whether an exercise of property rights might produce negative externalities damaging the property rights of others, as when people complain about noisy neighbours or the effects of fishing upstream on the fishing rights of those below. Indeed, similar issues arise with any attempt to designate a certain set of rights as 'basic' or 'absolute'. Thus, to take the strongest case, banning certain punishments as 'degrading', such as torture or the death penalty, potentially might lead to more crimes being committed and thereby produce more rights abuses than they prevent. Implementing such policies, therefore, involves an implicit calculation that fewer, or no more, equally important individual rights will be damaged because of a resulting rise in the number of murders and acts of violence. For example, it is standardly argued that these methods have no greater deterrent effect over other less brutal forms of punishment, that there is a danger of people being wrongly convicted, and so on.

Third, and following on from this last observation, rights cannot be isolated from collective decisions of a utilitarian or communitarian nature. Rights are sometimes claimed to protect the individual from tyrannous majorities by 'trumping' decisions made in the name of the public interest or common good (Dworkin, 1985: 91, 199–200). However, such social considerations are intrinsic to how we define and interpret rights. Indeed, rights are generally valued not because of their worth for particular individuals *per se*, for whom they may be of no interest and burdensome, but because of their contribution to certain collective goods and the more diffuse benefits that result from living in a community where they exist (Raz, 1994: Ch. 3). For example, journalists and politicians apart, few individuals personally make use of freedom of speech. However, all benefit from a society which enjoys this right and the role it plays in protecting against the abuse of power, disseminating information, and so on. These factors come into play when interpreting or resolving conflicts between rights, as in US debates over whether pornography counts as 'speech' or when considering possible limits to freedom of speech in cases such as incitement to racial hatred or the diffusion of state secrets.

Communitarians acknowledge this collective dimension to rights and consequently stress the primacy of upholding community values. But sociological (e.g. Walzer, 1983) and perfectionist (e.g. Raz, 1986) versions of communitarianism overestimate the homogeneity of communities and the degree of agreement on the good life. As a result, they end up downgrading the role of politics in parallel ways to rights-based theories. Thus, the former seek to segregate politics to a bounded political community, the nation-state, where 'language, history and culture come together ... to produce a common consciousness' (Walzer, 1983: 29) while the latter, espouse a form of ethical naturalism that suggests that all values can be ordered within a full vision of how the good society will foster human interests (Raz, 1986: 215). Though communitarians give more weight to political deliberation than rights-based models, both versions hold such deliberation assumes and promotes consensus on the good through explicating shared understandings, thereby abstracting from the very circumstances of dissent that make politics necessary. Indeed, they are apt to treat division as suspect, the product of factions and sinister interests. Where they endorse judicial review, this too is seen as the explication of supposedly common community values.

Fourth, and in this context most importantly, all three of the aforementioned sources of conflicts between rights or interpretations of them are related to disagreements over the four dimensions of politics. As Table 3.2 reveals, each of these models of citizenship assumes a different view of the sphere, appropriate scope, subjects and styles of politics. Yet these are far from settled, with political debate turning on precisely how they should be interpreted.

As we have seen, room for conflict exists even between proponents of the same model. The problem with either rights-based or community-based conceptions of citizenship, therefore, is that they rest on agreement on precisely those issues citizens most disagree about.

Finally, none has adequate political resources to cope with the disagreements that, for the reasons rehearsed above, inevitably arise. As we remarked, communitarians take consensus as the basis, logic and outcome of deliberation. Even if the first two elements held in theory, however, practically decisions often have to be made long before all the parties have managed to agree. Meanwhile, dissent frequently arises precisely because disputants do not share common experiences or a normative framework. Real politics must provide procedures for conciliating conflict in the face of continued disagreement. Rights-based theorists also assume a pre-political consensus, in their case produced by constitutionally trimming the areas of value disagreement from the political agenda. The residue supposedly comprises far more tractable interests that can be traded and modified in mutually beneficial ways. However, we have seen disagreements over the right and the good remain, being intrinsic to most policy decisions. Nonetheless, rights-based theorists are correct to fear the consequences of settling such disputes by political or economic horse-trading. Amongst purely instrumentally rational agents,

Table 3.2 The political dimensions of three models of citizenship

	Libertarian	*Social Democrat*	*Communitarian*
Subjects	All autonomous agents capable of entering legally recognized contracts, particularly in the economic sphere	All autonomous agents capable of entering legally recognized contracts, including the social and political sphere	Cultural and national groups
Spheres	Political sphere is a narrowly defined public framework for social interaction. Political discussion and intervention, if not regulation, inappropriate within a broad private sector	Political sphere is a more broadly defined public framework for social interaction. Political discussion and intervention, if not regulation, inappropriate within a narrower private sector	Political sphere is the nation-state
Scope	To protect the natural negative freedom and formal equality of individuals	To foster autonomy by preserving the broader negative freedom and more substantive equality of individuals and classes	To preserve communal self-determination and group solidarity
Styles	Constrained maximization to achieve mutual advantage via market trading	Constrained maximization to achieve mutual benefit via pluralist bargaining	Collaborative pursuit of shared goods

the interests of others will only be acknowledged if concessions are necessary, whilst the collective interest is liable to be sacrificed to the personal whenever free-riding or defection appear possible. Moreover, interests may remain in play connected to ideals and identities that people are unprepared to trade. In sum, this style of politics makes majoritarian tyranny and myopia all too likely. Of course, constitutional courts are invoked to guard against these dangers. Yet if there is no clear 'right' or 'principled' answer, as I have suggested, then their deliberations will not differ in kind to those of citizens. Indeed, they may be worse. The judiciary possesses a narrower range of experience than is available within a legislature, is comparatively poorly placed to consider the resource and other implications of a particular decision for the total package of government policies, and lacks the electoral legitimacy of political representatives (Sunstein, 1993: 145–9).

A political approach to constitutionalism attempts to overcome these difficulties by establishing practices through which citizens may agree on ways to disagree whilst making mutually acceptable decisions in areas requiring collective action. In the republican original of this thesis, the body politic is assumed to contain conflicting classes whose interests need to be balanced and mixed by dividing and dispersing power (Bellamy, 1996). Such balancing and mixing serves to check the adoption of purely self-serving positions and promotes a propensity to heed the views of others and take account of them in collective decision-making (Bellamy, 1999: Ch. 5). Traditional devices have included creating two legislative assemblies with different forms of representation and election, separating the legislature from the executive, and forms of federalism ranging from regional autonomy to self-governing functional associations. In other words, multiple spheres, subjects, scopes and styles of politics are employed to secure the mutual recognition of diverse groups.

As we noted, the underlying rationale of this system was to avoid domination by encouraging civic freedom. The crux is Rousseau's dilemma in the Social Contract: namely how can one be subject to the collective rules required for social life without being enslaved by the will of another (Rousseau, 1762, Bk I Ch: IV: 174)? As with Rousseau, the answer lies in taking part in a regular form of collective self-determination that assures the decisions are not products of the arbitrary will of particular individuals or groups but reflect the general will. This response is often believed to work only for relatively homogeneous and simple communities, and is rejected as anachronistic today. This objection is certainly justified in the case of those communitarian and deliberative democracy theorists criticized earlier, who do assume a common good or universal principle must underlie and provide the goal of self-government. By contrast, the neo-Roman and renaissance republican tradition I am drawing on makes no such assumption. On the contrary, these thinkers regarded conflicting conceptions of the right and the good as the norm. Instead, they conceived the political process as a dialogue through which agreed positions are constructed rather than discovered.

The key to this view is the injunction 'to hear the other side' (*audi alteram partem*). As Quentin Skinner (1996) and James Tully (1995: 115–16) have shown, dialogue was valued within humanist culture precisely because moral and political concepts were regarded as capable of being applied and interpreted in a variety of ways, so that any case can be described and evaluated from numerous and differing perspectives. The purpose of dialogue was to weigh these different points of view and find an accommodation between them. The dialogue neither assumed nor aimed at consensus in the sense of finding a fact of the matter or a set of general principles underlying or common to all their positions. Instead, the disputants exchanged interpretations in order to find connections, draw contrasts and construct compromises that build on these comparisons. To 'hear the other side', therefore, disputants must drop purely self-referential or self-interested reasoning and look for considerations others can find compelling, thereby ruling out arguments that do not involve a degree of reciprocity and mutual respect. They must strive to accommodate the clashes of preferences and principles associated with pluralism by seeking integrative compromises that view the concerns raised by others as matters to be met rather than constraints to be overcome through minimal, tactical concessions. In line with the classic logical principle *omnis determinatio est negatio*, the upshot is a negotiated compromise built upon multiple affinities and analogies between the views in play. Gradually an evolving practice of coexistence develops, founded not in the application of common abstract principles but in the experience of collectively reasoning about and making numerous particular decisions.

This culture of dialogue can be likened to a scheme of procedural justice within which different substantive conceptions of justice are discussed (Hampshire, 1999). For justice to be done it must be seen to be done. Thus, the openness of the dialogue is crucial, both in terms of the accessibility of the proceedings and their transparency. Citizen involvement guards against false negatives by trying to give all voices a hearing, and against false positives by allowing proposals to be contested. Rights get defined, refined, protected and respected through various political processes, which allow them to be tailored to particular contexts through primary and secondary legislation and more specific rules and regulations (Pettit, 1999: Postscript).

It is commonly raised that these processes themselves imply rights (e.g. Cohen, 1996). Clearly, any political practice institutionalizes a set of rights detailing who can participate, how, when and why. However, these rights do not reflect underlying general norms common to all legitimate democratic systems but are the products of citizens organizing themselves so as to be able to contest the ways the polity is structured. For example, workers' interests have been furthered more from their becoming unionized than as a result of the recognition of their rights *per se*. Indeed, the mobilization of workers has been crucial not only to those rights being recognized in the first place but also to how effectively they have been implemented. Moreover, because workers' rights have to vie with the property rights of capitalists and the interests of consumers, amongst other values, their defence and extension necessarily remains an ongoing political struggle. Nor are the norms governing the conduct of these struggles themselves constituted by pre-political rights. Instead, practice leads citizens to develop various dispositions of civility, tolerance and reciprocity, which facilitate their ability to hear and learn from others and live with difference. These appear in some form within most accounts of disputation and public reasoning, though their modes vary between cultures. Both fuller and less rigid than any set of principles or rules could ever be, such qualities can no more be acquired from a book of rules than can a sense of humour. They develop through practising citizenship and having to engage with others in conditions where the circumstances of politics apply. Moreover, they evolve and are enriched as the dimensions of politics get reinterpreted through new voices entering the dialogue and current ones changing.

Such a system resembles a democratic, common law *Rechtsstaat*. It contrasts with the two commonest versions of democratic politics associated with modern conceptions of constitutionalism – legal positivist notions that insist on the absolute authority of the author of the law, standardly the legislative assembly, and principled rights-based notions that seek to respond to the dangers of majoritarian and executive tyranny created by such views. Given the role that citizenship practice has undoubtedly played in the making of modern states, these theories have clearly never accorded totally with reality. However, they do constrain the available possibilities. The next section argues that within the EU context, they will exacerbate rather than placate the Union's legitimation problems. To remedy these requires encouraging the modest developments of European citizenship practice that currently exist.

CITIZENSHIP AND THE CONSTITUTION OF EUROPE

Earlier in this chapter, the EU was described as involving multiple spheres, subjects, styles and scopes for politics, with considerable contestation over their respective powers, character and relations. If true, this circumstance poses serious difficulties for both rights-based constitutionalism and the majoritarian decision-making that commonly accompanies it. The Charter of Fundamental Rights of the European Union reveals the likely pitfalls of the first.[3] Taking its cue from the Treaty of European Union as amended at Amsterdam (Article 6, formerly F), this proposal is premised on the member states and 'peoples of Europe' sharing a 'spiritual and moral heritage' made up of certain 'common' and 'universal values' intrinsic to 'the principles of democracy and the rule of law' (Charter, Preamble). Though the diversity of their political and constitutional 'cultures', 'traditions' and 'national identities' is acknowledged, this is alleged to pose no problem (Charter, Preamble). First, these are supposedly variations on a core set of fundamental rights (Charter, Preamble). Second, the Charter applies to the institutions and decisions of the Union, which allegedly complement and provide an additional layer to the domestic arrangements of the member states (Charter, Articles 51 and 52). To the extent the EU and member-state levels interact, the principle of subsidiarity will ensure the Charter's implementation and fine tuning will also be in large part a domestic matter.

Both these assumptions are misplaced. With regard to the first, we have seen how the possibilities for reasonable disagreement over rights extend even to the most basic provisions. Constitutional democracy has developed in quite different ways and under very different pressures within Western Europe, whilst in the East the differences are even more dramatic. Thus, the Italian constitution reflects the presence of Communist and Catholic traditions, the reaction against fascism and the experiences of the resistance which are largely foreign to Britain and which played out in quite different ways in the writing of the postwar German constitution. Likewise, the French constitution reflects a revolutionary republican tradition that accords a constituent power to the sovereign people that is absent or considerably weaker in other constitutions. These distinctive civic cultures have led multiculturalism to be handled very differently within the various member states, for example producing important variations in the interpretation of rights to freedom of thought, conscience and religion, discrimination and freedom of expression. With regard to the second assumption, we noted before how the EU interacts with – indeed is in part a manifestation of – the changing political dimensions of the member states. The economic and associated legal and social regulations stemming from the EU are not discrete. They affect core functions of government policy and the state's very *raison d'être*.

Because of this complexity, the Charter is likely to prove far more problematic than its proponents assume. Although the ECJ has consistently asserted the supremacy and direct effect of European law, this has never been entirely accepted when it affects constitutional essentials peculiar to the member states. Indeed, as the decisions of the French Conseil d'Etat in *Nicolo*, the German Federal Constitutional Court in *Internationale Handels-gesellschaft* and *Brunner*, the Italian Constitutional Court in *Frontini* and *Granital* and the House of Lords in *Factortame* all indicate, member-state courts have consistently grounded the validity of Community law, including its claims to supremacy, in the domestic legal order.[4] When the two seem to collide, therefore, a constructive constitutional dialogue has got under way. Despite some posturing by both sides, mutual accommodations have always been found and outright conflicts side-stepped. Most importantly in this context, the ECJ has come to recognize a patchwork of rights claims and generally been sensitive to national peculiarities (e.g. *Nold, Rutili*). This is not to say that there are not difficulties. In *Cinéthèque*, for example, the ECJ tried to distinguish its role in ensuring the compatibility of community law and rights and the role of national courts in upholding rights within domestic legislation. But as *ERT* revealed, that distinction becomes problematic when a domestic rights-based judgment becomes the basis of a derogation from fundamental Treaty rules. Similar problems emerged in *Grogan*.

These difficulties are not evidence of a lack of human rights protection within the EU, however, but evidence of its strength. The Charter simply adds an unnecessary further tier which lacks the subtlety and flexibility of the current system of negotiation. Instead, it is a highly conservative document which gives a *status quo* approach. The articles on citizenship are particularly telling in this respect (Charter, Chapter V Articles 39–46), since they now appear to raise to the status of Fundamental Rights what has been a limited policy reflecting the lowest common denominator of what can be achieved given existing institutions and member-state sensibilities. For example, the key right on the present account is the right of citizens to define their rights and hold accountable those empowered to defend and serve them. In its place, however, we get the far from fundamental shadow of this essential entitlement – the right of every citizen of the Union 'to vote and stand as a candidate in elections to the European Parliament in the member state in which he resides, under the same conditions as nationals of that state' (Charter, Article 39).

Of course, this chapter has argued that such a flexible system of rights negotiation ought to be carried out by political rather than juridical bodies. The European Parliament (EP) might be thought the appropriate place for this. Yet its legitimacy as a proto-European legislature is weak. Indeed, its attempt to gain that legitimacy through promoting the Charter and enshrining its place within it is a testimony to that weakness. It is now commonplace to acknowledge that no European demos exists (Chryssochoou, 1996; Weiler, 1996: 110–13). Support for the EU is largely mediated through its being beneficial for national, regional and other interests rather than because of a straightforward allegiance to the European idea.[5] Similarly, the EP is thought by most people to represent national views rather than pan-European interests *per se*.[6] Put another way, a European demos only exists through its links with various other demoi. This relationship has been conceived in the following ways: as an additional and complementary civic identity; as an overarching civic identity within which others – the national and the regional, for example, are nested; or as interacting and occasionally conflicting with other civic identities (Weiler, 1999: 344–8). Though national governments favour the first and Eurocrats the second, it is the last that best captures the actual situation. For though the EU does add to and reinforce many aspects of national and sub-national governance, the various cases referred to earlier indicate that it also rivals, conflicts with and potentially shapes these too. Yet it is the first and especially the second position that would be necessary for any common Charter or unitary legislative body to have legitimacy. As Weiler has pertinently remarked, in the absence of a unified European demos, asking the European peoples to accept legislation by majoritarian voting in the EP would be like expecting the Danes to acknowledge the legitimate authority of a German Bundestag to which they had been granted voting rights (Weiler, 1996: 111).

A situation of multiple European demoi requires a scheme that explicitly recognizes and seeks to promote dialogue between them and the various ways in which they debate the changing dimensions of the proto-European polity. To a remarkable degree, the actual structure of the EU does in fact reflect this concern. Thus, there are multiple channels of political representation for different sorts of political subjects: member states in the Inter-governmental Conferences and Council of Ministers, national political parties in the EP, selected functional interests in the Economic and Social Committee (ESC) and sub-national territorial units in the Committee of the Regions. In addition there are an increasing number of national and transnational interests, professional and campaigning associations and firms located in Brussels, many of which play a part in formal decision-making process through the obscure process of comitology. Though states retain a primary role in high politics and control the integration process through the Treaties, the EU's institutions have begun to develop a degree of autonomy which has encouraged a variety of sub- and trans-state organizations to deal with them directly. As a result, decision-making has become diffused across several tiers of government with ill-defined and shifting spheres of competence (Marks, Hooghe and Blank, 1996).

This diffusion of power provides the basis for the sort of political dialogue republicans advocate and that seems all too necessary in a system trying to balance regional, sectoral, state, transnational and supranational concerns. Both Neil MacCormick (1997) and Paul Craig (1997), for example, have argued that just such a republican rationale informs the sharing of legislative authority between the EP, the Council and the Commission. Thus, Craig (1997: 116–19) argues that though the extension of codecision procedure rightly reflects the EP's standing as the only directly elected European body, it is nonetheless appropriate that the power of legislative initiative rests with the Commission. On the one hand, this arrangement recognizes the need to accord due weight to the Council given that the democratic legitimacy of the Community remains largely state-based and grounded in an international agreement. On the other hand, it also acknowledges the legitimacy of the Commission's powers as guardian of the Treaties and the most likely body, given the Community's current stage of development, to direct policy towards fostering the collective goods they embody rather than sectional interests.

Of course, as Craig emphasizes, there is no denying the shortcomings of these arrangements from a republican perspective either. For example, Philippe Schmitter (2000: Ch. 4) has made proposals on representation within both the EP and the Council which would create a consociational system that would guarantee and improve on the current balance in decision-making power between large, medium and small states. He and Weiler also both suggest grafting a referendum on key legislative proposals on to elections for the EP in order to generate a European-wide public sphere to counteract the current tendency for voting to reflect national rather than European issues (Weiler, 1999: 350–1; Schmitter, 2000: 36–7). More importantly, the role of national parliaments and regional assemblies remain inadequately addressed, as do the concerns of a whole series of non-business interests – from the unemployed, through ordinary consumers to public interest movements, including trans-national coalitions of these groups. Since this last category is particularly pertinent to the active approach to citizenship advocated in this chapter, I shall close by reviewing certain developments in this area. For it is precisely here that citizen struggles are emerging that are reshaping the four dimensions of politics in ways that have potentially profound consequences for the constitution of Europe.[7]

At one level, there is already considerable scope for a wide range of interest representation within the EU. The Economic and Social Committee has provided a forum for consulting nationally based economic and social interest groups since the EEC's inception in 1958. However, this body has only an advisory and somewhat marginal consultative role within a limited number of policy areas, with its membership drawn from nominees submitted by the member states to the Council. Consequently, organized interests have taken advantage of the multiple channels for access opening up within the EU's many-layered decision-making processes in order to exert greater influence at the pre-proposal and implementation stages of any regulation. Examples include Articles 136 and 137 of the Treaty on European Union (TEU) (formerly Articles 117 and 118), that were introduced at Amsterdam and replace the Maastricht Social Protocol. These entrust the Commission with 'the task of promoting the consultation of management and labour at Community level' and of taking 'any relevant measure to facilitate their dialogue by ensuring balanced support for the parties' (Article 138, formerly 118A). These dialogues not only inform policy, they can lead to contractual relations and agreements between the social partners. There has also been the spread of the 'comitology' process whereby various advisory committees composed of scientific experts or affected social and economic interests have proliferated to aid the fleshing out of numerous regulative schemes in areas such as foodstuffs or health and safety.

Assessments of these structures are mixed. Certain commentators have highlighted the deliberative character of these bodies, arguing that national interests are obliged by the constraints of primary Community legislation and the presence of the Commission to focus on supranational concerns. As a result, they become more appreciative of the need to address those negative externalities of their activities that affect foreign subjects more than domestic ones (Joerges and Neyer, 1997). Other scholars, however, focus on the selectiveness of the groups they represent, their often informal and mainly advisory powers, their lack of openness and accountability to the public at large, and their preference for technocratic and managerial solutions (Weiler, 1999: 277–8, 283–5).

More encouraging, therefore, is the growth of specifically European 'public interest' organizations, which now comprise over 20 per cent of European groups (Greenwood, 1997). These are non-profit, nongovern-mental and self-governing bodies that cover a broad spectrum of issues and ideological perspectives, with a focus that goes from the local to the global. They tend to be polity- rather than policy-centred in that the concerns they raise, such as abortion rights, discrimination, environmental protection and the like, involve reinterpretations of basic norms or institutions. At the Amsterdam IGC some 50 such organizations came together at the initiative of the International European Movement to form a Civil Society Forum running parallel to the official conference (Curtin, 1997: 56–9). Hundreds of NGOs also submitted written observations as well as participating in the EP's public hearings with 'civil society' both prior to and following the IGC. A number of proposals have emerged from this activity that aim at creating a European public sphere. These include: a demand for the right to form European-wide organizations at the EU level rather than being subject to the legal and tax regime of a particular member state; the provision of more formal rights of consultation by such measures as broadening the ESC into an 'associative parliament', granting citizens opportunity structures for a direct input in the legislative process via a right to initiate referenda, and the passing of an American-style Administrative Procedure Act to ensure the participation of all interested parties in the framing of regulations; and finally increasing transparency and freedom of information, often through the use of new information technology (see Curtin, 1996: Part V for a summary. Craig, 1997: 119–24 draws out their republican potential. For parallel arguments in the US context see Seidenfeld, 1992).

Improvements along these lines have so far been hesitant. General consultative fora have been established for social policy and the environment. These involve regional and local authorities as well as a variety of interest groups and are explicitly conceived as a 'place of consultation and dialogue' between these parties and the Commission. However, the representativeness of the membership remains open to question and its standing and competence unclear and largely consultative. Amsterdam also saw the granting of a Treaty-based right of access to the documents of the EP, the Council and the Commission (Article 255, formerly Article 191A). Though the initiative was undertaken in the name of 'having decisions taken as openly as possible and as closely as possible to the citizen' (Article 1, amended former Article A), it is not formally part of the citizenship provisions. Some see this fact as implying the right to be an issue internal to the functioning of the institutions rather than a product of the democratic values to which the Union is now formally committed under TEU Article 6. Yet one advantage is the entitlement's extension beyond Union citizens to 'any natural or legal person residing or having its registered office in a member state'. Many problems remain, however. Though general principles are to be laid down by the codecision procedure, each institution will devise its own rules for transparency and openness. As Gregory and Giddings reveal in their analysis of responses to the Ombudsman's own initiative enquiry in this area, action on such matters often falls considerably short of their formal statements of support. As it is, plenty of leeway remains for member states or the institutions to deny access. Meanwhile, the more general issue of full information about and entry to the proceedings not just of these but of other bodies of the Union, not least the ECJ, remains blocked.

Whatever their shortcomings, the significance and potential of these first tentative steps towards extending citizenship practice should nonetheless not be overlooked. In many respects, these measures can be assimilated to the earlier analysis of the constitutive character of citizenship. The actions of public and other interest groups reflect the emergence of a new trans-European subject of politics. This development, however, is not occurring within a settled political framework, for in the process it is bringing about the creation of new styles and spheres of politics whilst expanding its scope. The demand for new rights of association, participation and access is part and parcel of the creation of new types of governance that supplement, cut across and occasionally subvert and supplant current systems of representative democracy in order to create a European public sphere. Yet these innovations should not be read in a teleological manner as heralding an 'ever closer Union of European peoples' or a deepening consensus on liberal democratic values. For the key to this new form of politics is dialogue and negotiation between a widening range of actors and agencies. The aim is not to achieve some pre-established goal but to set up a process within which different voices can be heard and their concerns taken into account.

The central dynamic is the further dispersal of power to preserve freedom from domination and promote reciprocity and compromise.

As innovations such as the pillar structure introduced at Maastricht indicate, deepening integration often goes hand in hand with enhanced flexibility and the introduction of new checks and balances (Shaw, 1999). Increasing citizenship participation within the Union is sometimes advocated as a way to overcome what many regard as a dilemma prompted by the self-interest of member states and the unwillingness of their élites to lose power. But within a very diverse community such as the EU, where differences and conflicts are likely to be profound, enhancing democracy may require even more differentiated structures if collective goals are to be pursued in ways that increase legitimacy as well as efficiency. Opening up Europe to its citizens represents the start rather than the culmination of a constitutionalizing process (Shaw, 2000).

CONCLUSION

Citizenship is frequently identified with mere membership of a given system and possession of the entitlements that follow. However, the most important entitlement is the leverage such membership gives for changing its terms and conditions. Though citizenship activity is conditioned and often facilitated by prevailing structures and the norms they embody, it also challenges and seeks to modify them, for the demands of existing and aspirant citizens alike involve implicit and often explicit reinterpretations of the general shape of the polity. However, there is no necessary telos towards an ever-expanding and fuller system of rights that is to be regarded as somehow more just or better than what went before. Rather, citizenship practice is a continuously reflexive process, with citizens reinterpreting the basis of their collective life in new ways that correspond to their evolving needs and ideals. The role of constitutionalism lies in promoting the civic freedom for such activity to unfold in ways that avoid dominating others. As we have seen, this is best achieved through the dispersal of power and the promotion of dialogue over common rules and arrangements.

The EU offers especially fertile ground for such an approach. Its boundaries, competences, membership and character are all in the process of negotiation. What remains as yet undeveloped are precisely those structures necessary to ensure the resulting accords promote rather than diminish the freedom of citizens. Endowing citizens with rights will not remedy this situation if these reflect highly contestable visions of Europe which they might wish to debate and dispute. An active European citizenship requires citizens having a say in the constitutional dialogue so that they can shape the Union for themselves. As we have seen, there are encouraging signs that this is beginning to happen. The result of their involvement may make the Union less uniform and more flexible than some would like but will also mark an important step in bringing the Union closer to the peoples of Europe.

ACKNOWLEDGEMENTS

I am grateful to Miriam Aziz, Jo Shaw, Jim Tully, Neil Walker, Alex Warleigh, Danilo Zolo and audiences in Leeds, Pisa and Vienna for their comments on earlier versions of this chapter.

NOTES

1. I borrow this phrase and some of the inspiration behind my argument from Lefort, 1988, p. 37, who takes it in turn from Hannah Arendt. See too Jeremy Waldron's parallel notion of political participation as the 'right of rights' (1999: Ch. 11), a phrase he borrows from William Cobbett, although I distinguish my view from his below.
2. Although there are certain parallels between my view of citizenship practice and the view of Wiener (1998) and Wiener and Della Sala (1997), as well as Tilly (1996) on whom they draw, I tend to see citizenship 'practice' in the more Wittgensteinian sense pioneered by Tully, that is as a series of language games, though I set the resulting dialogue in a more republican framework than he standardly employs (though see Tully, 2001).
3. References are to the draft of 28 September 2000 (Charte 4487/00) – the most recent at the time of writing.
4. These cases have been crucial to the evolving constitutional pretensions of the ECJ. They reveal how it has been forced by challenges from the constitutional courts of the member states to gradually assert the supremacy and direct effect of European law and its competence to decide such issues. However, these claims have not as yet been accepted in their entirety by any national constitutional court, although certain concessions have been made. Space prevents a full discussion of the details of these cases here, but for a useful outline see Craig and De Búrca, 1998, pp. 264–94.
5. See, for example, the criticisms in the Common Statement of the Platform of European Social NGOs and the European Trade Union Confederation (ETUC) participating in the public hearing on 27 April 2000 (Charte 4286/00 Contrib 158) and that presented at the same hearing by 'European Citizens and their Associations' (ECAS) (Charte 4294/00 Contrib 166).

6. When asked in a recent poll how they describe themselves – by nationality only, nationality and European, European and nationality, or European – respondents divided 45%, 40%, 6% and 5% respectively (Eurobarometer Report No. 48, March 1998). Thus there is little evidence of a European demos or a shared political culture.

7. It is noteworthy that in a 1989 Eurobarometer poll, 59% preferred the idea that the EP be organized around national criteria rather than the current political ones.

8. The paragraphs that follow are deeply indebted to Curtin, 1996, Parts 4 and 5, and 1997.

CASES

Internationale Handelsgesellschaft Case 11/70 [1970] ECR 1125, p. 1134.
Internationale Handelsgesellschaft [1974] 2 CMLR 549.
Nold v. Commission [1974] ECR 503.
Frontini v. Ministero delle Finanze [1974] 2 CMLR 372.
Rutili v. Minister for the Interior Case 36/75 [1975] ECR 1219.
SpA Granital v. Amministrazione delle Finanze [1984] 21 CMLR 756.
Cinéthèque v. Fédèrations nationales des cinémas français Cases 60-1/84 [1985] ECR 2605.
ERT v. Dimotiki Etairia Piliroforissis Case C-260/89 [1991] ECR I-2925.
Factortame Ltd v. Secretary of State for Transport [1990] 2 AC 85.
Nicolo [1990] 1 CMLR 173.
SPUC (Ireland) Ltd v. Grogan Case C-159/90 [1991] ECR I-4685.
Brunner [1994] 1 CMLR 57.

REFERENCES

Ackerman, B. (1991) *We The People: Foundations* (Cambridge: Harvard University Press).

Austin, D. and O'Neill, M. (2000) *Democracy and Cultural Diversity* (Oxford: Oxford University Press).

Barry, N. (1990) 'Markets, Citizenship and the Welfare State: Some Critical Reflections', in R. Plant and N. Barry (1990), *Citizenship and Rights in Thatcher's Britain* (London: Institute of Economic Affairs), pp. 34–77.

Bellamy, R. (1996) 'The Political Form of the Constitution: the Separation of Powers, Rights and Representative Democracy', in R. Bellamy and D. Castiglione (eds), *Constitutionalism in Transformation* (Oxford: Blackwell), pp. 24–44.

Bellamy, R. (1999) *Liberalism and Pluralism: Towards a Politics of Compromise* (London: Routledge).

Bellamy, R. (2000) *Rethinking Liberalism* (London: Pinter).

Chryssochoou, D. (1996) 'Europe's Could-be Demos: Recasting the Debate', *West*

European Politics 19, pp. 787–801.

Cohen, J. (1996) 'Procedure and Substance in Deliberative Democracy', in S. Benhabib (ed.), *Democracy and Difference: Contesting the Boundaries of the Political* (Princeton: Princeton University Press), pp. 95–119.

Craig, P. (1997) 'Democracy and Rule-making Within the EC: An Empirical and Normative Assessment', *European Law Journal* 3, pp. 105–30.

Craig, P. and De Búrca, G. (1998) *EU Law: Text, Cases and Materials*, 2nd edn (Oxford: Oxford University Press).

Curtin, D. (1996) 'The European Union, Civil Society and Participatory Democracy', *Collected Courses of the Academy of European Law* (Florence: EUI).

Curtin, D. (1997) *Postnational Democracy: The European Union in Search of a Political Philosophy* (The Hague: Kluwer Law International).

Dworkin, R. (1985) *Taking Rights Seriously* (London: Duckworth).

Dworkin, R. (1995) 'Constitutionalism and Democracy', *European Journal of Philosophy* 3, pp. 2–11.

Foweraker, J. and Landman, T. (1997) *Citizenship Rights and Social Movements: A Comparative and Statistical Analysis* (Oxford: Oxford University Press).

Fraser, N. (1997) *Justice Interruptus* (London: Routledge).

Gagnon, A. and Tully, J. (2001) *Recognition in Mutinational Societies* (Cambridge: Cambridge University Press).

Greenwood, J. (1997) *Representing Interests in the European Union* (London: Macmillan).

Hampshire, S. (1999) *Justice is Conflict* (London: Duckworth).

Held, D. (1989) *Political Theory and the Modern State* (Cambridge: Polity).

Janoski, T. (1998) *Citizenship and Civil Society: A Framework of Rights and Obligations in Liberal, Traditional and Social Regimes* (Cambridge: Cambridge University Press).

Joerges, C. and Neyer, J. (1997) 'From Intergovernmental Bargaining to Deliberative Political Process: The Constitutionalisation of Comitology', *European Law Journal* 3: 3, pp. 274–300.

Lefort, C. (1988) *Democracy and Political Theory* (Cambridge: Polity Press).

Linklater, A. (1998) *The Transformation of Political Community: Ethical Foundation of the Post-Westphalian Era* (Cambridge: Polity).

Lyons, C. (1996) 'Citizenship in the Constitution of the European Union: Rhetoric or Reality?', in R. Bellamy (ed.), *Constitutionalism, Democracy and Sovereignty: American and European Perspectives* (Ashgate: Avebury) pp. 96–110.

MacCormick, N. (1997) 'Democracy, Subsidiarity, and Citizenship in the "European Commonwealth"', *Law and Philosophy* 16, pp. 331–56.

Marks, G., Hooghe, L. and Blank, K. (1996) 'European Integration from the 1980s: State-Centric v. Multi-level Governance', *Journal of Common Market Studies* 34, pp. 341–78.

Marshall, T. H. (1950) *Citizenship, Social Class and Other Essays* (Cambridge: Cambridge University Press).

Nozick, R. (1974) *Anarchy, State and Utopia*, Oxford: Blackwell.

O'Leary, S. (1996) *European Union Citizenship: Options for Reform* (London: IPPR).

Pettit, P. (1999) *Republicanism: A Theory of Freedom and Government* 2nd edition

(Oxford: Clarendon Press).

Plant, R. (1990), 'Citizenship and Rights', in R. Plant and N. Barry, *Citizenship and Rights in Thatcher's Britain* (London: Institute of Economic Affairs) pp. 1–32.

Rawls, J. (1971) *A Theory of Justice* (Cambridge: Harvard University Press).

Rawls, J. (1993) *Political Liberalism* (Chicago: Chicago University Press).

Raz, J. (1986) *The Morality of Freedom* (Oxford: Oxford University Press).

Raz, J. (1994) *Ethics in the Public Domain: Essays in the Morality of Law and Politics* (Oxford: Clarendon Press).

Rousseau, J.-J. (1762) *The Social Contract and Discourses*, ed. and trans. G. D. H. Cole, (London: Dent, 1973).

Seidenfeld, M. (1992) 'A Civic Republican Justification for the Bureaucratic State' *Harvard Law Review* 105, pp. 1511–76.

Schmitter, P. C. (2000) *How to Democratize the European Union . . . And Why Bother?* (Maryland: Rowman and Littlefield Publishers, Inc.).

Shaw, J. (1998) 'The Interpretation of European Union Citizenship', *The Modern Law Review* 61: 3, pp. 293–317.

Shaw, J. (1999) 'Constitutionalism in the European Union', *Journal of European Public Policy* special edition 6: 4, pp. 579–97.

Shaw, J. (2000) 'Relating, Constitutionalism and Flexibility in the European Union', in G. de Búrca and J. Scott (eds), *Constitutional Change in the EU: From Uniformity to Flexibility?* (Oxford: Hart Publishing) pp. 337–58.

Skinner, Q. (1996) *Reason and Rhetoric in the Philosophy of Hobbes* (Cambridge: Cambridge University Press).

Soysal, Y. (1994) *Limits of Citizenship. Migrants and Postnational Membership in Europe* (Chicago/London: University of Chicago Press).

Sunstein, C. (1993) *The Partial Constitution* (Harvard: Harvard University Press).

Tilly, C. (1996) 'Citizenship, Identity and Social History', in C. Tilly (ed.), *Citizenship, Identity and Social History*, Supplement 3 of *International Review of Social History* (Cambridge: Cambridge University Press).

Tully, J. (1995) *Strange Multiplicity: Constitutionalism in an Age of Diversity* (Cambridge: Cambridge University Press).

Tully, J. (1999) 'The Agonic Freedom of Citizens', *Economy and Society* 28: 2, pp. 161–82.

Tully, J. (2000) 'Struggles over Recognition and Distribution', *Constellations* 7: 4, pp. 469–82.

Tully, J. (2001) 'La conception republicaine de la cityoennete dams la cadre des societes multiculturelles et multinationales', *Politique et sociétés* 21: 1, pp. 123–47.

Turner, B. (1990) 'Outline of a Theory of Citizenship', *Sociology* 24: 2, pp. 189–217.

Tushnet, M. (1999) *Taking the Constitution Away from the Courts* (Princeton: Princeton University Press).

Van Gunsteren, H. R. (1998) *A Theory of Citizenship: Organising Plurality in Contemporary Democracies* (Oxford: Westview).

Waldron, J. (1999) *Law and Disagreement* (Oxford: Oxford University Press).

Walzer, M. (1983) *Spheres of Justice: A Defence of Pluralism and Equality* (Oxford: Martin Robertson).

Weiler, J. H. H. (1996) 'European Neo-Constitutionalism: In Search of Foundations for the European Constitutional Order', in R. Bellamy and D. Castiglione (eds), *Constitutionalism in Transformation* (Oxford: Blackwell), pp. 105–21.

Weiler, J. H. H. (1999) *The Constitution of Europe: 'Do the New Clothes Have an Emperor?' and Other Essays on European Integration* (Cambridge: Cambridge University Press).

Wiener, A. (1998) *'European' Citizenship Practice: Building Institutions of a Non-State* (Oxford: Westview).

Wiener, A. and Della Sala, V. (1997) 'Constitution-Making and Citizenship Practice – Bridging the Democracy Gap in the EU?', *Journal of Common Market Studies* 35, pp. 595–614.

Part II

Internal Aspects of European Citizenship

4

Citizenship, Rights and the EU Ombudsman

ROY GREGORY AND PHILIP GIDDINGS

I. INTRODUCTION

Citizenship may be perceived in terms of the possession and exercise of a wide range of rights. In this context, rights take various forms, which can be considered in two categories: substantive and procedural. The substantive category consists of 'first generation' basic rights and fundamental freedoms, such as freedom from slavery, torture or cruel, inhuman or degrading treatment. Also part of the 'first generation' of human rights, but more narrowly civil and political in character, are the rights necessary for individual freedom, such as freedom of speech and association, to own property and to participate in the exercise of political powers. Next in the substantive category are the so-called 'second generation' of rights: social, economic and cultural rights, such as those to reasonable health care and welfare, the right to work and to equal pay and opportunities at work. More controversially, 'third generation' human rights, such as the collective rights of ethnic minorities, the right to economic development and the right to a good environment have been put forward (for example, Robertson and Merrills, 1996).

Our second category – 'procedural rights' – may usefully be divided into two: first, the citizen's right to 'good administration', that is, to receive fair, just, equitable and considerate treatment at the hands of officials who exercise public power in relation to any of the substantive rights listed above (Bradley, 1983: 96). And second, following Frank, the right to complain, to be heard, and to have corrective action taken if one has suffered harm from government (Frank, 1976: 122; cited in Caiden, 1983: 4). In their dealings with government, it is argued, on the principle of *ubi ius ibi remedium*, people have the right of appeal to an impartial arbiter. They must feel confident that public power is executed fairly and equitably in accordance with natural justice and the rule of law. This implies an entitlement to a fair hearing before a disinterested adjudicator with advice of the case to be made and a fair opportunity in which to meet it (Caiden, MacDermot and Sandler, 1983: 5).

The role of the Ombudsman institution, however, is not to determine whether these rights and entitlements of citizenship should apply, or even to campaign for them. That is the business of governments, political parties and pressure groups. The Ombudsman simply helps ensure that citizens are not denied the social and civil rights, both substantive and procedural, which the law and public policy confer on them. Insofar as the Ombudsman institution may help to secure and protect such rights, it helps promote a sense of citizenship (Oliver, 1991: 34–7; Marshall, 1950). A community's procedures for the protection of the rights of individuals can help to generate that sense of belonging to the community which is the social foundation for citizenship. Such procedures, by ensuring that the rights of citizens *qua* citizens are taken seriously by political, governmental and judicial institutions, give practical substance to the concept of citizenship for individual citizens.

II. RIGHTS, CITIZENSHIP AND THE OMBUDSMAN

In this section, therefore, we outline how the Ombudsman institution is involved with securing and protecting such rights, dealing first with 'substantive rights' and then with 'procedural' ones. With regard to substantive rights, we deal first with 'fundamental' or 'first generation' human rights. In mature liberal democracies, there is only a limited role for the Ombudsman in securing and protecting such rights because they are in the main protected by other well-developed procedures and institutions such as the courts of law. As Caiden (1983: 5) has argued, the courts, supplemented by administrative tribunals, are usually relied upon as the principal method of enforcing legal rights. For many of the basic human rights and fundamental freedoms, judicial processes can be an effective means of enforcement, at least in countries where the legal restrictions on these rights do not assume greater importance than the rights themselves.

In 'new' and 'emerging' democracies, however, after a period of totalitarian or authoritarian government, where the apparatus of legal safeguards is weak, insecure or non-existent, the Ombudsman institution has come to play a central role as a safeguard of freedom and protector of human rights in every sense of the term. An early and influential example of this development was the Spanish constitution of 1978 which explicitly included the principle of the defence of human rights in the Ombudsman's mandate, adding a new dimension to the conventional maladministration remit. This approach shaped the model of the Ombudsman institution (*Defensor del Pueblo*) that was subsequently to be adopted by many other new and developing democracies, particularly in Ibero-America and Africa (Alvarez de Miranda y Torres, 1999).

Turning to 'second generation' human rights, in mature democracies 'social, economic and cultural' rights often take the form of statutory entitlements which have to be delivered, directly or indirectly, by administrative authorities. The problem is that the ordinary machinery of law, and even administrative law, is not well suited to remedying many of the problems confronting individuals. It is, in Caiden *et al.*'s words, 'too costly, too slow, too inaccessible, too restrictive, too disruptive, too formal, too conservative, and in many instances, it has been deliberately excluded and no alternative is realistic or feasible in the circumstances' (Caiden *et al.*, 1983: 5).

Such a comment encapsulates the case for establishing the Ombudsman office in countries where the rule of law prevails, but the legal system leaves much to be desired as a means of dealing with the run-of-the-mill grievances of the ordinary citizen. The Ombudsman's concern with good and bad administration has therefore involved him continually in disputes about whether and how effectively such provision has been made for individual citizens. A commitment to protect 'third generation' collective human rights (for example, in relation to economic development, the environment and ethnic minorities), is not widely included in Ombudsman mandates but does feature in some of the more recently established offices, for instance in Argentina, Namibia and Hungary (Cuellar, 1999: 129–45).

As far as the second category of 'procedural rights' is concerned, 'good administration' and complaints are at the heart of most Ombudsman activity. The classical Ombudsman office, as it operates in mature liberal democracies, in Western Europe, North America and Australasia, for example, has traditionally been concerned with inquiries into complaints about maladministration and the redress of wrongs arising out of maladministration, thereby protecting citizens' rights 'to be heard' and to 'good administration'. In this role, the Ombudsman receives complaints from members of the public, investigates them, and reports his findings to the complainants and the organizations investigated. Should any wrong be uncovered, the expectation is that it will be put right. For the Ombudsman, protecting the citizen's right to good administration is thus very much a matter of investigating individual complaints, and righting wrongs on a case-by-case basis. This is the stock-in-trade of the Ombudsman's work. But a good many Ombudsman offices also concern themselves with 'systemic' defects in the administrative process, and offer explicit guidance to public authorities on what constitutes good administrative practice. Ombudsmen in Ireland, Hong Kong, New South Wales, British Columbia and England, for example, have all published documents setting out checklists for the benefit of public authorities seeking to ensure that they treat citizens 'properly, fairly, and impartially'.

In regard, therefore, to securing and protecting the rights and entitlements which flow from citizenship, we can see that an Ombudsman's role varies according to the category of rights (substantive or procedural) and the type of polity (e.g. mature or emerging democracies) as well as according to the presence and effectiveness of other mechanisms for rights protection.

III. THE EU OMBUDSMAN: CONTEXT AND ROLE

Background

Classically, the Ombudsman is an independent official appointed to investigate and report on individual citizens' complaints about administrative action and to recommend appropriate remedies. This concept has proved remarkably malleable. Originating in Scandinavia, it has spread, via New Zealand, through the Commonwealth, Western Europe and then globally (Gregory and Giddings, 2000). Its attractiveness lies in the key features of the institution – impartiality deriving from independence, accessibility, informality, speed and cheapness – at least in comparison to the courts.

In some states, such as the UK, the Ombudsman is strongly focused on maladministration; in others the focus is more on human rights. In some states the office is closely linked with the legislature; in others it is independent of both legislature and executive and in yet others, echoing its Swedish origins, it is linked to the Head of State. In some states the jurisdiction is limited to national government and its agencies; in other states it includes all governmental institutions, national, regional and local. In some states the Ombudsman is empowered to investigate and recommend; in other states the Ombudsman has powers to seek enforcement through the courts. In Europe the Ombudsman institution had been confined to Scandinavia until the UK adopted it in 1967, to be followed by France (1973) and Austria and Portugal (1976). With its adoption in Spain and Ireland in 1981 only four of the member states of the EU (Germany, Belgium, Greece and Italy) lacked a national governmental Ombudsman, and in the eleven regions of Italy the institution was to be introduced during the decade that followed (Gregory and Giddings, 2000).

The question of appointing a 'European Ombudsman' was raised several times during the 1970s, but support for the idea was by no means consistent in either the Commission or the European Parliament (EP) (European Parliament Debates, 1979: 23–4; Jenkins, 1989: 535–6). In June 1985 the EP passed a resolution stating that, because differences between national legal systems and the Community system made it impossible to transpose the Ombudsman institution into the Community system, it would be preferable to establish a parliamentary petitions committee (Marias, 1994a; Chanterie, 1985; Resolution adopted on 14 June 1985, OJ C175, 15 July 1985). Further exchanges in June 1987 confirmed the preference of some MEPs for the Petitions Committee method (European Parliament Debates, 1987: No. 2 – 353/91 and 353/92). Successful moves to adopt the Ombudsman institution thus had to await the citizenship initiatives within the European Council which were to be incorporated in the Maastricht Treaty in 1992.

The EU Ombudsman: role and functions

The Ombudsman institution created in 1992 owed its inspiration to a combination of Spanish enthusiasm for European citizenship and Danish concern for administrative efficiency and fairness. As it emerged in the early 1990s, the 'European Ombudsman' was a by-product of the former and a direct outcome of the latter.

The idea of introducing into the Treaty on European Union a chapter on European citizenship was launched in May 1990 by the Prime Minister of Spain, Felipe Gonzales, in a letter to his partners in the European Council. Spain felt it imperative to include as part of the drive for political union a 'European citizenship' which should be understood as 'a personal status' for all nationals of member states. The Spanish initiative was supported by Denmark, a member state where the Ombudsman has proved a highly successful institution. In a Memorandum issued in October 1990 the Danish government argued that, in order to strengthen the democratic basis for Community cooperation, an Ombudsman system should be introduced under the aegis of the EP (Ibanez, 1992: 106–8 and Laursen and Vanhoonacker, 1992: 293). Denmark's commitment was further underlined as a result of pressure from its parliament (Folketing, 1990). Spain and Denmark had different but complementary goals regarding the creation of a formal category of EU citizenship. Spain wanted to create a direct link between the individual and the EU as an explicit part of the democratization process in both Spain itself and the Union. Denmark wanted to enhance the Union's democracy as part of an attempt to convince the Danish people that integration was palatable. These two member states were able to ensure that citizenship remained on the IGC agenda and was included in the Treaty. However, in the struggle over institutional design, they were obliged to make concessions to those member states which, whilst able to accept EU citizenship as a gloss on freedom of movement, necessary for the single market, and to help 'sell' the

Union to the national publics, would not accept what they saw as the statist implications of a more substantive EU citizenship (see Warleigh, this volume).

However, the EP itself remained lukewarm to the suggestion of an EU Ombudsman, asserting that an Ombudsman would undermine the power of the Parliament and its Committees to supervise the Commission and its departments (Marias, 1994b: 74 and Reding, 1991). As a result, the Maastricht Treaty (TEU) did provide for an Ombudsman – but a legal basis was also created for the right to petition the EP, which until that time had been characterized as a 'custom'. Moreover, the Ombudsman Office was subordinated to the EP by the provision that the latter should elect the Ombudsman. This, with the development of codecision, seems to have been sufficient to persuade the EP that the Ombudsman would not be a threat. Thus, the reality that the European Ombudsman has had to face has been the need to coexist with the EP's Petitions Committee, the national Ombudsmen and the Petitions Committees of the parliaments of the member states. The Ombudsman has had to 'respect the functions of these bodies and … take care not to jeopardise them' (Marias,1994b: 75).

What emerged from Maastricht was not a 'pan-European Ombudsman' in the civic nationalist mode, but an Ombudsman with a remit limited to the particular institutions and bodies of the Union, grounded in the TEU itself and with the objective of enhancing a responsive administration. The Ombudsman's role is envisaged as engaging primarily with what we have categorized as 'procedural rights'. But the Office was also seen as having a supplementary role in support of the implementation of first and second generation substantive rights, although these rights are more directly protected by national courts, the ECJ and the ECHR. And because the Ombudsman's remit was limited to the actions or inactions of Union institutions and bodies, the Office is not able to intervene to protect Union citizenship rights against the actions or inactions of member states, such as for example in regard to consular protection.

The 'European' Ombudsman Office was created to examine complaints made by EU citizens, foreigners residing in the EU or legal persons with registered offices in the EU alleging 'maladministration in the activities of the Community institutions and bodies' with the exception of the ECJ and the Court of First Instance acting in their judicial roles. The Ombudsman, it is suggested, in effect equips the EP with 'an additional specialised form of scrutiny' (Westlake, 1994: 180). The Ombudsman's 'articles of government' secure the office's independence, grant it the power to conduct inquiries on his own initiative, and allow it to make reports to the EP.[1] Following a false start in the autumn of 1994, when it proved impossible to make an appointment owing to procedural difficulties (see Carvel, 1994;

European Parliament, 1994), the first EU Ombudsman, Jacob Söderman (Parliamentary Ombudsman of Finland from 1989), was elected by the EP on 12 July 1995 and began work in September 1995. He was re-elected for a second mandate on 27 October 1997.

IV. THE EU OMBUDSMAN AND CITIZENSHIP: AN ASSESSMENT

Given the form in which the EU Ombudsman emerged, the measure of the Office's success in promoting the concept of European citizenship has to be seen in the extent to which its work in relation to the activities of European institutions and bodies has had the effect of protecting the various categories of 'rights' discussed in the introduction to this chapter. We will consider substantive rights first before coming to procedural rights which have been the main focus of the Ombudsman's concern. Lastly, we will look at the Ombudsman's understanding of his role in relation to citizens' 'specific European Union rights'.

Substantive rights and the Ombudsman

Given the focus of his remit on alleged maladministration by the institutions and bodies of the Community, one would not expect that much of the Ombudsman's work would relate to protecting and securing fundamental human rights. The Community's institutions and bodies are not directly concerned with administration in those fields of activity (e.g. maintenance of law and order, prisons and the police) which most frequently give rise to alleged violations of such first generation rights. Nor are the Community's institutions and bodies directly concerned with second generation rights, other than the employment rights of their own employees. Here again the primary agent delivering Community policy is the member state. As regards third generation rights, the issue of environmental protection has stimulated two noteworthy cases – the Newbury By-pass and the French nuclear tests in Polynesia – but these were cases in which the heart of the complaint was the alleged failure of the Commission to take action against a member state which appeared not to be fulfilling Treaty obligations (EU Ombudsman, 1996: 10–11 and 28–32).

In the Newbury By-pass case the complainants took the view that the UK government had breached Community law by failing to carry out an environmental impact assessment of the Newbury By-pass. They alleged maladministration by the Commission in deciding not to open infringement proceedings against the UK under Article 169 of the European Commission Treaty, as it then was (as a result of the Treaty of Amsterdam's modifications of the TEU, Article 169 is now known as Article 226). The issue at stake was whether the relevant Council Directive 85/337/EEC, which came into effect on 3 July 1988, was applicable. The draft orders for the By-pass were published between 1986 and 1988 and the public inquiry began on 14 June 1988.

The complainants had first put their case to the Commission in 1994. The Commission replied via a press release on 20 October 1995 saying that, in the light of the ECJ's decision in the Grosskrotzenburg case (Case C431/92, *Commission v Germany*, judgement of 11 August 1995) it had decided to interpret the Directive as requiring an environmental impact assessment only for projects where the procedure for consent was started after 3 July 1988. This meant, in the Commission's view, that the Directive did not apply to the Newbury By-pass. The Commission also took the view that under Article 169 it had discretion whether to take infringement proceedings or not, and that this discretion was fully recognized by the ECJ.

The complainants then took their case to the Ombudsman, arguing that the Commission's decisions on the Newbury By-pass had been arbitrary and disingenuous. Moreover, by announcing its decision to the media in October, but not informing the complainants until December, the Commission had failed in its obligation to keep the complainants informed of the progress of their case. Although the Ombudsman did not find for the complainants in the sense of criticizing the Commission's substantive decision on the requirement for an environmental impact assessment, he did find the Commission guilty of maladministration. The Commission was found to have supplied inadequate reasoning for its decisions and had failed to inform the complainants of its decision before, or at least at the same time as, announcing the decision publicly through a press release.

As a result of the Newbury By-pass and several other complaints the Ombudsman concluded that he should carry out a more general examination – an own-initiative inquiry – into the procedural position of individual complainants in the Article 169 (now Article 226) procedure. His reasoning here is significant. He wrote:

> [A]n important part of the Ombudsman's mission is to enhance relations between the Community institutions and European citizens. The creation of the office of Ombudsman by the Treaty on European Union was meant to underline the commitment of the Union to open, democratic and accountable forms of administration ...
>
> On the basis of the complaints that the Ombudsman has received, it appears that the procedure currently used by the Commission causes considerable dissatisfaction amongst European citizens, some of whom regard the Commission's approach ... as arrogant and high-handed. Furthermore, the procedure appears not to promote the degree of transparency which

European citizens increasingly expect in the functioning of Community institutions and bodies (EU Ombudsman, 1996: 32).

Therefore, although the Newbury By-pass case did not result in an intervention by the Ombudsman to protect citizens' social or environmental rights, it does fully illustrate the use of the office to promote procedural rights and good administrative behaviour.

A second case in which environmental issues were raised was the case of nuclear tests in French Polynesia. In this case, the Ombudsman found that the Commission had not failed to discharge its responsibilities under the Treaty or exercised its powers incompletely or incorrectly. However, the inquiry obliged the Commission to demonstrate that its procedures had been correct, a point of some concern to many complainants.

Turning from environmental to human rights issues, it is also worth noting that the Ombudsman is able to apply 'human rights norms' to issues under review, where these norms arise from international agreements to which the member states are party – as, for example, his own-initiative inquiry into the use of age limits, where he examined the question of 'discrimination' in the light of the ECHR and the 1966 UN Covenant (EU Ombudsman, 1998: 259 ff.). In this respect it is significant that Article 6 of the TEU binds EU institutions and bodies to respect ECHR provisions. Nevertheless, the EU Ombudsman, following the classical Ombudsmanship tradition of Scandinavia and Northern Europe, is a 'human rights Ombudsman' only by extension. His principal remit is the quality of administration and the procedural rights connected with it to which we now turn.

Procedural Rights and the Ombudsman

In the Introduction to this chapter we subdivided these rights into the rights to (a) good administration; and (b) to have one's complaints properly investigated, and where appropriate, remedied. The Ombudsman's performance in this regard can, to some extent, be assessed by reference to the statistics of his case-work.

From the beginning of his mandate in 1995 to the end of June 2000, the Ombudsman received 6,092 complaints, about 30 per cent of which were within this mandate – 906 inquiries were begun. The Ombudsman has reported (EU Ombudsman, 2000a) the following outcomes:

- 181 cases were settled by the institution after the Ombudsman had opened an inquiry, of which one was an own-initiative inquiry
- in eleven cases the complainant withdrew the complaint

- in 388 cases no maladministration was found (including four own-initiative inquiries). (Thirty-nine of these concerned the French nuclear tests at Muroroa and 27 the Newbury By-pass in England)
- in eight cases the Ombudsman achieved a 'friendly solution'
- 116 inquiries were closed with a critical remark to the institution concerned (27 of these concerned one case, the Newbury By-pass in England)
- seventeen inquiries (four of them own-initiative inquiries) resulted in draft recommendations to the institutions and bodies concerned. In nine of these cases the body accepted the recommendations. In three other cases, all own-initiatives, the Ombudsman presented a special report to the EP.

In successive Annual Reports the Ombudsman has pointed out that the main types of maladministration alleged were lack of transparency, discrimination, unsatisfactory procedures, unfairness, avoidable delay and failure by the Commission to carry out its role as 'Guardian of the Treaties' (EU Ombudsman, 1996: 18; 1997: 30–1; 1998: 26; and 1999a: 22).

To what extent the outcomes achieved can be considered 'satisfactory' is a moot point which cannot be answered without very detailed research. One could perhaps assume that the 181 cases 'settled by the institution after the Ombudsman had opened an inquiry' and the eight in which a 'friendly solution' was achieved were settled satisfactorily. That would amount to about a quarter (25 per cent) of the 'closed cases'. On the other hand, it is worth noting that in some of the large proportion of cases which are ruled as inadmissible by the Ombudsman, he is able to advise complainants about alternative courses of action which they might take. Thus he reports (EU Ombudsman, 2000a) that he has advised complainants to:

- complain to a national or regional Ombudsman or to petition a national parliament (1189 cases)
- petition the EP (506 cases – the Ombudsman transferred 101 complaints directly to the EP, with the consent of the complainant)
- address the European Commission (504 cases, including cases where a complaint against the Commission was declared inadmissible because appropriate administrative approaches had not been made)
- address the ECJ (five cases), the Court of Auditors (two cases) or other bodies (364 cases)

Nevertheless, whatever the actual figures/proportions in these categories turn out to be, in relation to the total population of the EU member states, they are minuscule – and inevitably will remain so.

By contrast, own-initiative, comprehensive across-the-board, systemic inquiries which have figured quite prominently in the Ombudsman's activities benefit large numbers of citizens. Since the effect of such inquiries is likely to be 'preventive', by their very nature it is impossible to quantify the extent to which citizens' rights to good administration are protected. Nevertheless, four of the own-initiative inquiries undertaken by the Ombudsman illustrate this aspect of his work and in particular how it operates as a mechanism for protecting the citizen's right to good administration on a systemic basis. Other own-initiative inquiries include secrecy in the Commissioner's recruitment procedures and late payments by the Commissioner. These inquiries have concerned the Commission's role as guardian of the Treaties under Article 226; lack of transparency; the use of age limits in recruitment; and a code of 'good administrative behaviour'. These will be considered in more detail.

Article 226: the Commission's role as guardian of the Treaties

In 1996 a third of complaints that led to an inquiry by the Ombudsman's office concerned the way in which the European Commission exercised its responsibilities as the guardian of the Treaties, i.e. supervision of the fulfilment by member states of their obligations under Community law. On the basis of these complaints it appeared that the Commission's procedures caused considerable dissatisfaction among European citizens. The Ombuds-man therefore began an own-initiative inquiry into the matter (Case 303/97/PD. EU Ombudsman, 1997: 280). In the event the Commission's reply to the Ombudsman's inquiry satisfied him that its procedures appeared to be adequate for ensuring both that the citizen was being kept informed about the processing of his complaint and that the complaint would be processed within a maximum period of one year unless there were special reasons. Although the 1997 inquiry did not reveal any instance of maladministration, Mr Söderman subsequently argued that its significance lay in establishing the Ombudsman's role in this aspect of citizens' rights. The Commission's response had established that complainants had a place in the infringement procedure, a place which entitled them to certain procedural rights, such as being kept informed and given an opportunity to put forward views and criticisms concerning the Commission's point of view before the Commission committed itself to a final conclusion. Mr Söderman concluded:

> Despite these improvements, the administrative stage of the Article 226 procedure is still not a normal and transparent administrative process in which the complainant becomes a party. Until it becomes such a process,

there will remain a quite widespread belief amongst citizens that the rule of law at Union level is subject to arbitrary suspension by powerful political forces. This belief weakens citizens' confidence in the rule of law in the European Union. (Söderman, 1999)

Lack of transparency

The EU Ombudsman has defined 'transparency' to mean that the processes through which public authorities make decisions should be understandable and open; the decisions themselves should be reasoned; and, as far as possible, the information on which the decisions are based should be available to the public (Söderman, 1998: 40). Transparency is not only fundamental both to accountability and the possibility of participation; it is also necessary for the citizen's ability to protect his or her private interests. For this reason, the citizen needs to have access to the information on which public authorities base decisions affecting those interests. From this perspective, access to information necessitates fair procedures and two sets of rights: to defence and to individual privacy (Söderman, 1998).

Mr Söderman has argued (Söderman, 1999) that the EU's commitment to transparency (made at Maastricht and renewed at Amsterdam) imposes two requirements in relation to the provision of information: first, to take the initiative in providing information to citizens – to have, in other words, a targeted information strategy – and, second, to react properly when citizens take the initiative by asking for information and in particular for access to documents which have not already been put in the public domain. Prompted by several complaints, the Ombudsman began an inquiry into EU transparency, addressed to fifteen Community institutions and bodies. Its subject was not the 'quality' of the rules but their existence and public availability.

In their replies most but not all of the institutions and bodies informed the Ombudsman that they 'envisaged the adoption of rules on public access'. None claimed that adopting such rules would be impracticable or unduly burdensome (Söderman, 1998: 40). The Ombudsman accordingly concluded his inquiry with a recommendation that rules on public access to documents be adopted within three months (EU Ombudsman, 1996. OJ 1997 C 272/40). After some considerable delay, this was taken up by all the EU bodies except the ECJ, which argued that it was too difficult to separate documents relating to its judicial role from those which do not. EU bodies set up later, such as the European Central Bank, responded similarly, although Europol has adopted alternative temporary methods of transparency, pending formal regulations for the other EU bodies. The Commission's delay in producing a draft regulation on transparency is clearly beginning to irk the Ombudsman, especially in the light of the resignation of the Commission in 1999 on this very issue. This is made clear in the Foreword to the EU Ombudsman's Annual Report for 1999:

> The reason which is often given for maintaining traditional confidentiality – efficiency – seems rather paradoxical. Was it really efficient for the Santer Commission to collapse in March, leaving the Union's activities badly hampered for half a year in the absence of a lead from an active Commission? An important reason for the collapse was what had been done behind the curtain of confidentiality. Furthermore, experience shows that open administration . . . seems to be an effective tool against fraud and corruption, while a closed and confidential handling of public affairs appears to provide opportunities for fraud and corruption. I find it disturbing that those who oppose the increasing demands for more openness overlook this important point. (EU Ombudsman, 1999a: 12–13)

Age Limits

Many complaints have been made to the Ombudsman about the use of age limits as recruitment criteria for EU institutional staff (see EU Ombudsman, 1998: 259–68). Accordingly, in July 1997 the Ombudsman began an own-initiative enquiry into the use of age limits for recruitment. Simultaneously the Union was deciding that age should be explicitly included in the list of matters upon which action may be taken to combat discrimination. The responses to the Ombudsman's inquiries revealed the varying practices and policy stances of the institutions. The Commission decided as a matter of policy to abandon the use of age limits but, recognizing the need for common agreement between the institutions, adopted as a temporary measure the EP's limit of 45 years for its forthcoming competitions. By contrast, the Council's Secretariat reaffirmed its view that age limits, varied as they were according to the nature of the department's needs, were not 'discriminatory' in the sense the ECHR and ECJ give to that term.

Given that age discrimination was not explicitly prohibited, the Ombudsman argued that age limits need to be justified objectively, finding that the practice within the Community institutions of setting various age limits with differing grounds and without sufficient justification could not be considered as a correct application of age limits (EU Ombudsman, 1998: 267). However, the slowness with which the Amsterdam provisions have been enacted, and the Commission's failure to set up an inter-institutional agreement on this issue, have reawakened the Ombudsman's official interest in this matter, and Mr Söderman has demanded action from the Commission. As a result, a final judgement on the matter is not yet possible.

Code of good administrative behaviour

In November 1998 the Ombudsman began an own-initiative inquiry into the existence and public accessibility of a code of 'good administrative behaviour' (EU Ombudsman, 1999a: 19–20). In his inquiry the Ombudsman asked each of the nineteen institutions or bodies of the Union if it had adopted a code of good administrative behaviour for its officials in their relations with the public which was easily accessible to the citizens; and, if not, if it would agree to take the necessary steps to adopt one. Substantively, the Ombudsman sought to ensure lawfulness; equal treatment; proportionality; avoidance of abuse of power; abstention in cases of personal interest; legal certainty; fairness; and consistency. His suggested procedural principles are primarily concerned with keeping people properly and fully informed; giving them full opportunities to make their case; the need to give reasoned decisions; and the requirement to inform people of their rights of appeal or remedy (EU Ombudsman, 1999a: 19–20).

The Commission's response was broadly constructive, but promise was not made reality owing to the problems caused by the departure of the Santer team. The EP and Council were less responsive. Both institutions have so far failed to produce the codes of conduct they declared themselves to support in response to the Ombudsman's inquiry (EU Ombudsman, 1999b: 3–5). The Ombudsman thus concluded that in fact none of the institutions, bodies or decentralized agencies had yet adopted a code of good administrative behaviour as he had proposed. He thus made further draft recommendations:

- Each institution or body should adopt rules concerning good administrative behaviour by its officials in their relations with the public, taking guidance from the provisions of the Ombudsman's recommended code.
- In order to ensure that the rules could be easily understood by citizens, they should deal only with relations with the public. Other rules for staff should be dealt with in a separate document.
- The rules on officials' relations with the public should be adopted in the form of a decision and published in the Official Journal so as to be accessible to citizens (EU Ombudsman, 1999b: 10).

As a result, by March 2000 only six out of eighteen EU bodies had adopted such a code. The Ombudsman was far from satisfied with the progress made, arguing that rhetoric about commitment to good governance in the EU had not been made good (EU Ombudsman, 1999c). In April 2000, he issued a Special Report to the EP in which he recommended the enactment of a European administrative law to ensure that officials of all the EU bodies observe the same principles of good administrative behaviour in their relations with the public (EU Ombudsman, 2000b: 10).

The slow progress of this inquiry well illustrates the complexity of decision-making within the EU's structures. Formally there was a clear welcome for the Ombudsman's initiative and a recognition of the part it could play in the objective of bringing institutions closer to the Union's citizens. In that project comprehensibility and transparency are crucial, hence the Ombudsman's insistence that the code should be authoritative (adopted by a formal decision), accessible (published) and easily identifiable (a self-contained document, not tucked away in a staff guide compendium). Progress towards that end has been inhibited by the need to ensure that a common version of the code is adopted and that proper consultation with staff interests has been undertaken. It was also clearly delayed by the crisis arising from the Commission's resignation. There are signs that the Ombudsman is making some, albeit slow, progress towards what would be a real achievement. He cannot force adoption of the code, only persuade.

EU 'specific' rights and the Ombudsman

Under this heading it is necessary at the outset to remind ourselves that the Ombudsman's remit is limited because he is authorized to investigate allegations only against Community institutions and bodies. Alleged violations of rights 'specific' to the EU which are perpetrated by member states rather than by the Community institutions fall outside the Ombudsman's jurisdiction. When he receives complaints of this kind, the Ombudsman's procedure is normally to advise the complainant to petition the EP and, if the infringement seems to be a serious one, also to notify the Commission (EU Ombudsman, 1995: 30). Thus, for example, in relationship to freedom of movement within the Union, most of the obstacles identified result from the incorrect implementation and application of Community law by national, regional and local administrations and as such are outside the Ombudsman's remit. The present Ombudsman, being a firm believer in the principle of subsidiarity, insists that national Ombudsmen and similar bodies should be encouraged and assisted in dealing with complaints from European citizens concerning breaches of Community law (EU Ombudsman, 1998: 11).

Under the heading of EU specific rights, for which of course the courts are the major protectors, the Ombudsman's role is focused on two areas: the application of these rights as part of the entitlement to 'good administration' and monitoring complaints about the Commission's powers of enforcement under Article 226, both of which have been dealt with in a previous section. However, this does not mean that the Ombudsman has played no role in developing EU specific rights. In fact, the reverse may be true. The creation of an EU Charter of Rights (still under negotiation at the time of writing) has given the Ombudsman a further opportunity to promote the concept of a right to good administration, as his views were officially requested. Through lobbying and advocacy, the Ombudsman has been able to secure the inclusion of a right of the citizen to good administration (open, accountable and service-minded governance) in the proposed Charter (Charte 4170/00, Convent 17). He has also urged the drafting of the Charter to allow citizens alleging infringement of their fundamental rights by an EU body to appeal to Community Courts, and reiterated his readiness to 'supervise respect for fundamental rights as an extra-judicial remedy' (EU Ombudsman, 2000c). It remains to be seen what will finally emerge from the Convention's work but the lobbying success of the Ombudsman clearly demonstrates his role as promoter as well as defender of citizens' procedural rights in the sphere of public administration.

V. CONCLUSION

Although the creation of the Office of European Ombudsman was explicitly linked to the idea of strengthening European citizenship, it is obviously unrealistic to expect the Office to bear too much of the weight of expectations with regard to demonstrating the benefits of 'EU citizenship' for the citizens of member states and making the EU more popular. That is not only because the citizenship project is very wide-ranging. It is also because the Ombudsman institution is a very small player on the EU stage. That is most apparent from the 'scale-differential' between a Union of 250 million citizens, 15,000 officials and a budget of 86.5 billion ecus and an Office with 24 posts and a budget of 3.9 million ecus (EU Ombudsman, 1999a: 296). That differential alone demonstrates the limited impact which could be expected from the institution of the EU Ombudsman as at present constituted.

But that is, of course, to perceive the Ombudsman institution in isolation, whereas in fact the Office is one of many mechanisms which exist for facilitating effective relations between the Union, its institutions, the member states and citizens: the EU Ombudsman plays his modest part alongside courts, tribunals, parliaments and other intermediaries at European, national, regional and local levels. In this respect the Ombuds-man Office well illustrates the mixed model of citizenship and its multi-layered nature which have been pointed up in the other chapters of this volume.

The need to view the EU Ombudsman in the wider context is no surprise to Ombudsman-watchers, for Ombudsman institutions are very rarely if ever 'stand-alone' institutions. The role of an Ombudsman is to supplement other mechanisms for dealing with citizens' grievances and injustices, particularly those which are not best handled by political or judicial mechanisms. Typically (but not exclusively) the Ombudsman specializes in providing remedies for injustices inflicted upon individual citizens in consequence of maladministration, *where these have not been resolved by other means.* The role of the Ombudsman is to deal with those relatively rare (as they ought to be) cases in which 'internal' complaint-resolution processes go awry and resort to judicial or political process is inappropriate.

For most citizens, then, contact with the Ombudsman should be expected to be relatively rare. And in the case of the EU the individual citizen's direct contact with the Community's institutions and administration is also very limited. For the most part the citizen (in contrast, perhaps, to the entrepreneur) encounters national, regional and local administrations administering European laws, directives, and so on, rather than the European institutions directly. Moreover, the EU Ombudsman's remit extends beyond 'citizens': it includes legal as well as natural persons and persons residing or having a registered office in a member state – a provision which perhaps indicates a greater (and proper?) concern with promoting good governance than with effective citizenship.

Given the above, it is not surprising that a positive assessment of the EU Ombudsman's role in promoting citizenship has to be somewhat narrowly focused on three aspects: the citizen's entitlement to good administration; systemic improvements rather than individual cases; and drawing out the implications for administrative processes of the Union's declared commitment to international human rights standards. In these areas the evidence to date is that a beginning has been made, and to that limited extent the Ombudsman has made a contribution to facilitating 'European citizenship'.

Though it is limited, the significance of this contribution should not be under-estimated. Through his insistence on more transparency and the code of good administrative behaviour, and his advocacy of a Right to Good Administration, the Ombudsman is helping to develop the broader concept of a more service-minded and accountable administration. In common with the work of all Ombudsmen, such operations serve to enhance and underpin the legitimacy of governments. If officialdom does not behave correctly towards the individual, or if the shortcomings of officialdom are not subject to correction, then the foundations of government itself may be weakened. As Marten Oosting has put it:

Legitimacy is fundamental to every government; it is, if you will, its working capital. And it is on this capital that the government can draw in devising and implementing effective policy. However, it must make a continual effort to add to this capital by working in a manner that will add to the people's acceptance. (Oosting, 1995: 151–6)

In this respect, the European Ombudsman office, along with other oversight bodies within the Union, clearly has an important role to play. The political and administrative leadership of the EU commands limited confidence among citizens of the member states. Rightly or wrongly, the central institutions of the Community are widely seen by a significant group of citizens as bureaucratic, excessively secretive, sometimes venal and insufficiently accountable.[2] If there is one governmental structure that manifestly needs to add to its working capital of legitimacy and reinforce a sense of allegiance to its political institutions, that structure is surely the European Union.

ACKNOWLEDGEMENTS

The authors wish to acknowledge the assistance Dr Anthea Harris and the Nuffield Foundation have given in the preparation of this chapter.

NOTES

1. For accounts of the origins of the 'European citizenship' concept and the EU Ombudsman scheme, see Closa, 1992; Hummer, 1995; Marias, 1994b, 1994c and 1995; Wincott, 1994; European Parliament, 1995.
2. It should be noted, however, that according to the latest Eurobarometer survey (No. 53, Spring 2000), the average level of trust in the European Commission across the fifteen member states is 45%, and in nine of the member states, trust levels reached or exceeded 50% (Belgium, Greece, Spain, France, Ireland, Italy, Luxembourg, the Netherlands and Portugal). Trust is lowest in the UK (24%), Sweden and Germany (both 34%).

REFERENCES

Alvarez de Miranda y Torres, F. (1999) 'Human Rights and their Function in the Institutional Strengthening of the Ombudsman', in International Ombudsman Institute and Linda C. Reif (eds), *The International Ombudsman Yearbook Volume 2* (The Hague/Boston/London: Kluwer Law International).

Bradley, A. W. (1983) 'The Ombudsman and the Protection of Citizens' Rights', in Gerald E. Caiden (ed.), *International Handbook of the Ombudsman: Evolution and Present Function* (Westport, Connecticut: Greenwood Press).

Caiden, G. E. (ed.) (1983) *International Handbook of the Ombudsman: Evolution and Present Function* (Westport, Connecticut: Greenwood Press).

Caiden, G. E., MacDermot, N. and Sandler, A. (1983) 'The Ombudsman Institution', in G. E. Caiden (ed.), *International Handbook of the Ombudsman: Evolution and Present Function* (Westport, Connecticut: Greenwood Press).

Carvel, J. (1994) 'Ombudsman to Right EU Wrongs', *The Guardian*, 3 November 1994.

Chanterie, R. (1985) 'Report of Mr R Chanterie on Behalf of the Committee on the Rules of Procedure and Petitions', European Parliament, Doc. A2-41/85.

Closa, C. (1992) 'The Concept of Citizenship in the Treaty on European Union', *Common Market Law Review* 29: 6, pp. 1137–69.

Cuellar, J. M. (1999) 'The Ombudsman and his Relationship with Human Rights, Poverty and Development', in International Ombudsman Institute and Linda C. Reif (eds), *The International Ombudsman Yearbook Volume 2* (The Hague/Boston/ London: Kluwer Law International).

EU Ombudsman (1995) *Annual Report 1995*.

EU Ombudsman (1996) *Annual Report 1996*.

EU Ombudsman (1997) *Annual Report 1997*.

EU Ombudsman (1998) *Annual Report 1998*.

EU Ombudsman (1999a) *Annual Report 1999*.

EU Ombudsman (1999b) *Draft Recommendation of the European Ombudsman in the Own Initiative Inquiry OI/1/98/OV*.

EU Ombudsman (1999c) *Press Release No 14/99*.

EU Ombudsman (2000a) *Statistics concerning the Work of the European Ombudsman on 30 June 2000*.

EU Ombudsman (2000b) *Special Report to the European Parliament following the Own-Initiative Inquiry into the Existence and the Public Accessibility in the Different Community Institutions and Bodies, of a Code of Administrative Behaviour*, Brussels, April 2000.

EU Ombudsman (2000c) *Speech at the Public Hearing on the draft Charter of Fundamental Rights of the European Union*, Brussels, 2 February 2000.

European Parliament (1994) *Info Memo 150*, 24 November 1994.

European Parliament (1995) *Info Memo 115*, 27 June 1995.

European Parliament Debates (1979) 'Debates of the European Parliament', 10 December 1979.

European Parliament Debates (1987) 'Debates of the European Parliament', 16 June 1987.

Folketing (1990) 'Contribution of the Folketing', DOC EN/BUR/98450, 27–30 November 1990.

Frank, B. (1976) 'The Ombudsman and Human Rights – Revisited', *Israel Yearbook on Human Rights 6* (Tel Aviv: Faculty of Law, Tel Aviv University).

Gregory, Roy and Giddings, Philip (2000) 'The Ombudsman Institution: Growth and Development', in Roy Gregory and Philip Giddings (eds), *Righting Wrongs: the Ombudsman in Six Continents* (Brussels: International Institute of Administrative Sciences).

Hummer, W. (1995) 'The Position and Duties of the Ombudsman of the European Parliament', Opinion from 3 September 1995 by Order of the European Ombudsman Institute (Innsbruck: European Ombudsman Institute).

Ibanez, A. G. (1992) 'Spain and European Political Union', in Finn Laursen and Sophie Vanhoonacker (eds), *The Intergovernmental Conference on Political Union* (Maastricht: European Institute of Public Administration).

Jenkins, R. (1989) *European Diary 1977–1981* (London: Collins).

Laursen, F. and Vanhoonacker, S. (eds) (1992) *The Intergovernmental Conference on Political Union* (Maastricht: European Institute of Public Administration).

Marias, E. A. (1994a) 'The Right to Petition the European Parliament after Maastricht', *European Law Review* 19: 2, pp. 169–83.

Marias, E. A. (1994b) 'The European Ombudsman', *EIPASOPE*, European Institute of Public Administration, No. 1994/2.

Marias, E. A. (1994c) 'The European Ombudsman', *EIPASOPE*, European Institute of Public Administration, No. 1994/1.

Marias, E. A. (1995) 'Mechanisms of Protection of Union Citizens' Rights', in A. Rosas and E. Antola (eds), *A Citizens' Europe. In Search of a New Order* (London: Sage).

Marshall, T. H. (1950) *Citizenship and Social Class* (London: Pluto Press).

Oliver, D. (1991) *Government in the United Kingdom: The Search for Accountability, Effectiveness and Citizenship* (Milton Keynes: Open University Press).

Oosting, Marten (1995) 'Essential Elements of Ombudsmanship', in Linda C. Reif (ed.), *The Ombudsman Concept* (University of Alberta, Edmonton: International Ombudsman Institute).

Reding, V. (1991) *Report on the Deliberations of the Committee on Petitions during the Parliamentary Year 1990–91*, European Parliament, Doc A3-0122/91.

Robertson, A. H. and Merrills, J. G. (1996) *Human Rights in the World. An Introduction to the Study of the International Protection of Human Rights* (Manchester and New York: Manchester University Press (4th edition)).

Söderman, J. (1998) *The Citizen, the Administration and the Law: General Report prepared for the 1998 Fide Congress* (Strasbourg: Office of the European Ombudsman).

Söderman, J. (1999) 'Speech delivered to the Court of First Instance', Luxembourg, 19 October 1999.

Westlake, M. (1994) *A Modern Guide to the European Parliament* (London and New York: Pinter).

Wincott, Daniel (1994) 'Is the Treaty of Maastricht an Adequate "Constitution" for the European Union?', *Public Administration* 72: 4, pp. 573–90.

5

Market Citizenship: Functionalism and Fig-leaves

TONY DOWNES

I. INTRODUCTION

Significant expectations have been placed upon the establishment in the Treaty on European Union (TEU) of citizenship of the EU. For the European Commission (1993), 'the introduction of these new provisions underscores the fact that the Treaty of Rome is not concerned solely with economic matters'. It was to be a central element, perhaps the keystone, in the building of 'a People's Europe' (European Commission, 1975, 1984). Commentators have remained unconvinced, dismissing the Treaty's language of citizenship as 'rhetoric' (Lyons, 1996) and as failing to provide the hoped-for counterbalance to the EU's institutions in the quest for legitimacy (Armstrong, 1996). This chapter examines arguably the most effective dimension of the limited bundle of rights within the concept of citizenship established in TEU: 'market citizenship' (Everson, 1995). The term was always provocative and it will be argued here that the understanding of it was unduly narrow. Everson describes the 'market citizen' as posing few problems for academic analysis. This may be attributable to the fact that although the market citizen is understood as enjoying core rights derived from all of the four freedoms (of establishment/ movement of services, and of movement of persons, goods and capital), the significant analysis attaches to the market citizen as consumer, in particular as a beneficiary of the freedom of movement of goods. Everson recognizes that this is not a particularly fruitful line of investigation in terms of European rights of citizenship, since she sees citizenship rights as essentially comprising 'entitlements' (Dahrendorf, 1992) while consumer rights are much more about choices or, in Dahrendorf's terminology 'provisions'. In short, the rights attached to market citizens derived from the single market law relating to the free movement of goods do not look much like the kind of rights we would normally associate with the status of citizenship as such, even if they are rights of a kind which citizens as members of a free market society enjoy in their role as consumers.

If the analysis of the rights of market citizens is carried out in the case of the single market law relating to the free movement of workers and other persons, then the results are more fruitful. Here too it is possible to regard the market citizen as being 'instrumentalized', to borrow Everson's expression, not least by the European Court of Justice (ECJ). The significant difference is that the rights developed by the ECJ and attaching to market citizens are much more like the kinds of rights that we associate with the status of citizenship. Freedom to come and go throughout the territory is a classic 'entitlement' of the citizen, even if in the case of the European Community, as we shall see, the rights in question were originally restricted to *economic* actors. Even before the TEU it was doubtful if a person had to be engaged in true market activity to benefit from the rights in question, and this investigation seeks to identify whether the economic imperative once attached to these rights remains in place. Nevertheless, it is the case that the rights themselves are economic or market-related at least in origin, and that when first they were recognized they did not arise out of any identified status of citizenship. As such, they are more properly to be regarded as having started life as rights akin to citizenship rights, although through time their status may have changed so that they are now genuinely rights of citizenship.

This chapter is based upon an empirical and realist legal analysis. It focuses in particular on the role of the ECJ in the development of this dimension of EU citizenship. The reason for so doing is that it was largely as a result of the purposive and allegedly improperly activist (Rasmussen, 1986) jurisprudence of the ECJ that it was possible to argue as early as 1976 that the law relating to free movement of persons offered 'an incipient form of European citizenship' (Plender, 1976).[1] The ECJ is generally accepted to have been a catalyst for integration at several key stages in the short history of the Treaty of Rome, for example in recognizing concepts of supremacy and direct effect of EC law, and in breaking the legislative logjam in the *approximation* process. As is noted by Weatherill and Beaumont (1999: 622), it is an instinctive reaction for Community lawyers to turn to the ECJ for leadership when a new concept appears. It may be helpful to begin by setting out the evidence of what the ECJ has done in the past to create a 'form of citizenship', before examining more recent judgments which appear to reveal some reluctance on the part of the ECJ to go beyond certain limits in relying upon the notion of citizenship as established by the TEU. In this respect, not for the first time, there are signs that the Advocates General are pushing at the frontiers of the concept but so far failing to carry the ECJ with them.

II. 'CITIZENSHIP' BEFORE THE TEU

The contributions of the ECJ to the elaboration of a catalogue of practical rights which might be regarded as associated with a form of citizenship fall into two broad categories. First, and the subject of this chapter, are the substantive rights themselves: the expansive interpretation of rights of free movement, the corresponding restrictive interpretation of the limits on those rights, and the development of a general principle of non-discrimination. Second, beyond the scope of the chapter, are those elements of adjectival law which contribute so-called 'effective remedies' by which citizens may vindicate their EU law rights through national courts.[2]

Decisions relating to the first category are numerous, and it must suffice here to restate some well-known examples to illustrate the point. Let us begin with the concept of free movement of workers, provided for in Article 39 EC (ex Article 48). The provision is one of the key ingredients of the common market, allowing for free movement of one of the four factors of production. As such, it is inevitably limited to economic actors within the labour market, and the concept of 'worker' might have been interpreted restrictively to embrace only those making a measurable contribution to the goal of creation of a common market. In *Levin v Staatssecretaris van Justitie* (1982) the ECJ took the opposite approach: the concept of 'worker' is interpreted widely and inclusively, so that any person falls within its scope provided the work consists of 'the pursuit of genuine and effective activities' and is not so minimal as to be 'purely marginal and ancillary'. The ECJ refused to take account of the fact that the remuneration for the amount of work in question fell below minimum subsistence level in the host state. In *Kempf v Staatssecretaris van Justitie* (1986) the ECJ subsequently included within the definition of 'worker' a person whose activities only produced an income sufficient to live on by virtue of supplementary benefits paid by the host state. What are we to make of these decisions? To begin with, the fact that in *Commission v France* (1974) the right of free movement for workers was held to be directly effective (that is, enforceable by the individual through legal action in a national court) is itself an indication that the ECJ is not simply concerned with macro-economic issues of the labour market. It would have been possible to say that the free movement rules are addressed only to member states, and to reason that individuals did not need the rights which correspond to the member state duties in respect of free movement, since no individual will have a measurable impact on market integration. The ECJ rejected that route: free movement is an *individual* right at least akin to a citizenship right. But the ECJ goes further: although an element of 'market' activity remains a prerequisite of this right of free movement, it is set at a minimal threshold and it is difficult not to conclude that the ECJ's clear intention was to include as many as possible within a general right of free movement. The motive appears to have been to capture the involvement of individuals in the development of the Economic Community through an embryonic ideal of citizenship.

The ECJ's approach to limits on the free movement of workers is consistent with this view. Article 39(3) (ex Article 48(3)) allows limitations to be placed by member states on the free movement of persons on grounds of public policy, public security and public health. Here too it is possible to conceive of the legal control of such member-state action being left to the Commission under Article 226 (ex Article 169), and for the ECJ to have taken a broadly economic approach which reasoned that restrictions on particular individuals will rarely if ever have measurable consequences for integration, so that there would be no reason to interfere in respect of individual decisions as opposed to tackling national measures which would impede the free movement rights of significant classes of persons. The reality was otherwise. In *Van Duyn v Home Office* (1974) the ECJ recognizes the direct effect of Article 48(3), imposing strict due process safeguards of a 'civil rights' nature,[3] and although it allows a degree of discretion to the member states it requires national courts in applying Article 48(3) to individuals to take account of the attitude of the national law towards its own nationals in a similar position.[4] The facts of *R v Bouchereau* (1977) serve as a good example: a French national working in Britain was twice convicted of drug offences; the ECJ said that in so far as a second conviction showed some tendency to reoffend there was potentially evidence of a present threat to public policy, but that there must also be 'a genuine and sufficiently serious threat to ... one of the fundamental interests of society'.[5] In due course, the English magistrate imposed a fine but did not recommend deportation,[6] presumably because the attitude of the British courts to a British person found in possession of drugs would not have been to impose a very serious sentence commensurate with a threat to a fundamental interest of society. Clearly, the deportation of one French national with a criminal record relating to drugs offences would not have imperilled the economic success of the common market in labour; indeed, it is hard to imagine that there would be any such risk if each and every national of another member state, convicted of any criminal offence more serious than speeding or breach of parking regulations, were to be deported from the host state. If that is the case, it raises questions about the ECJ's motives in granting individuals rights in this way. Although the rights are built upon the foundation of economic activity, and so can be described as 'market rights' or rights pertaining to 'market citizenship', their extent and implementation by the ECJ goes far beyond the needs of the integrated labour market. Here again it is difficult not to conclude that the right of free movement of workers is being developed as a quasi-constitutional entitlement, and that the motive has more to do with the ECJ's recognition of the EU's need to win hearts and minds than it has to do with any direct economic imperative.

The *Adoui*[7] test embodies the beginnings of what may be seen as a principle of non-discrimination: although states may not deport their own nationals, so that direct comparison is impossible, the right to deport the nationals of other member states is contingent upon the host state having seriously repressive measures which it deploys against its own nationals in corresponding situations. In this form, the principle of non-discrimination is essentially negative in scope; it enables the person within the scope of the rule (in this case employees, but it might equally be a provider of services or a person seeking to exercise the right of establishment) to resist exclusion from another member state where such exclusion might be regarded as discriminatory by comparison with that state's treatment of its own nationals. The ECJ has gone significantly further in expressly adopting the principle of non-discrimination in Article 12 EC (ex Article 6) as the basis for granting positive entitlements to nationals of other member states. The context in which it did so can be regarded as developing a general right of free movement for all member-state nationals, although it is in a technical sense still predicated upon some economic (market) activity. The facts of *Cowan v Le Trésor Public* (1989) are probably well known: Cowan, a British national visiting Paris, was attacked near a Metro station; he applied to the French authorities under a criminal injuries compensation scheme, but was turned down on the basis that he was neither a French national nor the holder of a French residence permit nor a national of a state with which France had a reciprocal agreement in respect of such claims. Cowan's challenge to that decision was referred to the ECJ, which ruled that Cowan was entitled to the same degree of protection, on the basis of the non-discrimination rule in Article 12 EC, as a French national or a person resident in France. The decision rests upon two fairly bold interpretations of the Treaty. The first related to Cowan's entitlement to invoke EC law at all, since it had already been established in *Sagulo, Brenca and Bakhouche* (1977) that the non-discrimination principle set out in the Treaty did not apply in the abstract, but could in fact only apply in the context of a specific policy provision of the Treaty. In other words, Cowan had to show that he was in some way participating in the economic/market function of the Treaty. That he was treated as a consumer of services was not in itself surprising, because although the Treaty is drafted only in terms of providers of services being able to move freely in order so to do in other member states, the ECJ had already recognized in *Luisi and Carbone v*

Ministero del Tesero (1984) that in the case of some services it is not realistic for the provider to move, so that a single market for such services can only be created by interpreting the Treaty as allowing free movement for consumers. The remarkable element in Cowan is the minimal threshold the case seems to imply as governing the right to invoke the provisions of Community law at all. Cowan, it seems, was a 'tourist', but was staying with a relative in Paris,[8] and so presumably was not consuming hotel services and may only occasionally if ever have consumed restaurant services. Indeed, it is not certain he consumed any services other than those of the transport which seems to have led to his unfortunate experience! The second remarkable interpretation of the Treaty is the ruling that the right of free movement coupled with the right not to be discriminated against by comparison with host-state nationals included positive entitlements which were by no means directly related to the exercise of the right of free movement in question. This is not to question the general idea of secondary rights which are 'parasitic' upon primary rights of free movement and which can be said to be necessary to give substance to the primary right – for example, the right for a spouse and children to have rights of residence and social provision as necessary concomitants of the right of free movement of a worker;[9] without such ancillary rights not many workers would choose to exercise the primary right in question. But it seems unlikely that the right of access to criminal injury compensation is determinant of the choice made by a tourist whether or not to visit a particular destination. The decision leaves unanswered the question of whether there are any (and if so which?) rights which are not available by virtue of the principle of non-discrimination.

The decision in *Cowan*, then, appears to create something close to a general right of free movement for nationals of member states, since it seems that by the mere fact of moving the citizen will inevitably satisfy the minimum threshold for the consumption of services so as to fall within the scope of the Treaty. That right of free movement includes negative rights, or immunities, such as the right not to be prevented from entering the host state and the right of movement within the state, and the right not to be excluded or deported on trivial grounds related to public policy or security. It also includes an as yet ill-defined catalogue of positive (or claim) rights available by virtue of the principle of non-discrimination. Although there is a residual economic/market criterion for the right to exist, it has been defined in such a way as to be almost meaningless. It appears impossible to argue that such an interpretation of the Treaty was inevitable: on the contrary, the argument here is that by what it has done (if not always by what it has expressly said) the ECJ has deliberately and progressively elaborated a right of free movement akin to a citizenship right. It appears equally impossible to argue that such an interpretation, if not inevitable, was essential to the purposes of creating a single market for labour or for services. What, then, was the ECJ's motivation? Two possibilities come to mind: to force the pace of integration at the level of individual rights, or to disguise the absence of any real engagement of the individual in the constitution-building process by creating rights which are at best peripheral to the issues of democratic deficit and legitimacy.

Secondary legislation on rights of residence

In the course of the legislative programme initiated to bring about the completion of the single market three Directives were adopted relating to rights of residence for, respectively, member-state nationals generally,[10] retired persons[11] and students.[12] This legislation contains mixed messages from the point of view of ascertaining whether the dominant element in the identification of effective citizenship rights is that of economic/market activity. All three Directives were drafted in a form which did not demand market activity to fall within their scope: they require only that the individual have sickness insurance and sufficient resources to avoid becoming a burden on the social assistance system of the host state.[13] Moreover, originally in each case the legal base of the Directive was Article 308 (ex Article 235), which is the residual legislative power rather than a power linked to a specific Community policy. That suggests that the 'market' element is no longer dominant: in this field as in the others the Commission persuaded the Council to pick up the law-maker's baton from the previously activist ECJ. However, the European Parliament challenged the legal base adopted for the students' Directive,[14] and the ECJ ruled that Article 235 could not apply as the legal base because a more specific legal base was available (namely, Article 12(2) EC (ex Article 6(2), coupled with the provisions on vocational training – Article 149 (ex Article 126)). The ECJ, therefore, appeared to decline the opportunity for further development of rights akin to citizenship rights, and to adopt a solution which expressly espoused an economic/market basis for the creation of rights.

III. MARKET CITIZENSHIP AFTER THE TEU

Article 8 EC (now Article 17) established citizenship of the Union, comprising such rights as are conferred by the Treaty, including according to Article 8a (now Article 18) rights of free movement and residence 'subject to the limitations and conditions laid down in this Treaty and by the measures adopted to give it effect'. In the light of the analysis thus far it should be apparent that the scope of these rights is complex and perhaps deceptive. In the case of free movement, the Treaty places a general condition of economic activity on the existence of such a right, but even before the drafting of the Treaty the ECJ had all but circumvented that requirement by its decision in *Cowan*. So, the existing Treaty-based right of free movement, now attached to the new status of Union citizen, is pretty well a general right. In the case of residence, the right is expressed by implementing legislation to be 'general', which it is in the sense that no economic activity is required, but it is subject to a seemingly stringent financial threshold.

What is interesting to examine is what the ECJ has made of rights akin to citizenship rights since the establishment of Union citizenship. One possibility was that a court which has not been afraid to make ground-breaking decisions of a constitutional nature would be spurred on to further bouts of activism. The alternative view is that the ECJ's activism has been stimulated by what the members of the ECJ perceive to be unacceptable inaction on the part of the Community's legislators, most especially the Council of Ministers. On that view, once citizenship was openly on the political agenda, the ECJ might be expected to take rather more of a back seat. The reaction has been more of the latter kind, although there is at least potential for further development. The ECJ has been unwilling, in the main, to accept arguments for extension of the rights of individuals based simply on the new status of Union citizenship. So, in *Skanavi* (1996) the ECJ refused to determine a dispute about the exchange of driving licences by reference to the citizenship provisions, rather than by the more traditional, economic activity-based rules on the right of establishment.[15] And in *Uecker and Jacquet* (1997) the ECJ refused to depart from its previously established position that the free movement rights do not apply in the case of a national of a member state in his/her home state: the fact of being a citizen of the Union was of no assistance when the matter had no Community dimension and was therefore said simply to be one of the internal law of a member state. In these decisions, at least, there is little sign of judicial activism: the orthodox economic/market activity basis has apparently been reasserted.

More recently, however, the ECJ has linked the non-discrimination principle to the citizenship provisions of the Treaty in a decision which may prove to be just as far-reaching as *Cowan* appears to be. *Maria Martinez Sala v Freistaat Bayern* (1998) involved a claim for social security benefits (namely, a child-raising allowance) for migrant workers, and as such it might have been determined simply by reference to the traditional rules. The likelihood was that the claimant would qualify under either the rules relating to employment or those relating to social security, but the ECJ did not have access to enough facts to know for sure which regime, if either, applied. The ECJ therefore considered whether there was any right to the benefit claimed on the basis of a legally established residence, which the German authorities in question did not seek to challenge, without reference to either legislative regime. The Commission had argued, in its submission, that such a right did exist by virtue of Article 18 (ex Article 8a) coupled with Article 12 (ex Article 6), and effectively this argument was accepted by the Court. It will be remembered that Article 12 cannot be applied as the direct source of rights,[16] but can only be deployed to establish the extent of rights enjoyed under some positive Community law policy (so, for example, in *Cowan* the principle of non-discrimination in Article 12 applied by virtue of Cowan falling within the scope of the Treaty provisions on freedom of movement in respect of the provision and consumption of services). According to the ECJ, in this case the claimant fell within the scope of the Treaty by virtue of the provisions on citizenship, because she was a national of one member state lawfully resident in another member state. Once within the scope of the Treaty, the non-discrimination principle could be called into action in order to ensure that she was treated no differently from a national of the host state in respect of the benefits in question.

This decision offers a tantalizing prospect of Union citizenship as the source of wide-ranging social rights which are not directly related to economic/market activity. It does so by challenging previous assumptions about the scope of Articles 17 and 18 (ex Articles 8 and 8a). To begin with it had been thought that the reference in Article 18 to the rights to move and reside freely being 'subject to the limitations and conditions laid down in this Treaty' meant that those rights were no greater in scope as part of the status of citizen than they had been previously. The decision in *Sala* appears at first to raise the citizenship provisions to the same constitutional potential as the core market-based provisions relating to free movement, in as much as the ECJ appears willing to allow the ancillary deployment of the non-discrimination principle in respect of citizenship in just the same way as it had previously allowed it in respect of free movement. This certainly appears to be the express view of Advocate General La Pergola, who describes his reasoning in favour of the solution adopted as 'a logical development' of the decision in *Cowan*, and to be the forerunner of recognition by the ECJ of a broad principle of non-discrimination in respect of all benefits based upon the status of citizen. The Advocate General expressed similar views in *Stober and Pereira v Bundesanstalt für Arbeit* [1997]. However, it would be wrong to get too carried away at this stage, since the ECJ stresses that it has not in this case recognized that the right of residence itself derived from the status of citizen, despite the wording of Article 18, for the simple reason that the German authorities did not seek to challenge whether the claimant was lawfully resident there. Its decision, for the time being at least, is only that one of the 'conditions' of lawful residence is, by virtue of the citizenship provisions, a right to rely upon the non-discrimination principle. It remains to be seen whether it will take the next step of declaring a general right of residence with associated benefits purely on the basis of citizenship and without reference to any form of market/economic activity or to any secondary legislation creating such a right. For it to do so would, of course, seem to contradict Directive 90/364, which creates such a right but only under much more stringent conditions.

IV. THE AMSTERDAM TREATY AND MARKET CITIZENSHIP

The Maastricht Treaty left the concept of market citizen relevant if only because the key rights of free movement and residence (said by Article 8a to be enjoyed by every citizen of the Union) were defined entirely in terms of the limitations and conditions laid down by the Treaty and by secondary legislation; at the time those limitations and conditions reflected the market orientation of the Community, even if the ECJ had already made inroads into a narrow interpretation of the market focus. The previous analysis would, however, only have been of historical interest if the Amsterdam Treaty had introduced a more substantial catalogue of citizenship rights which are independent of any market dimension. In practice, the impact of the Amsterdam Treaty is less than clear-cut, but it is probably the case that market-based rights akin to citizenship rights will continue to have a role.

There are clearly elements of the Amsterdam Treaty which can be regarded as creating or at least having the potential to create citizenship rights in a real sense, which are independent of any market dimension. Thus, Article 13 provides the legal base for legislation to combat discrimination based on sex, racial or ethnic origin, religion or belief, disability, age or sexual orientation, without there being any express restriction of such legislation to discrimination related to the exercise of economic rights. Any such legislation would create genuine citizenship rights. However, the Treaty does not itself create any new rights under this head, and Article 13 is very unlikely to be found to be of direct effect.[17] Moreover, the opening proviso to Article 13 (which states that it applies 'without prejudice to the other provisions of this Treaty *and within the limits of the powers conferred by it upon the Community*' (emphasis added)) leaves open the possibility of argument that Article 13 cannot be the basis for the creation of generic rights against discrimination, but is – like Article 12 (ex Article 6) – parasitic upon the substantive (and market-based) provisions of the Treaty.[18]

The other significant development in the Amsterdam Treaty relating to citizenship is the so-called 'communautarization' of the Schengen agreement.[19] Here also the developments are less successful than might at first appear in getting away from the notion of market citizenship. The translation of the Schengen arrangements away from an intergovernmental and ultimately public international law basis to a firm foothold in the Treaty has the potential to provide a guarantee of the rights of free movement associated with the status of Union citizenship in Article 18 EC (ex Article 8a) without any reference to economic activity. This remains the case, even if the Community version of Schengen and the wider idea of an area of freedom, security and justice is subject to a second-class form of legal protection by comparison with other species of Community rights for individuals. However, by definition it would seem that citizenship rights are rights which adhere to all citizens by virtue of that status. As Wagner (1998) points out, the opt-out provisions in the Protocol on the Position of the United Kingdom and Ireland mean that the newly communautarized Schengen arrangements do not in fact guarantee rights of free movement to all Union citizens because nationals of the UK and Ireland are excluded from their ambit. On the other hand, this chapter has already argued that there is an all-but-general right of free movement arising from the market-based Treaty law; nationals of the UK and Ireland will continue to enjoy these rights which in practical terms will be difficult to distinguish from the rights of free movement under the Schengen arrangements. Not for the first time, flexibility (or enhanced cooperation or multi-speedism or variable geometry) may result in technical differences with political significance without actually having a significant impact on the rights of individuals. The example of the UK opt-out from the Maastricht Treaty Social Chapter is as salutary as it was predictable. Faced with two-tier development in the field of social protection the member states empowered to press ahead were rarely willing to do so, and some of the most significant developments occurred on the basis of a previously existing legal base which applied to all member states.[20] We should not be altogether surprised, therefore, if the old regime of rights akin to citizenship rights, based on single market law, continues to play an important role, not least because in this field the powers of the ECJ to define the rights of individuals are unimpaired.

V. CONCLUSIONS

Although it is over-simplistic to equate the Treaty of Rome and the ECJ with the American Constitution and Supreme Court, even brief study of the latter reveals an evident and, it is suggested, transferable lesson: it is wrong to assume that constitutional or quasi-constitutional texts are set in stone and have immutable meanings. There is no doubt that in its original conception the Treaty established rights of free movement and residence as adjuncts only of market activity. Since these rights were in the beginning among the most effective rights attached to the new status of citizen, it was understandable that the establishment of citizenship was dismissed as window dressing, limited to economic actors and not creating general civic or constitutional rights. That judgement, however, did not take account of the ability of the ECJ to redefine key terms and reinterpret the Treaty's provisions. Even before the establishment of Union citizenship the market component had been significantly reduced in practice by the decision in *Cowan*, and by secondary legislation on residence. Subsequently, the ECJ has exploited the dynamic potential of the citizenship provisions themselves; now, it seems, they may be more than simply declaratory of existing rights under other provisions of the treaty and secondary legislation. They may actually be the source of general social rights by virtue of the non-discrimination principle, and even of a less restrictive general right of residence than that created by Directive 90/364. As such, they stand in a position to fulfil O'Keeffe's (1994) prediction that 'if change will come, it will be as a result of the success of the Union and of the internal market, accompanied by an ever-increasing bundle of rights attached to Union citizenship'. On the other hand, these newly developed and still developing rights are built upon relatively flimsy foundations, with links which still go back to the narrow concept of market citizen, and the ECJ at least seems powerless or reluctant to develop citizenship rights outside that framework. This may be attributable to the fact that the ECJ is no longer the activist court that it was twenty years ago, or to the fact that the ECJ has now conceded the initiative in this area to the legislators since there is at least some indication of a willingness to move forward. For those who believe that 'the new citizenship' based on economic and social rights[21] is a sufficient concept in a postnational construct such as the EU, this may be of no concern. For those who would find in the concept of citizenship not merely rhetoric but a claim of democratic legitimacy, the work of the ECJ until now is unlikely to be more than a fig-leaf barely hiding the inadequacies of the Treaty.

NOTES

1. Those inclined to believe a realist interpretation of the Court's jurisprudence may be interested to note that Richard Plender, although writing in a personal capacity, was a legal secretary (or *référendaire*) at the ECJ.
2. For an up-to-date account, see Weatherill and Beaumont, 1999: 423–32.
3. See Dir. 64/221 and see Case C-175/94 *R v Secretary of State for Home*

Department ex p Gallagher [1995] ECR I-4253.

4. Cases 115 & 116/81 *Adoui v Belgian State, Cornuaille v Belgian State* [1982] ECR 1665: 'Although Community law does not impose upon the Member States a uniform scale of values as regards the assessment of conduct which may be considered as contrary to public policy, it should nevertheless be stated that conduct may not be considered as being of sufficiently serious nature to justify restrictions on the admission to or residence within the territory of a Member State of a national of another Member State in a case where the former Member State does not adopt, with respect to the same conduct on the part of its own nationals, repressive measures or other genuine and effective measures intended to combat such conduct.' (para. 8).

5. *Bouchereau* (1977), para. 35.

6. (1977) 2 CMLR 800, 801.

7. Note 4 above.

8. This fact is not disclosed in the official report, but was reported by his solicitor in a communication to the Solicitors' European Group.

9. See, for example, Reg. 1612/68.

10. Dir. 90/364.

11. Dir. 90/365.

12. Dir. 93/96, replacing Dir. 90/366 which was annulled on the ground that the Council had adopted the wrong legal base: Case C-295/90 *Parliament v Council* [1993] ECR I-4193.

13. This, admittedly, remains a significant obstacle to a truly general right of residence.

14. See Note 12 above.

15. The issue has now been superseded by legislation.

16. See above, *Sagulo, Brenca and Bakhouche* (1977).

17. For a general discussion, see Flynn (1999).

18. See further Barnard (1999).

19. The communautarization of Schengen is, of course, of wider significance in that it also brings the possibility of a common visa, asylum and immigration policy. This aspect is beyond the scope of this chapter, except to note along with several others that it means that Union citizenship is defined by the exclusion of others as much as by inclusion. The literature is already voluminous: Schrauwen (1998); Wagner (1998); O'Keefe and Twomey (1999).

20. The best example is the 'Working Time' Directive affair: *UK v Council* (1996). And see generally McGlynn (1998).

21. See Schnapper (1997) esp. at 204–5.

REFERENCES

Armstrong, K. (1996) 'Citizenship of the Union? Lessons from Carvel and the Guardian', *Modern Law Review* 59, 582.

Barnard, C. (1999) 'Article 13: through the Looking Glass of Union Citizenship', in D. O'Keeffe and P. Twomey (eds), *Legal Issues of the Amsterdam Treaty* (Oxford: Hart Publishing).

Dahrendorf, R. (1992) *Der Moderne Soziale Konflikt* (Stuttgart: DVA).

European Commission (1975) *Towards a Citizens' Europe*, Bull. EC Supp 7-1975, 11.

European Commission (1984) *A People's Europe*, COM (84) 446.

European Commission (1993) *First Report on Citizenship* COM (93) 702 final.

Everson, M. (1995) 'The Legacy of the Market Citizen', in Shaw, J. and More, G. (eds), *New Legal Dynamics of European Union* (Oxford: Clarendon Press).

Flynn, L. (1999) 'The Implications of Article 13 EC – After Amsterdam, Will Some Forms of Discrimination be More Equal than Others?', *Common Market Law Review* 36, 1127.

Lyons, C. (1996) 'Citizenship in the Constitution of the EU: Rhetoric or Reality?', in Bellamy, R. (ed.), *Constitutionalism, Democracy and Sovereignty: American and European Perspectives* (Aldershot: Avebury).

McGlynn, C. (1998) 'An Exercise in Futility: The Practical Effects of the Social Policy Opt-out', *Northern Ireland Legal Quarterly* 49, 60.

O'Keeffe, D. (1994) 'Union Citizenship', in O'Keeffe, D. and Twomey, P., *Legal Issues of the Maastricht Treaty* (London: Chancery Law).

O'Keeffe, D. and Twomey, P. (eds) (1999) *Legal Issues of the Amsterdam Treaty* (Oxford: Hart Publishing), especially Chs 16–21.

Plender, R. (1976) 'An Incipient Form of European Citizenship', in F. Jacobs (ed.), *European Law and the Individual* (Amsterdam: North Holland).

Rasmussen, H. (1986) *On Law and Policy in the European Court of Justice* (Dordrecht: Martinus Nijhoff).

Schnapper, D. (1997) 'The European Debate on Citizenship', *Daedalus* 126, 199.

Schrauwen, A. (1998) 'People in the Community: A Recurring Fraction', *Legal Issues of European Integration* 2, 93.

Wagner, E. (1998) 'The Integration of Schengen into the Framework of the EU', *Legal Issues of European Integration* 2, 1.

Weatherill, S. and Beaumont, P. (1999) *EU Law*, 3rd edition (London: Penguin).

6

Disintegrating Sexuality: Citizenship and the EU

CARL F. STYCHIN

I. INTRODUCTION

This chapter examines two different citizenship discourses: European and sexual citizenship. As the two increasingly come to intersect within the legal and political order of the European Union, I take this opportunity to interrogate how they can usefully inform each other. The history of EU citizenship has been tied largely to a particular conception of individual rights, which have been primarily socio-economic and market-oriented. The criticism of this citizenship form is that it has not been conducive to practices of citizenship which could be described as active or political. Rather, citizenship through rights has been linked to the disciplinarity of the market. However, rights also have been said to have the potential to exceed this disciplinarity, and to transcend the purely economic integrationist dimension of citizenship. In this chapter, I suggest that this 'excess' can form the basis of active, participatory citizenship. In other words, while the 'structure' of rights and the market may shape practices of citizenship in particular ways, those constraints are not totalizing, and the 'agency' of actors engaging with that structure can lead to unanticipated outcomes.

I go on to argue, though, that rights alone may be insufficient to create a meaningful European citizenship. Forms of active participation which go beyond the claiming of rights are needed as well. Gender- and sexuality-based rights struggles will be deployed to underscore this point. Struggles for rights in this context may be politicized, but the enjoyment of rights victories can remain private, passive, and market-centred. Thus, in this chapter, I advocate stronger connections between the language of rights and citizenship participation, in order to breathe active life into what may otherwise be largely static citizenship constructs. The lobbying efforts of the International Lesbian and Gay Association (ILGA) Europe will be deployed to exemplify this claim.

While the active/passive dichotomy of citizenship provides one central theme to this chapter, a second theme runs in tandem. This focuses on what 'lessons' can be provided by the experience of sexual citizenship politics in North America and elsewhere, not only for the emergence of sexual citizenship discourse within the EU, but also more generally for the development of a conception of European citizenship. The cautionary lesson which sexuality politics provides is the danger of attempting to construct and impose the disciplinarity of fixed identities in political life. 'Identity' increasingly has come to be eschewed in favour of a more open, less fixed, and less *essential* politics, which is often described in the language of coalition and affinity. This discourse suggests that while commonalities allow social actors to work together – to participate actively and collectively in the political arena – the connections between those actors remain informed by the differences between them. I argue that this insight is particularly important in understanding sexuality in a European legal and political context, where the commonalities which may exist around sexual object choice are exceeded by multiple differences which make a fixed, universalizable, politically informed sexual identity deeply problematic. But a politics of affinity and coalition is not only useful for understanding sexuality politics in Europe. It also may usefully assist in how we conceive of European citizenship: as an exchange across differences, where the language of networks, movements and flows replaces the dream of a unitary, fixed, and stable identity.

Thus, this chapter will examine two central challenges for European citizenship: that of creating an active, participatory, and democratic form; and the challenge of a citizenship grounded in a notion of 'belonging' where the conditions of membership are neither totalizing nor singular, and where the boundaries of membership remain sites of contestation.

II. CITIZENSHIP UNBOUND

I begin with a sketch of the ways in which the idea of European citizenship has been constituted of late in academic discourse, and I then go on to connect that to the construction of sexual citizenship. I interrogate the relationship between European and sexual citizenship, examining the ways in which theoretical work in these two areas interestingly relate, and how they might usefully inform each other. Such connections are appropriate to make, given the development of sexual identity politics in the arena of the EU, which is often articulated in the language of citizenship. The challenging of boundaries is central to this analysis, both in terms of national (and trans-national) citizenship, membership, and belonging, as well as to the ways in which the categories of sexual identity are conceived. There is an underlying tension between the need for boundaries, grounded in an inside/out dichotomy, and the potentiality of European (and sexual) citizenship for contesting those boundaries.

As a starting point, it bears reiterating that, although the idea of citizenship grounded in membership of the EU has been overwhelmingly rights-based, with little official conception of duty, the rights articulated have been primarily socio-economic market rights. Indeed, because of the often cited 'democratic deficit' within EU institutions, the political processes themselves are widely viewed as extremely distanced from individual citizens, and it is claimed that they do little to inculcate an 'active' form of citizenship (Armstrong, 1998; de Lange, 1995). There appear to have been few opportunities for active, democratic practices of citizenship, given the democratic deficit, the historically narrow focus of rights discourse, and the lack of citizen identification with European institutions. Citizenship in the context of the EU historically has been a legalistic, market-centred concept (Shaw, 1998). Perhaps as a consequence, rights discourse – because it is now an entrenched feature of EU law and politics – is considered a most productive site for the construction of an 'active' European citizen (de Búrca, 1995). Rights might be instrumental in creating a sense of European belonging. Another inversion of 'traditional' citizenship discourse thereby becomes apparent. Political processes are associated with passivity, distance, élitism, and corruption. Rights, by contrast, are associated with the active and involved citizen, relating to and making claims through the institutions of the EU, as well as within national institutions through the language of European law. European citizenship, as it emerges through these discourses, thus underscores how a simply active/passive dichotomy cannot unproblematically be deployed as a way of analysing rights and citizenship. As well, the claim that rights discourse can be located on the 'private' side of the public/private dichotomy also becomes problematic. While the enjoyment of rights may be centred in a private, depoliticized sphere, the *pursuit* of rights – the campaign, rather than the judicial result – can be an active, public, and potentially democratic endeavour. It now occurs, not only on the national stage, but in the trans-national sphere.

However, the language of rights in the EU has been historically tied to a particular conception of the good, namely, the promotion of the economic integration of the Union, and the creation of a 'transnational capitalist society' (Ball, 1996). Rights thus were constructed as a tool towards the achievement of an economically grounded, integrationist aim (de Lange, 1995). For example, the original justification for sexual equality rights – fundamental to European rights discourse – was not a broad-based concern with participation by women on equal terms in the public sphere, but a desire to ensure a level playing field in the cost of factors of production between the member states of the European Economic Community.

But the potential unruliness of rights discourse also may be apparent here, as rights now exceed narrow, economic integrationist conceptions of the good. In fact, the original economic impetus for equal rights has broadened out to include a political, normative rationale grounded in 'equality' as a fundamental tenet of EU citizenship in its own right. This potentiality of rights to grow roots deeper than the purely economic integrationist dimension of the Union has prompted some to claim that it could provide a counterbalance to the primarily economic focus of the EU: serving to ground a more explicitly 'political' citizenship (see Stychin, 1998: 115–30). Moreover, European citizenship inhabits a tension between the economic goal of 'free movement' between member states, which provides the original grounding for many EU rights, and a universalistic notion of *human* rights. The latter trajectory is demonstrated by the fact that the European Convention on Human Rights is one of the sources of law now recognized within the EU legal order. Thus, although citizenship of the Union is a concept still closely associated with the rights of rational, self-interested, economic actors, able to move factors of production freely across the national boundaries of EU member states (provided they possess nationality of a member state and are gainfully employed), the claim is that citizenship has the potential to mean something *more*, and it is this excess which potentially might be exploitable in the cause of active, democratic citizenship. At the same time, the EU certainly underscores how, in late capitalist societies, the paradigm of active citizenship increasingly is defined in terms of employment, rather than military service. It is the citizen employed in the trans-national marketplace who now claims a right to cross borders freely. This problematizing of national, sovereign boundaries through mobility may provide one of the keys to the invigoration of European citizenship.

The point here is that rights in the EU context may usefully problematize the active/passive binary of citizenship. Rights may be central to active participation in this trans-national polity, and also are key to the cultivation of an active, meaningful European identity. But rights discourse by itself may provide insufficient 'glue' to bind (or cobble) together such an identity, based around citizenship of the Union (Warleigh, 1998). In this way, the active/passive dichotomy re-emerges, as the claim is made that in order to be meaningful, citizenship demands not only supranational rights, but also active participation which goes *beyond* the claiming of rights in the name of citizenship. Thus, Jo Shaw (2000) argues that EU citizenship must be seen as emerging from the conjunction of membership and rights, but the assumption is that membership and belonging are more wide ranging than simply the claim to rights entitlement, which then can be enjoyed as a citizen. Implicit here again is the assumption (often correct) that the *enjoyment* of rights is ultimately private and passive – removed from the realm of citizenship.

Rights discourse around sexual and gender identities is being invoked with increased frequency. Claims to rights which emanate from the UK have been made before the European Court of Justice (ECJ) and thereby have entered the trans-national legal and political arena. In terms of strict legal outcomes, the results have been mixed. Litigants have argued that the guarantee of sexual equality in employment protects transgendered people from dismissal (*P. v S. and Cornwall County Council* (1996)) and, in another case, that it demands equal employment benefits be paid to same-sex couples as are paid to non-married heterosexual couples, when partnership benefits are an element of pay (*Grant v South West Trains* (1998)). The transgendered claim was successful, but the partnership benefits case was not. However, both claims involve employment and, in the case of partnership benefits, it seems far removed from the domain of active, political citizenship. Indeed, arguments for sexual equality are often normatively grounded in part in the importance of rights as a means to 'perfect' competition in the labour market.

But the cases both assumed considerable political significance amongst interested constituencies in the UK and trans-nationally in the EU, serving to some degree to energize and politicize communities. Defeat before the ECJ in *Grant* itself might be important to trans-national mobilization, particularly since the ECJ sent a clear message to the governments of the member states that concerted action on their part in the form of new European legislation was advisable.

The possibility of such legislation has been facilitated by the Treaty of Amsterdam. The Treaty *empowers* member states to enact European legislation to combat discrimination on the basis of sex, racial or ethnic origin, religion or belief, disability, age or sexual orientation. The inclusion of sexual orientation can be attributed to pressure from lobbyists in several member states, as well as active support from some governmental officials (Bell and Waddington, 1996: 333). The Treaty is seen as a means of enriching European citizenship more broadly. With respect to sexuality, claims which might originally appear to be passive, private, and even disciplined, have come to possess an active, public, political, and even potentially democratic component as they emerge in the political space of the EU.

In sum, sexual citizenship articulates sexuality in the public sphere through claims for rights and participation, while also cultivating (and claiming a right to) separate spaces for sub-cultural life. These spaces sit uneasily on the public/private divide, but historically have been subject to close surveillance by the state. At the level of the private sphere 'proper', sexual citizenship highlights the *relevancy* of sexuality in the private sphere

to public claims, while simultaneously creating the conditions for normal-
ization by bringing sexuality into the public sphere through the claim to
citizenship. Finally, the mobility dimension of European citizenship – free
movement – has impacted directly upon lesbian and gay Europeans, as it
has facilitated their ability to move between geographically based sub-
cultures, to create connections between them, and to re-imagine their
relationship to national space (Binnie, 1997; D'Oliveira, 1993). An
increasingly trans-national dimension to lesbian and gay communities
thereby may be emerging, in which migration is motivated not simply by
economic factors, but also by support and friendship networks and the
extent to which community and 'lifestyle' are entrenched and developed in
different member states. Whether these patterns of migration are
qualitatively different from those of other groups in the EU is debatable.
Bob Cant (1997: 1), for example, argues that 'lesbians and gay men differ
from other groups of migrants in that there is no homeland that can
validate our group identity'. At the same time, Cant recognizes that lesbian
and gay migration narratives underscore 'the extent to which the
invention of identities draws on both the lesbian and gay community
and the community of origin' (p. 1). My point here is simply that patterns of
independent migration by self-identified lesbians and gays, for reasons
related directly to sexuality, are significant, and they are fostered and
facilitated by Community legal rights.[1] With respect to European citizenship, this is all highly relevant, because historically 'the Community has
refrained from intervening in what are seen as controversial matters of
sexuality and gender relations, often associated with national identity and
specificity' (Kofman, 1995: 132). As trans-national institutions slowly
come to recognize sexuality issues, these dynamics become increasingly
salient. The 'private' no longer is characterized as 'national', but instead is
beginning to enter a trans-national 'public' sphere.

A more fluid notion of space and identification in this context also might
usefully challenge the normalizing power of rights and politicized identities
which has been identified by Wendy Brown (1995) and others, in that it
suggests a movement away from 'ethnicized identities' towards a 'wider
solidarity' (Weeks, 1995: 122). As we recognize multiple spheres with
more fluid boundaries, we can reject the possibility of a unitary subject. As
Morris Kaplan (1997: 68) has argued, drawing on the work of Hannah
Arendt, citizenship needs to 'avoid the homogenizing assumptions implicit
in unitary and exclusive conceptions of identity'. Public (and not so public)
spheres could be sites of democratic contestation both over European and
sexual identities, in which the term – be it 'European' or 'homosexual' –
'cannot fully or exhaustively perform its referent' (Butler, 1997: 108).

The implications of this more open and less fixed politics have been fairly widely considered in the context of sexual identities. Shane Phelan (1995: 345), for example, in her analysis of lesbian and gay politics, suggests that a recognition of the specificities of individuals who identify as non-heterosexual demands a rejection of an overarching and ultimately fictitious identity, to be replaced by the imagining of politics as grounded in 'affinities' and coalitions. The shift from identity to coalition underscores the importance of the *activity* of politics (p. 343). After all, a coalition must be continually reconstituted in order to survive, much more so than a fixed identity. Its precariousness and provisionality is explicitly acknowledged, as is its likelihood of shifting shape in the future. The creation of spaces for deliberation is emphasized by Phelan (p. 347); deliberation amongst people who may form an affinity because they have something in common, but who may not consider themselves as sharing an identity. This politics of affinity as a grounding for citizenship could inform European politics and citizenship discourse. Identification as 'European' would be grounded, not on identity, but on affinity, and it is also an invaluable way of conceptualizing trans-national social movement politics, such as an emerging European politics of sexuality. A politics of affinity differs from one centred on a fixed identity in that affinity suggests that the fictions of a homogeneous and totalizing group attribute have been rejected in favour of a recognition that a shared characteristic or experience – which may lead to (or require) common endeavours – cannot overwhelm the differences that exist between members of the group.[2]

For example, the *struggle* for the recognition of sexual orientation as an identity to which anti-discrimination rights attach in the EU may well involve *active* citizenship in the years ahead, provided that a broader notion of what constitutes politics is accepted. Through this and other developments, the trans-national arena may be facilitating an affinity which crosses national boundaries of the EU, partly fostered by legal and political struggles. Rights also have facilitated mobilization at the national level, and the EU context highlights the ways in which engagement at national and trans-national levels can intersect. That is, social movement politics locally and nationally feed into the trans-national sphere through rights. At the same time, recognition in the Treaty of Amsterdam might suggest cooptation to the European project. In that sense, EU institutions may seek to cultivate the *loyalty* of lesbians and gays through recognition, creating a mutually beneficial relationship.

However, these processes may result in a kind of colonization of sexuality by legal and political discourse. The expansion of the EU will make this of some importance in the future, as it raises the possibility of a movement towards a European-wide consensus around the *meaning* of sexuality, not only as warranting anti-discrimination protection, but also more fundamentally as a politicized identity. This dynamic might also produce a 'disintegrative' reaction, 'asserting the normative authority of the local and the national over the global and international' (Turner, 1990: 212). Equally importantly, European integration raises the role of identity politics across the EU, as it may well come to be superimposed on national contexts in which it has little by way of 'tradition' (see Valentine, 1996). For example, the construction of citizenship claims around sexuality – similar to those emerging from other identity-based social movements – may well sit uneasily with republican conceptions of *le citoyen* in France.

It is partly for these reasons that a citizenship model founded on a more fluid basis than 'identity' is important in terms of how both European and sexual citizenship are conceived. As for sexual citizenship, the transnational context underscores why a construction of fixed identities is problematic. The issues raised by rights discourse lend themselves to the imagining of a coalition-based model. It is through active, democratic political strategies that coalitions will continually emerge, change, and evolve, as individuals identify (or not) with particular trajectories of rights struggles. Issues of sexual identification in Europe seem particularly suited to Phelan's model of coalition and affinity, rather than identity. Sexual identification undoubtedly is a bond which may bring peoples together, but the differences between them seem far too great to establish anything like a fixed and stable identity. Indeed, to attempt to construct one is to engage in disciplinarity of the highest order. The idea of multiple public (and not so public) spheres seems apposite here, in which those publics have sufficiently permeable boundaries to facilitate coming together around particular issues, but also allow for separation (see also Laclau and Mouffe, 1985). An example could be common endeavours and mutual support around rights struggles between trans-gendered people and lesbians, gays, and bisexuals, which has been facilitated by the character of EU anti-discrimination law with its focus on 'sex' discrimination. While dialogue across identifications here may prove valuable, any attempt to construct a single, dialogic public sphere grounded in a fixed identity would not reflect the differently located subjects at issue.

But the *problems* of dialogue also need to be considered, and the transnational context may well exacerbate them. While civic republican forms of citizenship herald active participation in a dialogue over the common good, Nancy Fraser (1997: 78) quite rightly points out in response that politics and deliberation can become 'infected' by 'social inequalities'. Thus, she argues that a politics of recognition cannot be divorced from a politics of redistribution in order to foster the conditions of social equality – preconditions for a true dialogic situation (p. 80). This is extremely apt in the EU context, both in terms of the conditions for a dialogic overarching

European public sphere, and, no less importantly, for the identity-related spheres emerging trans-nationally, such as those around sexual identity. The enormous differences in material and other locations of individual subjects who may share an affinity around sexual object choice ensure that the conditions for dialogue are extremely difficult to attain, but should be struggled over nonetheless (see Valentine, 1996). For example, the dangers of dominance by Western, Northern, likely male, economically affluent (and historically politicized around identity) activists, located in cultural locations in which a strong support structure for litigation is present, must surely be a concern; not only because of the material differences between EU regions (differences which will be exacerbated by likely expansion of the EU eastward), but also because of the centrality of sexuality to politicized identity in those same parts of the EU which enjoy affluence. The extent to which economics is in large measure *constitutive* of sexual identities deserves consideration, for it suggests that East/West, North/South divisions may well be central – for economic reasons – to the way in which sexuality is constructed within Europe, especially given the historical focus of sexual citizenship on consumer consumption. The relationship between economic inequality and social movement politics thus should be an issue within trans-national sexual identity politics, and more generally in the construction of EU (and national) citizenship. It highlights the importance of attempts at economic redistribution as a necessary corollary of cultural recognition. It also exemplifies how the focus of rights struggles within the EU on same-sex economic benefits privilege the interests of those for whom such benefits are a realistic possibility.

To the extent that the political is constituted through relations of antagonism, as Chantal Mouffe (1992) suggests, there simply may be insufficient commonality amongst non-heterosexually identified people across national boundaries today within the European sphere to constitute – or galvanize – a shared political identity. It is difficult to imagine such a trans-national political identity developing, which reinforces my claim that a relatively 'loose' politics of affinity is more realistic than a politics of identity founded on an antagonistic moment.

Thus, my argument is largely a normative one, concerning how sexuality politics within the EU should mirror the claims currently being developed around EU politics and identification more broadly. Namely, it should aspire to be a site of exchange across differences, rather than becoming an arena for the colonization of difference through the privileging of particular experiences (Bankowski and Christodoulidis, 1999). The focus shifts from bounded identities to more fluid conceptions of space and identification. The language of networks, movements and flows is no less apt for social movement politics as it is for European politics more generally (Walker, 1999). But, at the same time, sexual citizenship might inform the ways in which European citizenship is itself imagined. A politics of affinity and coalition – in which the possibility of a singular and homogeneous identity is eschewed, or at least permanently deferred – may provide a useful antidote to attempts at forging a European identity, along with the exclusions wrought in the construction of such a bounded and fixed concept. The central tension between bounded space and more fluid conceptions of belonging is one which runs throughout this analysis, and I want now to consider on a micro level how these tensions play out in the context of citizenship struggles around sexuality in the EU.

III. FINDING A PLACE IN A EUROPEAN CIVIL SOCIETY

In this section, I look more closely at a particular example of trans-national politics in the EU, through a consideration of the role of ILGA Europe. The reasons why I have chosen ILGA Europe are straightforward. It is a European regional association within an overarching international NGO; it has been quite successful in being accepted at an official level within the institutions of the EU (it has consultative status with the Council of Europe and it is a member of the Platform of European Social NGOs); it has received funding from the European Commission to produce reports; it has carried out lobbying functions with the various institutions of the EU, including the European Parliament; and, most importantly for my immediate purposes, it has produced a recent report *Equality for Lesbians and Gay Men: A Relevant Issue in the Civil and Social Dialogue* (ILGA Europe, 1998), which illuminates many of the tensions around both European and sexual citizenship which I have examined. The report is part of a broader project supported by a grant from the European Commission (see also Bell and Waddington, 1996; Bell, 1998).

The title of the report foreshadows its central theme of 'mainstreaming' issues concerning sexual identity politics in the debates around European integration. More generally, ILGA Europe articulates its claims within a discourse of civil society popular in European citizenship debates. It provides an umbrella for the bringing together of national and local organizations across a range of issues which increasingly traverse the national boundaries of the EU. The Report, for example, focuses on youth, ageing, families, housing, poverty, disability and racism. It underscores the possibilities for the synthesis of rights discourse and citizenship participation. The importance of rights as *status* is emphasized, but so too is the crucial role of social inclusion of non-heterosexuals in all activities and programmes of the EU (so as to ensure their equal participation in society) (ILGA Europe, 1998: 14–24).

The report recognizes that sexuality does not amount to an uncontested identity in the sense of a clearly defined 'group' across the EU (ILGA Europe, 1998: 15). Rather, the importance of equality discourse around rights and participation stems from the interrelationship of the 'social, political, and economical environment' (p. 15). But the report also asserts the meaningfulness of sexual identity categories, particularly in the context of the Treaty of Amsterdam provision which recognizes sexual orientation. ILGA Europe demands that steps be taken trans-nationally to implement this empowering Treaty article.

Thus, ILGA Europe is forced as a matter of practical politics to assert a coherent identity which traverses Europe and, simultaneously, it neces-sarily claims a certain 'naturalness' to the identity 'European' from which claims to citizenship flow. In this way, the construction of rights appears to be founded on a belief in groups – 'lesbians and gays'; 'Europeans'. And the assumption is that an agenda for politics can be constructed for groups despite multiple differences of nation, gender, age, race, etc. But the report also recognizes the potentiality of the language of coalition, including coalitions with other movements focused on related issues in the EU (ILGA Europe, 1998: 7). Thus, ILGA Europe advocates something which resembles a politics of radical pluralism, with its emphasis on a 'principle of democratic equivalence' across partially sutured identities (Mouffe, 1992: 379).

There is a certain irony at work here, in that the institutions of the EU appear to be *facilitating* a fairly active form of citizenship around sexuality, while European citizenship has been predominantly perceived as a passive construct focused on status. This underscores how actors within civil society can always, through the language of rights *and* participation, breathe active life into what may appear to be static citizenship constructs. Furthermore, it is ironic that this form of active citizenship has been achieved largely through the financial support of the European Commis-sion; an institution of the EU widely thought to be distanced from its citizens.

The focus of ILGA Europe on both the achievement of legal rights, as well as 'mainstreaming' towards full participation in civil society, demonstrates the claim that a synthetic relationship between rights and participation in citizenship is possible. Rights and civic participation thereby can become mutually reinforcing through an active, democratic citizenship form.

IV. CONCLUDING THOUGHTS

The politics of sexuality in Europe provides a useful microcosm for analysing citizenship in the EU more generally. The tension between fluidity and exchange, versus the fixity and colonization of identity, runs throughout the politics of sexuality and the politics of European citizenship. It is foundational to the self/other dichotomy, and it underscores how an acknowledgement of difference and multiplicity – increasingly central as a normative matter to the articulation of European citizenship – still demands some final point of reference, some commonality, through which to make sense of difference. As Roberto Alejandro (1993: 206) suggests, while we might aspire to a citizenship grounded in 'competing traditions and competing languages', we also need 'a common vocabulary to deliberate about a shared life' (p. 225).

I have argued in this chapter that the politics of sexuality provides a laboratory for EU citizenship discourse, underscoring the potentiality and limitations of a trans-national public sphere. It highlights the problematic of the binaries of citizenship, while also sometimes reproducing them. Like sexual citizenship, European citizenship more generally is shaped by a tension between the need to construct meaningful categories of belonging and the need to 'live with' the differences that challenge and undermine the fixity of boundaries which contain the categorization. More fundamentally, this analysis raises the question whether citizenship and belonging need inevitably be bounded in order to be coherent and meaningful. Alternatively, can we apply the language of coalition and affinity as a means of moving away *from* identity *towards* identification? Affinity suggests a commonality – elements of a history that in some sense might be shared across difference – but in which ebbs and flows across and between spheres of politics occur, depending upon the issue at stake. Public (and not so public) spheres intersect and interact without merging, and a common public sphere of European citizenship remains a permanent site of contest over its meaning and future. This model can be described as recognizing communities characterized by rights and participation, but in which the boundaries of communities are always sites of contestation; sites of community in which discipline is resisted (despite its inevitable occurrence), and in which democratic politics is recognized as vital. The emphasis on active participation and the mutability and permeability of communities, as well as the recognition that rights discourse will itself lead to political antagonisms between diverse communities which will need resolution through agreement, underscore the connections between a politics of affinity and a model of citizenship described by Richard Bellamy and Alex Warleigh (1998: 463) as 'cosmopolitan communitarianism'.

For example, as I write this in July 2000, the first-ever lesbian and gay 'World Pride' celebration has just ended in Rome. This unprecedented event saw hundreds of thousands take to the streets, and resulted in a previously unheard of discussion and debate on sexuality in Italy. It brought together a disparate collection of peoples who clearly shared an affinity across an array of national, cultural and other differences. The apparent openness of the march to all, with its lack of rigid boundaries regarding who 'belongs', allowed difference to flourish and seemed to avoid the disciplining of identity that is often seen in analogous demonstrations of pride in North America. Moreover, pride marches themselves represent both a call for rights and a manifestation of active practices of citizenship. But what World Pride also produced was an active opposition to the event (strongly supported by the Vatican). Opponents characterized the event as an 'invasion' of Rome, underscoring how the march was constructed as emanating from 'outside' the community and threatening its integrity (a highly communitarian discourse). These political antagonisms were certainly not resolved in the process, but mobilization around sexuality – bringing it literally into the public sphere – draws those antagonisms into sharp relief, and demonstrates the need for resolution, compromise and ongoing dialogue. The public reaction in Italy to World Pride suggested to many a much greater willingness to engage in such a dialogue than was previously thought possible.

Affinity provides a model which may prove useful for other groups for whom the disciplinarity of a singular and totalizing identity is increasingly untenable. In fact, nationality itself could be seen in these terms, underscoring again the importance of multi-level political mechanisms for compromise and agreement, once it is recognized that disagreement and debate need not suggest disloyalty to any particular national or other group. Rather, a politics of affinity *assumes* the existence of cross-cutting cleavages which will pull in different directions on any political subject with respect to most issues of controversy (for example, gay Catholics). In that sense, a politics of affinity demands that communitarian ambitions be modified.

Finally, the 'political' remains itself a site of contest, challenging the historical construction of public and private, which has been so central to citizenship discourse. Just as the relation of public and private is problematized, so too is the distinction between active and passive citizenship, and the way in which rights have been constructed as a site of passivity. The possibilities of European citizenship lie in the potential to synthesize rights and belonging, in the creation of opportunities for democratic contestation in the interstices between liberal rights, the disciplinarity of the free market, and the differences between and within national identifications.

NOTES

1. Migration aimed at unification with a same-sex partner is also increasingly prevalent, but seems to me to replicate heterosexual migration practices in a much more obvious way (see Waaldijk, 1996).
2. The idea of affinity as a way of understanding this politics emerged from Phelan's (1995) observation and experience of lesbians working politically with gay men, where the fictitious character of a 'lesbian and gay' political identity was often all too apparent. Yet, a common struggle remained shared in the face of political differences.

CASES

Grant v. South West Trains Case C-249/96 [1998] ECR I-621.
P. v. S. and Cornwall County Council Case C-13/94 [1996] ECR I-2143.

REFERENCES

Alejandro, R. (1993) *Hermeneutics, Citizenship, and the Public Sphere* (Albany: State University of New York Press).

Armstrong, K. A. (1998) 'Legal Integration: Theorizing the Legal Dimension of European Integration', *Journal of Common Market Studies* 36: 2, pp. 155–74.

Ball, C. A. (1996) 'The Making of a Transnational Capitalist Society: The Court of Justice, Social Policy, and Individual Rights Under the European Community's Legal Order', *Harvard International Law Journal* 37: 2, pp. 307–88.

Bankowski, Z. and Christodoulidis, E. (1999) 'Citizenship Bound and Citizenship Unbound', in K. Hutchings and R. Dannreuther (eds), *Cosmopolitan Citizenship* (Basingstoke: Macmillan).

Bell, M. (1998) 'Sexual Orientation and Anti-Discrimination Policy: The European Community', in T. Carver and V. Mottier (eds), *Politics of Sexuality: Identity, Gender, Citizenship* (London: Routledge).

Bell, M. and Waddington, L. (1996) 'The 1996 Intergovernmental Conference and the Prospects of a Non-Discrimination Treaty Article', *Industrial Law Journal* 25: 4, pp. 320–36.

Bellamy, R. and Warleigh, A. (1998) 'From an Ethics of Integration to an Ethics of Participation: Citizenship and the Future of the European Union', *Millennium: Journal of International Studies* 27: 3, pp. 447–70.

Binnie, J. (1997) 'Invisible Europeans: Sexual Citizenship in the New Europe', *Environment and Planning A* 29, pp. 237–48.

Brown, W. (1995) *States of Injury* (Princeton: Princeton University Press).

Butler, J. (1997) *Excitable Speech: A Politics of the Performative* (New York: Routledge).

Cant, B. (1997) 'Introduction', in B. Cant (ed.), *Invented Identities? Lesbians and Gays Talk About Migration* (London: Cassell).

de Búrca, G. (1995) 'The Language of Rights and European Integration', in J. Shaw and G. More (eds), *New Legal Dynamics of European Union* (Oxford: Clarendon Press).

de Lange, R. (1995) 'Paradoxes of European Citizenship', in P. Fitzpatrick (ed.), *Nationalism, Racism and the Rule of Law* (Aldershot: Dartmouth).

D'Oliveira, H. U. J. (1993) 'Lesbians and Gays and the Freedom of Movement of Persons', in K. Waaldijk and A. Clapham (eds), *Homosexuality: A European Community Issue* (Dordrecht: Martinus Nijhoff).

Fraser, N. (1997) *Justice Interruptus* (New York: Routledge).

ILGA Europe (1998) *Equality for Lesbians and Gay Men: A Relevant Issue in the Civil and Social Dialogue* (Brussels: ILGA Europe).

Kaplan, M. B. (1997) *Sexual Justice: Democratic Citizenship and the Politics of Desire* (New York: Routledge).

Kofman, E. (1995) 'Citizenship for Some but Not for Others: Spaces of Citizenship in Contemporary Europe', *Political Geography* 14: 2, pp. 121–37.

Laclau, E. and Mouffe, C. (1985) *Hegemony and Socialist Strategy* (London: Verso).

Marshall, T. H. (1950) *Citizenship and Social Class and Other Essays* (Cambridge: Cambridge University Press).

Mouffe, C. (1992) 'Feminism, Citizenship and Radical Democratic Politics', in J. Butler and J. W. Scott (eds), *Feminists Theorize the Political* (New York: Routledge).

Phelan, S. (1995) 'The Space of Justice: Lesbians and Democratic Politics', in L. Nicholson and S. Seidman (eds), *Social Postmodernism* (Cambridge: Cambridge University Press).

Shaw, J. (1998) 'The Interpretation of European Union Citizenship', *Modern Law Review* 61: 3, pp. 293–317.

Shaw, J. (2000) 'The Problem of Membership in EU Citizenship', in Z. Bankowski and A. Scott (eds), *The European Union and its Order* (Oxford: Blackwell).

Stychin, C. F. (1998) *A Nation by Rights* (Philadelphia: Temple University Press).

Turner, B. S. (1990) 'Outline of a Theory of Citizenship', *Sociology* 24: 2, pp. 189–217.

Valentine, G. (1996) 'An Equal Place to Work? Anti-Lesbian Discrimination and Sexual Citizenship in the European Union', in M. D. García-Ramon and J. Monk (eds), *Women of the European Union: The Politics of Work and Daily Life* (London: Routledge).

Waaldijk, K. (1996) 'Free Movement of Same-Sex Partners', *Maastricht Journal of European and Comparative Law* 3: 3, pp. 271–85.

Walker, R. B. J. (1999) 'Citizenship after the Modern Subject', in K. Hutchings and R. Dannreuther (eds) *Cosmopolitan Citizenship* (Basingstoke: Macmillan).

Warleigh, A. (1998) 'Frozen: Citizenship and European Unification', *Critical Review of International Social and Political Philosophy* 1: 4, pp. 113–51.

Weeks, J. (1995) *Invented Moralities* (Cambridge: Polity).

7

The Social Citizen?

MITA CASTLE-KANEROVA AND BILL JORDAN

I. INTRODUCTION

European social citizenship is potentially a means of sustaining the member states' national systems for social protection that have been eroded by global market forces, and for balancing the competitive features of EU market-making by institutions for social cohesion and solidarity. However, the whole notion of social rights is currently under revision, through the influence of new approaches pioneered in the USA and UK. Our aim is to review these debates, and their implications for the development of EU citizenship, in the light of the accession of the post-communist Central and East European countries.

The new emphasis on citizenship in the EU's treaties, policies and aspirational documents raises a number of questions about the social dimension of the EU. Does the switch from the Maastricht commitments on the 'social rights of *workers*' to those of *citizens* betoken a substantive or merely a rhetorical change? If the former, does this in turn signify a shift from postwar notions of passive entitlements to benefits and services from a protective state, towards the more active version of 'rights-and-respon-sibilities' now pursued by Bill Clinton in the USA (Waddan, 1997) and Tony Blair, under *A New Contract for Welfare* (Department of Social Security, 1998) in the UK? And what influence, if any, has the shift in political thought towards an interest in citizens' duties, virtues and mutualities as members of a community had on the European Commission's thinking on social issues such as cohesion, redistribution and solidarity?

Since Maastricht, the development of tripartite agreements, regulating labour-market conditions and integrating groups previously outside such regulation, has been hailed as a new dimension in European corporatist social policy (Falkner, 1998). The idea of shoring up the 'European social model', through social partnership in establishing minimum standards, as the counterpart to the deregulatory Internal Market Programme, has been given substance through this process of policy-making under the Social

Protocol. However, at the same time, the Commission's own policy documents reveal ambivalence about how to find a balance between such measures and the Anglo-American agenda of labour-market flexibility, work incentives and welfare retrenchment. The German government epitomizes this ambivalence on social policy among the member states, with Chancellor Schröder's adoption of a joint manifesto statement with Tony Blair in May 1999 (Blair and Schröder, 1999) quickly followed by a set of interventions to prop up ailing industrial giants and forestall redundancies, as Schröder's modest welfare reform package collapsed.

One question that remains unsettled is whether European social policy will require *active* social citizens, who earn their entitlements and demonstrate their willingness to contribute. Part of the culture shift under way in the UK is a change from policies for 'equality of outcome' though redistribution towards 'equality of opportunity' through higher rates of participation in a 'flexible' labour market (Brown, 1997). Citizens have a duty to try to make themselves more 'employable' through education and training (even if they are lone parents with several children, or people with disabilities, long-term illnesses or handicaps). The state, in return, has responsibilities to sustain resources for 'lifelong learning' and create employment opportunities, as well as reforming the tax-benefit system so as to give better incentives for the increasingly fragmented, irregular, short-term, part-time and subcontract work that is available (Standing, 1999).

Equal opportunities therefore become the focus of more attention within the field of social rights, and as relevant to the terms of citizenship as those of labour-market participation. We will argue that this change in the significance of equal opportunities affects the European context in several ways. If the most important sphere for the performance of citizenship obligations (and conversely, for the power of the state to enforce these duties) is to be the labour market, this represents a major shift in the governance of civil society and the household, taking women, people with disabilities and other minorities out of the private sphere, and bringing them into the public sphere – but at the same time changing the terms on which all citizens interact as members of a community. It affects women's role especially, and the significance of informal and voluntary work for civic governance.

On the face of it, the new emphasis on labour-market activation of lone parents (almost all women) and people with disabilities in the UK might seem to move it nearer to Continental Europe, where the Bismarckian model of social citizenship was more clearly rooted in contributions through roles as workers than in the evolved form of the Beveridgian model. But of course this never applied to women, least of all in Germany, Italy, Spain, Austria and even the Netherlands, where female labour-market participation was traditionally lower than in the Anglo-Saxon countries (Esping-Andersen, 1990). These were not only employment-based social insurance systems but also 'breadwinner' models of social protection, in which social rights were earned for their wives by husbands (Lewis, 1998). Rather than moving the UK into line with the Continental European model of the 'social state', it would instead – if adopted as the EU's new orthodoxy on these issues – push the latter towards a new version of the social citizenship that has prevailed in the Scandinavian countries since the 1960s, with very high rates of employment for women, mainly in the service sector. The difference, of course, is that women would not enjoy the same levels of pay and conditions in the new 'flexible' labour markets of this decade, nor the security of public-sector jobs. Hence a shift away from Continental European principles of subsidiarity in the governance of the household and civil society would expose these groups to market forces (and to poverty) in a way already familiar to their counterparts in the UK and USA (Esping-Andersen, 1999).

The other relevant impact of this change is already affecting the applicant countries of Central-Eastern Europe. Equal opportunities for men and women are part of the framework of European legislation with which the legal systems of those countries are now required to harmonize (or approximate). The European Commission is involved in the process of reviewing its existing statutes and regulations with this objective in mind (Castle-Kanerova, 2000). We will discuss two aspects of this process, in the light of the previous analysis.

First, we examine the implications of West European-style equal opportunities legislation being imposed as part of the requirement for accession to the EU, and as a precursor to the other programmes of harmonization in relation to a much broader area of social, commercial and even cultural regulation. We analyse two sides of this process – the manner in which EU harmonization processes assume the desirability and even superiority of 'Western' notions of equal opportunities, without regard for the traditional and institutionalized versions of these concepts embodied in the former regime; and the response of the applicant countries, in terms of adopting the formal aspects of these rules, without substantive implementation of their outworkings in social relations. We ask whether this kind of formalism in issues of citizenship betokens a broader problem regarding the inclusion of the accession countries in meaningful member-ship.

Second, we discuss the difficulties in processes of 'cultural transplan-tation' of forms of governance that are not rooted in the civic or civil traditions of Central-Eastern Europe, where social benefits and services were regarded as the benevolent gift of the socialist rulers to the people. Is it possible to move straight from this tradition to the far more demanding notion of rights that are *negotiated* between a discretionary officialdom and an active, informed and *choosing* citizenry, able to substantiate its claims to welfare, inclusion and equality? If the EU trend is towards social citizens who are capable *both* of fending for themselves in a competitive economic environment, *and* of demonstrating the validity and genuineness of their claims to a bureaucracy with powers to enforce 'contracts' and conditions around benefits and services, this is a tall order for those who have been raised within the culture of state socialism. Indeed, these state powers might even (Heaven forbid) be implemented in a state socialist way.

Our argument links these two themes – the ambiguity of European social policy and the politics of enlargement – through the example of equality of opportunity for men and women. We show that political traditions and entrenched patterns of social interaction (social capital) are relevant for the development of social citizenship and the accession of postcommunist countries.

Developments in social citizenship in the EU

If the 'normative turn' in political thought, and the 'return of the citizen' (Kymlicka and Norman, 1994) as part of that development, have had any impact on public policy, it is in the field of social protection. The rise of the 'moral majority' in the USA, the brief triumph of Newt Gingrich's Republicans in the mid-term elections during Bill Clinton's first presidency, and their influence on Clinton's subsequent welfare reform programme, have all been well documented (Waddan, 1997). The 'collapse of the Centre' on social issues, such as the death penalty, Aid for Families with Dependent Children and compulsory workfare, was reflected in Clinton's Personal Responsibility Act (1995). These in turn have clearly influenced the New Labour government in the UK, which frequently proclaims that 'work is the only reliable route out of poverty', and asserts its intention to 'break the mould of the old, passive benefits system' (DSS, 1998: 24). In his own definition of the Third Way, Tony Blair emphasizes the principles of 'equal worth, opportunity for all, responsibility and community' (Blair, 1998a: 3) and the need for 'a new contract between the citizen and the state' (Blair, 1998b: iii).

What have been less well documented and analysed are important parallel changes in other EU member states. In some (but by no means all) of these, the 'activation' of claimants of unemployment-related benefits by government programmes, in the name of 'social inclusion' or even the 'right to employment', has led to significant changes in the governance of welfare. An American researcher, R. H. Cox, has captured the spirit of this change in Denmark and the Netherlands, probably the two most interesting and apparently successful examples, as a shift 'from safety nets to trampolines' (Cox, 1998). Claimants are required to enter into individual 'contracts' with officials charged with responsibility for preparing them for and placing them in employment, but also holding powers to disallow their benefits if they fail to cooperate in the implementation of these plans. The impact of these measures is rather different from those of workfare in the USA, and the various New Deals in the UK, partly because the minimum wage is so much higher in these EU countries (more than double the UK level in Denmark, for example); and partly because claimants come from a much less impoverished situation, because of far higher benefit rates in both countries, and minimal long-term unemployment in Denmark, which has the lowest rates in the EU (Goul Andersen, 1996; Loftager, 1996; Jordan and Loftager, 1999).

Cox explicitly links these developments with the ways welfare reforms are changing conceptions of social rights all over the developed world (Cox, 1999). He argues that the postwar European and North American welfare states were grounded in principles of entitlement, universality and solidarity, but that during the past twenty years changes in law and administration have challenged this version. A whole range of measures, including privatization, devolution to new agencies, decentralization and the 'attempt to revive the obligations of citizenship' have transformed policy and practice in the field of social benefits (Cox, 1999: 1). He specifically draws attention to the achievement orientation of the changes, the emphasis on rights and responsibilities, and the move from uniform rules to reviews on a case-by-case basis (Cox, 1998). 'These changes have introduced a more discursive view of rights, one where the formal legal conditions once thought the hallmark of progressive social policy are now seen to be inflexible and impersonal' (Cox, 1999: 19). Although he does not use the example of Ireland, Cox might also have included it, as it is a country in which phenomenal success in terms of economic growth rates and impressive reductions in unemployment have been achieved. The Irish reform programme has taken twenty years, involving a combination of wage restraint, tax reform, improved incentives and a low-key programme of activation, within a European-style 'social partnership' approach, under alternating coalition governments, and without a Blairite 'moral crusade' to change political and civic cultures (Jordan, 1999).

The picture is less clear within the other EU member states. Taking Germany, France and Italy as the largest examples of 'Continental European welfare regimes' within the Christian Democratic tradition (Esping-Andersen, 1990), there remains a serious problem of how generous social security schemes can remain viable with large and growing proportions of 'inactive' claimants (Scharpf, 1999). Along with other Continental countries, they adapted to the challenges of the past 30 years – the oil-price shocks of the 1970s and '80s and increased mobility of capital and tax-competition between states (Genschell, 1999) – by increasing social insurance contributions. These surcharges on wages now represent 20.4 per cent of GDP in France, 15.5 per cent in Germany and 13.2 per cent in Italy, compared with 6.2 per cent in the UK (Scharpf, 1999: Table 5); in Germany, they add 50 per cent to the costs of employing a worker on the minimum wage. It has proved impossible to stimulate cost-sensitive private-sector employment in services in the face of these barriers; but governments confronted massive political opposition to any measures they took to lessen this (such as increasing personal and corporate taxation or cutting benefits).

This issue has proved increasingly urgent because these regimes were characterized (in comparison with the USA and UK on the one hand, and the Scandinavian countries on the other) by low rates of total employment, low rates of women's labour-market participation, high rates of income-replacement for the economically inactive population, and limited social services for young, disabled and elderly people. This 'transfer-intensive' bias provided benefits to sustain the incomes of male breadwinners during unemployment, sickness and retirement, and relied on women to supply unpaid care. Hence the low rates of employment in social services of all kinds have been linked to the low participation rates for women. Indeed, the basis for the success of the Continental European model in the 1960s was a highly regulated labour market in which male industrial wages were able to rise because women were excluded, and taxation levels remained moderate because social service provision was so sparse. In recent years, manufacturing employment could only be sustained by improved productivity and, among these countries, only the corporatist industrial relations of Germany could consistently deliver this (Streeck, 1999). Even Germany's unemployment rose sharply in the 1990s in the face of these challenges, as high minimum wages and social insurance contributions proved insurmountable barriers to employment expansion. Whereas the Netherlands government was able to sponsor a 'jobs miracle' (Visser and Hemerijck, 1997) by integrating social insurance contributions with taxation, and the French decided in 1999 to relieve employers of social insurance contributions for low-paid workers (Scharpf, 1999), the Schröder coalition in Germany has proved unable to take even the first steps in such reforms, and is left with little prospect of the rapid expansion in service employment that it seeks.

This leaves the European Commission poised between the 'modernizing' and 'activating' policies of the UK on the one hand, and the 'defence of the

European Social Model' on the other. While countries like Denmark, the Netherlands and Ireland show that a mixed model is possible, there is a limit to the scope for assisting member states to reach such internal compromises. Some analysts argue that the Internal Market Programme is itself the best way in which the EU can assist national governments to regain relative autonomy under globalizing conditions because it allows member states to identify the requirements of adaptation with external (European) pressures (Fernandes, 1999). For instance, the Swedish coalition government achieved a considerable modification of its country's social protection system as part of the process of entry into the EU, thus defusing the crisis over rising unemployment and low growth of the early 1990s (Lindbeck, 1995). But at the same time, the EC must be *seen to* sustain social cohesion through characteristically Continental European policies for social security and health care insurance. Hence, for example, in the EC's *Communication on a Concerted Strategy for Modernising Social Protection* (European Commission, 1999) the first objective was 'to make work pay and to provide secure income', emphasizing labour-market flexibility, but insisting on a strategy for using resources better, not lowering social protection levels. 'A high level of social protection is an important factor for both social cohesion and for economic progress' (p. 3).

In the next section, we will consider the specific issue of equal opportunities for men and women in the context of these ambiguous developments in European social policy.

II. EQUAL OPPORTUNITIES AND EMPLOYMENT

The tension between these two approaches to social citizenship in Europe is well demonstrated by the different interpretations of policies for equal opportunities among member states. While there is a growing consensus at the micro level about how equal opportunities for men and women might best be pursued in the workplace and in public life (the Scandinavian countries having given a strong lead in these fields), there is still divergence about the macro-level of policy, especially over employment opportunities. In the UK especially, the New Labour government is committed to a continued expansion of women's employment from its already high level. The New Deal for Lone Parents is an important part of the activation programme, and the Working Families Tax Credits and Child Care Credits introduced in October 1999 are aimed at improving incentives for this group (Jordan, Agulnik, Burbidge and Duffin, 2000). This is part of the government's overall commitment to the ideas that 'work is the most reliable route out of poverty'; that education and training, as part of 'lifelong learning', are means to greater employability and a more adaptable workforce; and that low-paid and part-time work, supplemented by tax credits, can be the first steps on a ladder to good jobs, as the best path to sustainable equality between citizens.

By contrast, it is only necessary to look at the post-Maastricht social policy initiatives under the Social Protocol of November 1993 to see how the other member states adopted different priorities and methods (the UK having excluded itself from these processes through John Major's opt-out). Two of the first three subjects tackled by the European organizations representing employers and workers, under new corporatist institutions, were parental leave and 'atypical' (i.e. part-time) work, both issues of direct concern for women in employment. Here both the processes of negotiation and the outcomes reflected the social partnership approach of the Continental European model, with the regulation of the labour market as an essential counterpart to the deregulating aspects of the market-making (Falkner, 1998: 97). In the case of parental leave, this was seen as 'an important means of reconciling professional and family responsibilities, and promoting equal opportunities and treatment between men and women' (*ibid.*, p. 121). In practice this (the first collective agreement under the Social Protocol) largely consolidated existing practice, and was innovatory only in Germany, Ireland, Belgium and Luxembourg; it has been taken up by men to any significant extent only in Sweden, where they enjoyed earnings-related income protection. However, the same approach was shown in a more ambitious attempt to tackle a subject at the heart of the deregulation/flexibilization of employment debate, which resulted in the agreement on part-time work, aimed at preventing discrimination against part-time workers (mainly women). Even though the substantive achievements of the agreement were limited, the fact that the social partners were able to reach it, and become involved jointly in its implementation, is claimed by Falkner as evidence of a new European-level culture, and the continued effectiveness of the corporatist approach to governance.

Thus the agendas of the UK government and the rest of the EU have diverged on the whole topic of employment policy and equality of opportunity, and the access of the UK to the Social Protocol under New Labour does not resolve this tension, because the Blair government has in many ways consolidated its predecessor's approach. Iversen and Wren (1998) summarize the policy issues at stake as a 'trilemma' for nation-states; they can have any two of employment expansion in the service sector, equality of wages and budgetary restraint, but not all three. The Continental European states have opted for equality and restraint, the UK for employment expansion and restraint; the new EU institutions have so far adopted an approach in line with the Continental European model.

Iversen and Wren's careful analysis of employment and income statistics from five EU countries and the USA shows that the UK's levels of wage inequality are now comparable to those of the USA, with a parallel weakening of the trade union movement. Women in public-sector employment (which has actually declined, despite the large overall expansion of service work) have been the main sufferers, with wages of hospital cleaners (for example) declining by 30 to 40 per cent through privatization (Iversen and Wren, 1998: 536); yet overall there has been a substantial increase in women's employment. At the opposite end of the scale, in Germany wage inequalities have been reduced in the same period, but women (along with older workers) have been the main group suffering labour-market exclusion (*ibid.*, p. 516).

One field involving several aspects of social citizenship is that of social care. Their role as unpaid carers distinguishes women as citizens with inferior access to the public sphere (Lister, 1998). In the Scandinavian countries, around 25 per cent of the working population are employed in public services, and a major portion of these are jobs in social care, which supplement or replace informal care by families (Iversen and Wren, 1998: Table 2). This transformation of the care given to children and older people was accomplished mainly in the 1970s and 1980s, and based on high trade union membership and rising salaries for (mainly women) employees. In the UK, there are now over one million employees in social care (Department of Health, 1998: Ch. 5), but most of these are in private residential and nursing homes for elderly people, and have very low pay. Finally in Germany in 1990, public-service employment stood at around 10 per cent of the working population, with private-sector services also far lower as a proportion of the workforce (Iversen and Wren, 1998: Table 2), implying a continued reliance on unpaid care by women in households.

This situation has been slightly changed in recent years by the incorporation of the funding of old-age care into the social insurance system in Germany. However, this has not resulted in as large an expansion of employment in this field as some had anticipated or hoped. Most frail, old people have availed themselves of the opportunity, within the rules of the new system, to use the cash for household income, presumably shared with the kin who provide informal assistance (Pfau Effinger, 1999).

For those who regard employment as the key to equality of opportunity between men and women, the Scandinavian and British models of social care are both superior to the Continental European one, and especially that of Germany. Furthermore, as Esping-Andersen (1999) points out, the more women enter the labour market, the faster the *overall* growth in jobs and fall in unemployment. Hence the so-called 'inflexibilities' of European labour markets may have less to do with minimum wages and regulation of working conditions, and more to do with the gender relations under which women traditionally have lower rates of participation and where there is less provision of public or private social care. However, the persistence of inequalities between the earnings of men and women in the UK casts doubt on this interpretation. From the point of view of citizenship, the expansion in low-paid work in social reproduction services, consisting of 'dead-end' jobs which require long-term subsidization through the tax-benefit system, may be as exploitative and unjust as patriarchal domestic relations (Jordan, 2000; Jordan *et al.*, 2000).

III. EQUAL OPPORTUNITIES AND THE ENLARGEMENT OF THE EU

In this section, we turn to a rather different aspect of the future of European social citizenship, the accession of the Central-Eastern European applicant countries to membership, and the processes of 'harmonization' through which they are prepared for this by European Commission programmes. These can be seen as extending EU citizenship, and specifically social citizenship (Harlow, 1999), by adjusting these countries' national legislation to that of the EU. This section draws on experiences of being involved in a series of PHARE projects on one relevant aspect – equal opportunities between men and women – in the Czech Republic in 1996, and in Poland, Hungary and Slovenia in 1998–9 (Castle-Kanerova, 2000), designed to screen national laws and make recommendations to ease accession to a partnership of like-minded legal systems.

Equal opportunities for men and women was one of the earliest of such programmes, and we suspect that this was because everyone on both sides (in the applicant countries as well as the European Commission) assumed that it would be an easy, 'soft' subject to cover. After all, the old socialist constitutions were very clear on equality. Equal rights for men and women were written into the statute books, and generally men and women received equal treatment before the law (Fuchs, 2000). In addition, many surveys showed that neither men nor women perceived gender discrimination in their lives. Hardship was equally shared among all except the top élite. Furthermore, the kinds of issues that were raised in the previous section were absent under socialism. There was no part-time work that could be less well paid; all formal work for men and women was in some sense 'forced' and for the state; there were no 'housewives' who stayed at home, dependent on their husbands to bring cash and control the household budget; no dichotomy between paid and unpaid work; and no serious gender issues of social protection or redistribution, since there was no opportunity for the kinds of inequalities of wealth and income that generate male dominance and female powerlessness. So, to approximate equal opportunities legislation was seen as a relatively simple proposition.

Yet these projects revealed large differences in the hidden assumptions made by the two sides in the harmonization process. In the Central-Eastern European countries, some kind of collectivist notion of rights and responsibilities still holds, in the fundamental sense that legal and constitutional rules are seen as granted by the state, rather than residing in the citizens themselves, and certainly not negotiated between individuals, through their social relations. The Central-Eastern European countries have preserved (frozen, as it were, through the socialist period) a pre-World War Two version of the state and citizenship, in which the former is clearly the leading actor. In the Czech Republic, for example, the Prussian model of state–citizen and state–civil society relations still prevails; legislators are considered, and consider themselves to be, the guardians of a higher order, upholding it for the greater good, on behalf of a superior authority. They are not, in this sense, the servants of citizen-electors; rather the reverse. Even the currently debated reform of state administration in the Czech Republic relies heavily on this notion of a self-improving profession within self-evolving institutions, rather than a system that is accountable to citizens for the service it provides, to whom, and how.

By contrast, the EU version of equal opportunities at the micro level now portrays these as not being so much about legal codes as about a social climate that challenges disadvantage, and creates conditions in which citizens have the confidence to raise issues of injustice without hindrance or intimidation. In other words, it is not so much about prohibitions of certain actions, as about allowing the freedoms of individuals' potentialities to flourish without judgement or prejudice. In issues of job selection, promotion, how employees get on and get noticed, the criteria applied should not favour one sex over another. This operationalizes the Scandinavian approach to gender equality, that the social standing of men and women, including their positions in the labour market, needs to be problematized, not merely codified. Outcomes are thus the results of complex interactions, including disputes and negotiations, and standards are eventually sustained by consensual (but always provisional) coopera-tion, but usually after a long struggle, often involving battles both in the courts and within the legislative arm of the state.

That process has eventually built up a substantial stock of social capital, in the form of norms and patterns of interactions between men and women. This social capital inheres in the structure of relations between men and women in workplaces and other public-domain situations, and acts as a resource that allows women to pursue their interests in ways not previously available to them (Coleman, 1990, 2000). To some extent it has also spilled over into informal and private-sphere relationships

(Inglehart, 1997), relying on discourses of equality and sharing to reach negotiated solutions where interests conflict.

In the absence of such a history, and without the benefit of such invisible relational resources, representatives of applicant countries found it difficult to understand or accommodate to the EU approach. Participants in the projects emphasized that their national laws did not differ much from the EU where equal treatment was concerned, when equal opportunities were seen as absence of discrimination. Hence the whole exercise came to be less about legal approximation, and more about the attempt to impose this particular part of the 'European democratic heritage' on these countries. The Central-Eastern European officials emphasized that on these issues they provided reliable ministerial and legal expertise, and could thus communicate satisfactorily with member states and the EU without difficulties. It was therefore hard to extend the debate about equal opportunities beyond the legislative framework.

Equal opportunities provide a specific example of a general problem for accession countries. The doubt we wish to raise is about notions of social citizenship in EU member states that are already evolving, in some cases more rapidly than indigenous populations can readily handle. There are currently high demands on many EU citizens to exercise their civic competences, and demonstrate their civic virtues, in order to qualify for benefits and services; is this expectation of the accession countries too high? Given the very different traditions, and especially the absence of politically effective civil society organizations, self-mobilizing collective action and the sense of individual moral autonomy and empowerment in applicant societies, it is in traditional social protection and the availability of public-sector support that citizens' remaining security still resides.

It would be wrong to suggest that social capital in these states is deficient; rather it takes different forms. As Richard Rose has shown, the experience of organizational failure under the communist system led citizens to develop networks to protect themselves from official intrusion, or to exploit formal systems (Rose, 2000: 149). Individuals rely on a variety of such networks for getting things done, and there are substantial differences in choices of solutions between countries as well as between situations of state failure. For example, in the Czech Republic surveys reveal that citizens are far more likely to use personal contacts or pleading with officials to get a better flat, a permit or a hospital bed than in Russia or Ukraine, whereas they are much more likely to resort to bribery or side-payments in the latter two countries (Rose, 2000: 163–7). Rose concludes that 'this suggests that the heirs of Habsburg tradition, often dilatory or obstructive, are not corrupt to the degree of former Soviet officials' (pp. 164–5).

Yet this also raises, in an acute form, another central dilemma of

European citizenship in relation to the extension of membership to the postcommunist states. Are there any aspects of the political and social traditions of those countries that are seen as worth preserving, and can the version of EU citizenship adopted there support and sustain these? It is ironic if equal opportunities law and implementation can find nothing of value in societies that did, in many ways, prioritize equality over other political values, and produce social relations in which differences arising from occupation, education and earnings were so little reflected in differences in lifestyle and culture. In parts of Central-Eastern Europe (though increasingly not in Hungary, the Czech Republic and Poland) the intelligentsia, the professions, white-collar workers – both men and women – are scarcely distinguishable in terms of clothes, cars or leisure pursuits from their counterparts in manual roles. It seems perverse that societies as polarized and unequal in so many ways as those of Western Europe should impose their versions of equal opportunities (however advanced and enlightened in many of the aspects identified) on countries still in the grip of a very fundamental form of equality, equal misery.

Furthermore, it is by no means obvious that these societies have nothing to offer to the 'common European heritage' in their political histories and civil society traditions either. Despite the fact that much of it was a by-product of authoritarian politics and inefficient communist administration, the social capital generated by the former regime has many positive features. Among these phenomena, the dissidents' achievements, the successful revolutions of 1989, rather low crime rates, high levels of public safety and security, cultures of public civility and mutual respect, impressive cultural achievements, strong kinship and friendship networks, all represent features that might well, in another context, and with a political leadership that asserted them more forcefully, be seen as worthy of nurturance and protection. After all, it is well recognized that social capital is usually a by-product of activities and purposes other than its production (Coleman, 2000), and that any such capital is beneficial for some socially desirable ends, and harmful for others (Solow, 2000). Many aspects of the socialist legacy of entrenched behaviours can be seen to have their roots in forms of equality and social citizenship that are endangered by Western influences – threats which should arguably be taken more seriously than the EU currently takes them.

IV. CONCLUSIONS

Although it ranged on a continuum from the Austrian and Italian communitarian approaches to the German social democratic and British liberal variants, the social citizenship of postwar welfare states in Northern

Europe was located in a general framework of what Richard Bellamy and Alex Warleigh (1998: 461) call 'liberal cosmopolitanism' – universal and uniform rights, secured by compulsory financial contributions, and distributed according to principles of entitlement-based justice. The duties attached to these social rights remained vague; the role of beneficiary or service user was essentially a passive one. There were several uncriticized assumptions built into these institutions, such as that contributors were mostly men, that they contributed out of earnings from employment and (except in Scandinavia) that benefits were provided for their partners and children as 'dependants'.

In so far as there has been any clear version of European citizenship, it has until recently followed this tradition. Everson (1995) argues that citizen participation is no more than participation in the market, and hence a fundamentally 'thin' concept of citizenship, with little active content. On to this economic notion have been grafted the social rights of the Maastricht Treaty, and the institutions which include European employers' and labour organizations as partners in the process of euroregulation. We have shown that these continue to address workplace issues, but that the topic of equality between men and women has hitherto constituted the main 'social' element in these new processes.

Ideas about social inclusion through 'activation', emanating via the UK from the USA, are argued from within a communitarian tradition, but a very limited and partial one. The responsibilities of citizenship are imposed, through state officials, on one part of the population, and as an obligation to take paid employment or training, as a condition for receiving benefits. European Commission documents on social protection and social inclusion acknowledge the need for broader economic participation, greater flexibility and better incentives, but stop far short of adopting this approach. Indeed, they continue explicitly to endorse the 'European social model' of relatively generous replacement rates for inactive beneficiaries.

In the longer term, there may be scope for convergence between the two strategies around an issue that is currently ignored by both. Hitherto, the expansion of employment in social reproduction tasks (especially health and social care) has been seen as a strength of the US-UK strategy but – as we have hinted – this overlooks important issues about balance and choice over how to combine paid and unpaid work, formal and informal care. In the foreseeable future the reformed tax-benefit system will have to address the issue of support for family caring, voluntary work in social services, community activism, social entrepreneurship, and so on (Jordan *et al.*, 2000: Chs 2 and 3). Extending the tax credits to those participating in unpaid but socially valuable work roles – a 'participation income' (Atkinson, 1995) – would be the first step towards giving all citizens the right to an income that is not tied to employment duties (Fitzpatrick, 1999; Standing, 1999) – a basic income.

Conversely, in the Continental Europe tradition, resistance to both wage cutting and the creation of new in-work benefits or tax credits may require an approach that supports family care and other forms of informal work, including the expanding voluntary sector (Anheier, 2000), with its emphasis on volunteering. It is possible that new forms of social citizenship could emerge, eventually promoted by the same institutional systems, which made income support less rather than more conditional on paid employment. A basic income that was an individual entitlement of all citizens would create a radical form of equality between men and women, and allow an eventual redistribution of paid and unpaid work roles, based on negotiation and choice. Such a system could have both variable national and universal European elements.

It is far from clear that this change would have the same effects in all societies, or all parts of any one society. The outcomes would again depend on social capital, in the form of the resources available for men and women to pursue their interests in the public and private spheres. As we illustrated in the previous section, such relational resources can profoundly influence the results of interactions. In the absence of other changes, greater inequality (in income and power) could occur. Hence complementary policies for empowerment and inclusion, which might vary considerably between societies, would be required.

Any such long-term institutional convergence presupposes largely separate rather than coordinated developments in national social policies, but with some overall EU background principles, notably on equal opportunities. Meanwhile, other EU initiatives will continue to be of relevance. The Amsterdam Treaty attempts to give more substance to European citizenship, particularly in relation to the enforcement of rights by individual citizens. For example, a recent leaflet offers direct advice about how to obtain redress at the national and European level if 'single market rights' are infringed (European Commission, 2000). The Treaty also established procedures for protecting fundamental rights. Article 13 empowers the Council to take appropriate action to combat discrimination, including discrimination on grounds of gender, and the Community is given the opportunity to develop policies and proposals to prevent discrimination and violence.

We have argued – with examples from social protection and from equality of opportunity – that the progress of economic integration in the EU exacerbates tensions between competition in a free-market environment, and cohesion between members of a trans-national political association. The accession of the former socialist countries of Central-

Eastern Europe has already challenged the established systems by which the EU sought to mitigate these tensions. The Cohesion Funds and the various programmes to address uneven economic development (often accentuated by increased competition and free trade) have had to be reformed and modified to take account of the lower *per capita* incomes of these states. But we have raised a series of further questions about the 'social dimension' of the EU, and whether increased pressure to make labour markets more flexible, to increase levels of formal participation (especially among women), and to commercialize aspects of social care, indicate developments which are in line with the demands of a more competitive global economy, but in tension with parts of the European tradition.

On both income equality and equality of opportunity, the strong claims of the Commission's documents are counteracted by economic tendencies within the member states. The reality of decentralization and fragmentation resists the central thrust of European social policy-making. The enlargement process will increase these tensions. The accession countries, dealing simultaneously with processes of economic liberalization and political democratization, have little experience in how to resolve such conflicting pressures.

Poverty and gender inequality are becoming more visible targets of EU programmes, and moving up the agenda of policy-making (Fuchs, 2000). If the notion of European citizenship is to have substance, rather than being part of a 'legitimation theatre' for the Internal Market Programme, the ambiguities identified in this chapter will need to be directly addressed. Especially in the enlargement process, new versions of social citizenship, that better match new economic realities, will be required.

REFERENCES

Anheier, H. (2000) 'The Third Sector and Volunteering: What Are The Issues?' Paper given at ILO meeting on Global Income Security, Bellagio, Italy, 6–8 March.

Atkinson, A. B. (1995) *Public Economics in Action: The Basic Income/Flat Tax Proposal* (Oxford: Oxford University Press).

Bellamy, R. and Warleigh, A. (1998) 'From an Ethics of Integration to an Ethics of Participation: Citizenship and the Future of the European Union', *Millennium*, 27: 3, pp. 447–70.

Blair, T. (1998a) *The Third Way: Politics for the New Century*, Fabian Pamphlet 588 (London: Fabian Society).

Blair, T. (1998b) Preface to *A New Contract for Welfare* (London: Stationery Office).

Blair, T. and Schröder, G. (1999) *The Blair-Schröder Manifesto* (Internet).

Brown, G. (1997) 'Why Labour is Still Loyal to the Poor', *Guardian*, 15 August.

Castle-Kanerova, M. (2000) 'Equal Opportunities in the Czech Republic and Other Vysegrad Countries as Part of the Requirements of Accession to the EU', *Czech Sociological Journal*, Winter.

Coleman, J. S. (1990) *Foundations of Social Theory* (Cambridge, Mass: Harvard University Press).

Coleman, J. S. (2000) 'Social Capital and the Creation of Human Capital', in P. Dasgupta and I. Serageldin (eds), *Social Capital: A Multifaceted Perspective*, (Washington D.C.: World Bank), pp. 13–39.

Cox, R. H. (1998) 'From Safety Nets to Trampolines: Labour-Market Activation in the Netherlands and Denmark', *Governance: An International Journal of Politics and Administration*, 11: 4, pp. 397–414.

Cox, R. H. (1999) 'The Consequences of Welfare Reform: How Conceptions of Social Rights are Changing' (Norman, OK: University of Oklahoma, Department of Political Science).

Department of Health (1998) *Modernising Social Services: Promoting Independence, Improving Protection, Raising Standards*, Cm. 4169 (London: Stationery Office).

Department of Social Security (1998) *A New Contract for Welfare* (Green Paper) Cm. 3805 (London: Stationery Office).

Esping-Andersen, G. (1990) *The Three Worlds of Welfare Capitalism* (Cambridge: Polity).

Esping-Andersen, G. (1999) 'The Jobs–Equality Trade-off'. Paper given to the ECPR Summer School, European University Institute, Florence, 12 July.

European Commission (1999) *Communication on a Concerted Strategy for Modernising Social Protection, European Social Policy*, Supplement No. 100, October.

European Commission (2000) 'Enforcing Your Rights in the Single European Market', *Europe Direct: Dialogue with Citizens and Business* (Luxembourg: European Commission).

Everson, M. (1995) 'Economic Rights within the European Union', in R. Bellamy, V. Buffachi and D. Castiglione (eds), *Democracy and Constitutional Culture in the European Union* (London: Lothian Foundation Press), pp. 137–52.

Falkner, G. (1998) *EU Social Policy in the 1990s: Towards a Corporatist Policy Community* (London: Routledge).

Fernandes, L. F. (1999) 'Reregulation in the European Union'. Paper presented at an ESRC Network Meeting, University of Braga, Portugal, 17 November.

Fitzpatrick, T. (1999) *Freedom and Security: An Introduction to the Basic Income Debate* (London: MacMillan).

Fuchs, D. (2000) Interview with President of the European Women's Lobby (Denise Fuchs) *PHARE Consensus Social Protection News*, January.

Genschell, P. (1999) 'Tax Competition and the Welfare State' (Cologne: Max-Planch Institute for the Study of Societies).

Goul Andersen, J. (1996) 'Marginalisation, Citizenship and the Economy: The Capacities of the Universalist Welfare State in Denmark', in E. O. Erikson and J. Loftager (eds), *The Rationality of the Welfare State* (Oslo: Scandinavian University Press), pp. 155–202.

Harlow, C. (1999) *Citizen Access to Political Power in the European Union* (Florence:

EU Working Papers, Robert Schuman Centre) No. 99/2.

Inglehart, R. (1997) *Modernization and Postmodernization: Cultural, Economical and Political Change in 43 Societies* (Princeton: Princeton University Press).

Iversen, T. and Wren, A. (1998) 'Equality, Employment and Budgetary Restraint: The Trilemma of the Service Economy', *World Politics*, 50, pp. 507–46.

Jordan, B. (1999) *The Morality of Welfare Reform: An Anglo-Irish Comparison.* Paper given at a Conference on the Morality of Welfare, St George's House, Windsor Castle, 29 June.

Jordan, B. (2000) *Social Work and The Third Way: Tough Love as Social Policy* (London: Sage).

Jordan, B. and Loftager, J. (1999) 'Labour-market Activation in the UK and Denmark'. Paper given at a Conference on Unemployment and Labour Markets, Graz, Austria, 27 May.

Jordan, B., Agulnik, P., Burbidge, D. and Duffin, S. (2000) *Stumbling Towards a Basic Income: The Prospects for Tax-Benefit Integration in the UK* (London: Citizen's Income Trust).

Kymlicka, W. and Norman, W. (1994) 'Return of the Citizen: A Survey of Recent Work on Citizenship Theory', *Ethics* 104, 2, pp. 352–8.

Lewis, J. (1998) *Gender, Social Care and Welfare State Restructuring in Europe* (Aldershot: Ashgate).

Lindbeck, A. (1995) 'Objectives and Strategies in the Development of the Swedish Welfare State'. Paper presented at a Workshop on Objectives and Strategies in the Development of European Welfare States, Centre for Social Policy Research, University of Bremen, 24–5 April.

Lister, R. (1998) 'Vocabularies of Citizenship and Gender', *Critical Social Policy* 56, pp. 309–31.

Loftager, J. (1996) 'Citizen's Income – A New Welfare-State Strategy', in E. O. Eriksen and J. Loftager, *The Rationality of the Welfare State*, pp. 134–54.

Pfau-Effinger, B. (1999) 'Labour Markets and Personal Social Services in Europe'. Paper given at IFSW European Conference on Work, Economy and Social Welfare, Helsinki, Finland, 20 June.

Rose, R. (2000) 'Getting Things Done in an Antimodern Society: Social Capital Networks in Russia', in P. Dasgupta and I. Serageldin (eds), *Social Capital: A Multifaceted Perspective* (Washington D.C.: World Bank) pp. 147–71.

Scharpf, F. W. (1999) 'The Viability of Advanced Welfare States in the International Economy: Vulnerabilities and Options', Working Paper 99/9 (Cologne: Max-Planc Institute for the Study of Societies).

Solow, R. M. (2000) 'Notes on Social Capital and Economic Performance', in P. Dasgupta and I. Serageldin (eds), *Social Capital: A Multifaceted Perspective* (Washington D.C.: World Bank) pp. 6–9.

Standing, G. (1999) *Global Labour Flexibility: Seeking Distributive Justice* (Basing-stoke: MacMillan).

Streeck, W., (1999) 'Comparative Solidarity: Rethinking the "European Social Model"', Working Paper 99/8 (Cologne: Max-Planck Institute for the Study of Societies).

Visser, J. and Hemerijck, A. (1997) *'A Dutch Miracle': Job Growth, Welfare Reform and Corporation in the Netherlands* (Amsterdam: Amsterdam University Press).

Waddan, A. (1997) *The Politics of Social Welfare: The Collapse of the Centre and the Rise of the Right* (Cheltenham: Edward Elgar).

Part III

External Aspects of European Citizenship

Part II

The Political Economy of European Citizenship

R. J. BARRY JONES

I. INTRODUCTION

The issue of citizenship has become increasingly salient as the EU has moved slowly, and often hesitantly, towards greater integration. Citizenship is, however, a surprisingly elusive concept, as contributions to this, and related, studies demonstrate. Equally problematical is the issue of the entity, or entities, to which notions of citizenship may properly be applied.

The Shorter Oxford English Dictionary defines citizenship as the possession of the status of a citizen, and a citizen as 'an inhabitant of a city or (often) a town' and/or as 'a member of a state' or 'an enfranchised inhabitant of a country'. Neither definition is particularly helpful in the case of putative 'European citizenship' as Europe, however defined, is clearly considerably more than a city or a town and its status as a state or a country, actual or potential, remains highly contentious. Moreover, the latter state/country focus moves the issue of citizenship directly into the troubled waters of 'sovereignty': its substance and possession. At its very least, the notion of European citizenship coexisting with citizenship of the member states of the EU requires some notion of mixed or shared sovereignties – the full implications of which have yet to be worked out in theory or revealed in practice.

What is clear is that any notion of citizenship must relate to membership of a polity of some kind and, indeed, discussions of an emergent European citizenship commonly refer to the crystallization of a new EU polity. Unfortunately the notion of a polity also remains stubbornly vague and imprecisely related to notions of citizenship. At one extreme, it is rare to use the term citizen to refer to an elector for a parish council and, at the other extreme, terms like 'world citizen' can only be used as a very loose metaphor, precisely because the 'polity' in question is relatively insignificant in the first case and no more than embryonic in the latter.

The maze generated by the definitional and practical difficulties of both the notions of citizenship and of polities will be navigated in this Chapter through two procedures. First, to develop an analytical distinction between three facets of 'citizenship': formal citizenship; instrumental citizenship; and affective citizenship. Second, to analyse polities in terms of the collective goods that they provide, or that they might provide, if they functioned effectively. The interrelationship between the three facets of citizenship is, it will be argued, ultimately critical to the substance and robustness of any instances of 'citizenship'. The ability of polities to supply 'legitimate' collective goods effectively will in turn be critical to the ability of any polity to establish and maintain a durable link between the three facets of citizenship and, hence, ensure its own ultimate survival.

There is growing interest in 'constructivist' approaches to the European Union (specifically *Journal of European Public Policy*, 1999), and to politics and international relations, more generally (Ruggie, 1998). The basic proposition that the social realm is constructed by, and on the basis of, the ideas that underlie human activity opens up a range of possibilities. At one extreme, constructivism can drift into extreme variants of philosophical idealism and/or postmodernism. Less dramatically, constructivism provides one component of the attempted resolution of the structure–agent debate (Hollis and Smith, 1991) through structuration theory (Giddens, 1984). However, as Margaret Scotford Archer (Scotford Archer, 1988) has argued, persuasively, that the retention of structural perspectives is essential if coherent explanation of change within the social (and political) is to be possible in terms other than 'spontaneous' changes in human subjectivity. Methodologically, then, only a hybrid variant – structural constructivism (Jones, 1999) – can preserve a constructivist perspective, in combination with a significant measure of structural analysis. The analysis presented in this chapter is thus largely 'rationalistic' in its tenor and tone (Keohane, 1988) by emphasizing conditions and developments that are located at the structural level of social and political life and examining the responses that they might reasonably be expected to evoke from the individuals upon whom they impact. Many contemporary attempts to construct a European polity and, with it, a reality of European citizenship reflect strenuous efforts to talk new 'realities' into existence: a constructivist project (Ruggie, 1998: Introduction) in being. The argument in this chapter, however, will be that the success of such efforts to construct the new Europe will be qualified by the ability of the EU to generate affective citizenship through effective forms of formal and instrumental citizenship, that formidable obstacles continue to face such efforts, and that the record to date, despite some successes in specific spheres, remains far from encouraging.

II. CITIZENSHIP – FORMAL, INSTRUMENTAL AND AFFECTIVE

'Rights' and 'duties' are central to most discussions of the substance of citizenship. However, it is important to differentiate between those 'rights' and 'duties' that are concerned with the institutions and formal constitution of any polity, on the one hand, and those 'rights' and 'duties' that are concerned with the actual goods and services that are provided by the polity to its citizens, individually and collectively. With the former approach, an account of citizenship might be constructed in terms of the 'right' to vote for the government of any polity and the 'duty' so to do on prescribed occasions (O'Keefe and Bavasso, 1998; Lippolis, 1998). However, such a constitutional focus of citizenship would say nothing about much of the functional significance of the relevant polity for individual citizens, or its ultimate durability, because it fails to address the wider purposes for which the polity exists, or is supposed to exist, beyond those of the structures and procedures that define its form and ensure its institutional functioning. Thus, the sets of legal definitions and provisions that endow individuals with formal membership of a polity are important (Welsh, 1993; Marias, 1994), but remain only a small part of the picture of substantive and meaningful citizenship.

Citizenship within any polity thus has to be defined in two ways. First, in terms of the rights and duties of citizens that concern the institutional functioning of the policy. Second, by a specification of the range of wider instrumental purposes that the policy fulfils for its members (Meehan, 1993). Such instrumental citizenship is significant in two ways: it defines, as will be seen, the nature and significance of the polity, itself; and it establishes much of the substantive relationship between the polity and its members. The provision of security from external or internal threats to life and property, or the supply of material benefits in kind or cash are both instrumental relationships between polity and population that are likely to give substance to notions of citizenship.

Extensive or intensive features of instrumental citizenship are, in turn, likely to foster positive popular sentiments towards the polity that provides valued goods and services and that, indeed, embeds such provision within a structure of law and well-functioning institutions. Affective citizenship, with populations viewing the polity of which they are members with affection and loyalty, is thus likely to develop where valued forms of instrumental citizenship have been developed and sustained for any length of time, as witnessed by popular sentiments towards victorious states at the end of major wars.[1]

Affective citizenship is, moreover, no mere matter of sentiment or of vague notions of identity. Affective citizenship, where well developed, is the bedrock upon which the polity rests and upon which it has to call when it is confronted by serious challenges and potentially costly decisions and courses of action. The willingness of 'citizens' to pay taxes to support collective objectives, even when they may not be immediate beneficiaries or even appreciate fully all the uses of those taxes, is evidence of the existence of such affective citizenship. Even more significantly, the willingness of 'citizens' to defend their polity with armed force and, if necessary, place their lives in jeopardy, is the ultimate test of a deep-seated and robust affective citizenship.

III. THE NATURE AND IDENTITY OF POLITIES

The discussion of the three facets of citizenship provides some indication of the foundations of effective polities. Such polities, to be worthy of serious consideration, must exist for purposes other than their mere survival or to satisfy an emotional need to proclaim membership of something called a polity. What substantial polities do in practice is to provide valued public goods for their members. Such public goods are those forms of collective goods that can only, or best, be ensured through the operations of agencies of public governance; that is, private arrangements will be insufficient to secure their generation, or generation at levels sufficient to meet the general need. Collective goods are, in turn, goods and/or services that are characterized by *lumpiness* in provision – with distinct thresholds of resources required to bring them into existence – *non-excludability* – where members of the collectivity in question cannot readily be excluded from enjoyment of the collective good once it is supplied to all – and *indivisibility* – with the collective good not being divisible into small portions for consumption by individuals or subsets of the collectivity (Frohlich, Oppenheimer and Young, 1971; Olson 1982).

All institutions of governance must thus exist to define and/or supply one or more credible collective goods. Institutions of public governance ultimately differ from those of private governance only in two respects. First, the potential scope (i.e. the number and variety) of collective goods that are (or might) be addressed and, second, the domain (i.e. the number and variety of constituents) over which authoritative action is exerted to define and supply such collective goods. The resources and legitimacy of effective institutions of public governance, or polities, should thus be considerably greater than those of agents of private governance. Substantive public governance, and hence a significant polity, is thus absent where pertinent collective goods are not at stake, or cannot realistically be expected to come under active consideration.

The shaping of a polity, and its work in identifying and providing valued collective goods, is the substance of politics. Politics is thus essentially a three-level activity (Jones, 1995a). At the foundational (or constitutional) level, politics defines the nature, membership and legitimate scope of any collectivity and its legitimate authorities – i.e. the polity. Thus, the

Constitution of the USA identifies both individuals and the member states of the 'Union' as legitimate 'constituents'. Within modern international 'politics', states have been defined as the primary, legitimate constituents of the 'international' system. The second – institutional – level of politics consists of the complex sets of practices and institutions – some formally prescribed, others the products of habits and conventions – through which the legitimate members of the polity act and reach decisions. The third and final level of politics is then composed of the day-to-day activities, dealings and decisions of those engaged actively in any polity (the 'politics' of newspaper reports and electoral pundits).

Political debate and disputation takes place at all three levels of 'politics' and, through them, the identities of appropriate collective goods are defined and the means of their supply established. The identities and relative 'rights' of the constituents of a polity can be disputed at the foundational level, as in the case of the American Civil War. The institutions of a polity can also give rise to debate, as in the case of contention over electoral systems in contemporary Britain. Day-to-day political debates and deliberations conventionally concern the means of supply of acknowledged collective goods, but may also extend into attempts to redefine the collective goods that should be the purpose of the polity, as in recent attempts to 'roll back' the state in a number of Western democracies.

IV. CITIZENSHIP AND PUBLIC GOODS

The relationship between those special types of collective goods that constitute public goods – their definition and supply – and the various facets of citizenship is at the heart of the problem of citizenship, in general, and that of European citizenship, in particular. For a polity to create viable institutional citizenship two things must happen: first, appropriate public goods must be defined and supplied; and, second, the putative 'citizens' must be persuaded that these are valid public goods, are best supplied by the polity in question, and have a reasonable chance of being supplied in practice by that polity. These requirements are closely connected (possibly in a 'chicken-and-egg' manner) with issues of identity; of patterns of political and social identification.

The issue, here, is whether there is a widespread belief that there are collective (or public) goods that can only be supplied, be best provided or most credibly be expected from the polity that seeks to establish institutional citizenship. A formal identification as citizens of the EU, and rights to participate in direct elections to the European Parliament, have been accorded to the peoples of the EU by successive treaties. These, however, remain at the level of polity-maintenance and do not encroach far into areas of substantial interest to the majority of the population of the EU.

The EU has encountered considerable difficulties with regard to substantive public goods. Protection from external threats probably involves the creation of a common defence structure and capability. Such a possibility, however, remains intensely controversial, arouses the deep-seated opposition of considerable numbers of European 'citizens', and has been confined, thus far, to the modest revitalization of the Western European Union (which is not identical in membership with the EU) and a new rapid reaction force to allow European members of NATO to undertake actions in areas of particular interest to themselves. Internal security remains predominantly in the hands of the member states, with the partial exception of EU-wide networks to combat drug-smuggling and terrorist activity. This partial exception on the domestic security front, however, is muted in its popular impact by the very fact that it operates, necessarily, in the covert domain and is therefore largely hidden, in action and effect, from the public.

One, much vaunted, contribution of the EU to the security of its 'citizens' does, however, remain. A popular claim for the EU is its contribution to postwar peace within Western Europe. Such a claim has proved to be persuasive amongst a portion of the region's population, but has always remained vulnerable to the qualifications that the primary sources of postwar peace in Europe were the comprehensive military defeat, and armed occupation, of the major revisionist powers and the rapid emergence of a common external threat from the Soviet Union and its Eastern and Central European satellites. In the former case, the collective good of collective peace was delivered by the Allied Powers and in the second case, it was generated by the Soviet threat.

The economic realm has offered an increasingly powerful potential source of public goods to substantiate the emergent European Union polity.[2] The force of mobility provisions within the EU derives, primarily, from the economic opportunities that it gives to those with such rights (Wouters, 1994). Indeed, economic and trade issues provided the practical cement for the early decades of the European Economic Community and its successor the European Community. The earlier Coal and Steel Community was motivated by a desire to tie together the heavy industry of Germany and France and render it less feasible for them to go to war with one another in the future. The Common Agricultural Policy (CAP), however, was justified, formally, as a means of guaranteeing a sufficiency of agricultural commodities for the population of the member states. The status of the CAP as a genuine public good for the whole European Community and its peoples has, however, been increasingly challenged by those who perceive it to be a partial good directed at agricultural interests and lobbies.

Industrial strength and general economic prosperity has, however, become a growing concern of the EU. With the growth of economic competition within the international economy from the late 1960s onwards, the EU has been increasingly promoted as the appropriate level at which to focus polices aimed at preserving and enhancing industrial competitiveness. A number of early programmes designed to encourage technological innovation (Swan, 1983) have been complemented by policies (and corresponding directorates within the European Commission) in such areas as industrial competition, European-wide transport, education and training. Most significantly, however, the member states of the EU agreed to negotiate collectively in the Uruguay Round of the General Agreement on Tariffs and Trade: protracted negotiations which produced, not only significant measures of trade liberalization, but also the creation of the new World Trade Organization. Moreover, a number of subsequent trade disputes with the USA – the disputes over the EC's banana import-regime and the dispute over the EU's desire to restrict the importation of beef treated with growth hormones – have been managed by the EU rather than member states.

Such concerns with economic, industrial and trade policy clearly reflect the intrinsic importance of such matters to the EU and its member states. They are also of potential pertinence to the material well-being of the EU's population and the creation of general support for the EU and its institutions. There are two difficulties here, however. The first is that economic and industrial policies tend to have a differential impact upon the populations for which they are devised. The market integration and harmonization that has been increasingly the focus and effect of the European Community certainly has varying implications for those in different socio-economic situations. Detailed statistical analysis of attitudes and opinions amongst the population of the EU has, indeed, revealed clear correlations between economic advantage/disadvantage from the integrated European market and patterns of support/opposition with regard to integration within the EU and sentiments of identification with the wider European polity and society (Gabel, 1998). In general, it is the more highly skilled and the wealthier who support European integration and affect a European identity and the less skilled and poorer citizens who remain more sceptical. The advent of monetary union within the EU is likely to compound this differential experience and response, as the rich and skilful increase their personal mobility and the poorer and less skilled are increasingly exposed to the effects of increased intra-EC competition upon the conditions and prospects of worthwhile employment.

It is also the case that a range of measures adopted to promote and consolidate the single European market have created new complications for its citizens. Rules and regulations have impacted extensively upon producers, distributors and consumers of a wide range of goods and services. Some of these rules and regulations reflect the real requirements of market harmonization; others, however, owe more to bureaucratic inertia and/or to the philosophy that what can be regulated ought to be regulated.

The Recreational Craft Directive (RCD) exemplifies the latter impulses as much as the former. The purpose of the RCD was to promote a single market within the European Community for leisure craft, and was prompted by a belief that different national standards for the safety and construction of leisure craft constituted an obstacle to the free importation and exportation of such vessels from one member country to another. With standards for the construction of recreational boats being set by national authorities and imposed unevenly upon boats constructed and sold within the various national jurisdictions, boat producers were faced with widely varying legal obligations in different European markets and boat owners were exposed to the danger of purchasing unsafe vessels. However, prior to the promulgation of the Recreational Craft Directive, there was very little evidence of unmanageable obstacles confronting boat builders that wished to trade in other EU member states or that boats were being manufactured and sold that were seriously unfit for their prospective, and usually self-evident, usage. The practical effect of the RCD, however, was to drive out of business a number of smaller boat builders who, despite long records of building sound vessels, could not generate the revenues to cover the considerable costs of establishing compliance with the RCD.

Earlier measures taken under the Single European Act also demonstrated the uneven effects upon 'citizens' of policy-making within the European Community. The single European market entailed the regularization of Value Added Tax (VAT) collection procedures throughout the European Community, particularly for goods and services that were to be traded and/or transported across 'national' frontiers. The general rule was that the authorities of the country from which a good or service was transported would be responsible for the imposition and collection of VAT (and subsequent shipments treated as VAT-paid at their destinations). There were, however, to be two exceptions to this general rule in the cases of transportation 'equipment': motor vehicles and pleasure boats. In these two cases, the responsible VAT authority would be those of the country into which the completed vehicle or boat was shipped. This opened up the possibility that boats currently in use might have VAT imposed upon them whenever they arrived in the ports of another EU member state unless they could establish that all due VAT payments had already been made within some other EU member state.

The promulgation of these new VAT collection rules under the Single

European Act, however, had a number of curious features. First, the rules were not finally clarified until the 14 December 1992 (Royal Yachting Association (RYA) Information Leaflet, 17 December 1992) and not made public until after the Single Market came into existence on 1 January 1993. Second, the 'home country' taxation authorities could certify VAT-paid status of a boat only by issuing a Single Administrative Document (SAD) (see RYA Leaflet 'Applying for a VAT Status Certificate'). Third, the tax authorities could issue SADs only in respect of older (Council Directive) boats actually located within the EU (though not necessarily their own countries) on 1 January 1993, even if it could clearly be established that all due VAT payments had been made on the vehicle or boat when new, or when subsequently resold. The effects of such retrospective 'legislation' were to place a number of boat owners in a particularly difficult situation. If, as might be the case, the vessel was temporarily outside EU waters on 1 January 1993, its VAT-paid status could not be established by home country VAT authorities in the form that would be automatically acceptable to the VAT authorities of other EU member states (i.e. they could not be issued with a SAD). Such boat owners, when contemplating a return to EU waters, thus faced the danger (very real in some cases) that VAT authorities in the country of their landfall might declare the VAT status of their boats to be uncertain and hence impose a new VAT bill, possibly at the prevailing rate on the current market value of the boat. In the case of boats of any size, such a VAT bill could have been substantial. The returning boat owner was thus faced with the unhappy choice of contriving to avoid arrival in any EU member country whose VAT authorities might be thought to be unsympathetic or risking a substantial VAT bill, which could be challenged only within the courts of that country: an inherently costly and risky undertaking.

The negotiation of the VAT elements of the implementation of the Single European Act, it should be noted, had involved the 'representation' of the boat owners of the various member states by their respective national boating associations (the Royal Yachting Association in the case of the UK). However, this 'representation' had done nothing to secure the promulgation of the relevant rules in sufficient time to allow vulnerable boat owners to relocate their boats before 1 January and had only achieved modest modifications in the length of retrospective VAT obligations. 'Citizenship' for many EU boat owners at the time of the introduction of the Single European Market was thus a pretty feeble creature. Influence to secure a sensible and timely policy was minimal. Retrospective and capricious legislation could not be resisted or challenged. The consequences of the 'legislation' could be confronted only through costly and highly risky individual legal action in the courts of the relevant member state. The need for robust citizenship rights and processes had certainly been demonstrated, but the introduction of the Single European Market has, however, demonstrated many of their practical weakness. For boat owners, more-over, it has also done nothing to enhance their personal mobility, as the imposition of substantial tax by Greek authorities in mid-2000 upon arriving recreational vessels, including those owned by EU 'citizens' ('Greece Gets Ready', *Practical Boat Owner* No. 404, p. 40) demonstrates.

The case of private boat owners, and many of the builders of smaller leisure craft, thus indicates the gap that has often emerged between the expectations of equal and equitable treatments, which might well be prompted by talk of a new European 'citizenship', and the sorry practical experience of cost, uncertainty and the prospect of complex legal process to establish, or even restore, reasonable treatment.

The growing role of the EU in the external trade relations of its constituent states does, however, suggest one significant public good, or set of public goods, that might substantiate the credentials of an EU polity. The management of the EU's external trade relations complements a range of intra-EC measures in economic and industrial policy that are designed to respond to, and even establish a measure of control over, aspects of contemporary globalization. While the nature and extent of such globalization remains highly controversial (Jones, 1995b; Hirst and Thompson, 1996; Jones, 2000) many of the features that are associated with increasing internationalization/globalization within the international political economy clearly do create problems that need to be addressed and opportunities for agencies like the European Community/Union to establish their role and enhance their attraction to their 'citizens'.

Here again, however, there are some difficulties confronting the EU's ability to underpin its role and impact in a world of intensifying competition and advancing internationalization/globalization. The impact of issues of trade policy upon individual citizens are often somewhat muted, unless those citizens are directly affected by new regulations or the consequences of a trade dispute, and their general significance is not generally appreciated. Moreover, there are many who still believe that the divergence in the economic and industrial structures and interests of the member states are such as to qualify the desirability of the EU's role in such matters and to reduce its ultimate effectiveness. Finally, true believers in the principles of free trade would deny that an interventionist trade policy (or indeed any other kind of industrial policy) constituted a legitimate public good for supply at the EU or at any other level. Internationalization/globalization might or might not, in short, create problems for states; and might or might not be suitable for joint action within, and by, the European Community/Union.

Overarching the issue of moving from formal citizenship to instrumental and thence to affective citizenship is thus the problem that public goods, in general, cannot be defined in an uncontentious manner: While one individual might believe that a 'good' like nuclear deterrence must be provided, and provided on a collective basis, others might dispute the very need for the provision of such a good by any society or polity. There are also continuing disputes about the best level at which collective and/or public goods should be provided: should policies directed towards economic and industrial stability be generated at the level of the EU as a whole, or at more local levels? The debate about subsidiarity within the EU has exemplified such debates and uncertainties about the level of supply of various public goods.

In practice, many valued public goods continue to be provided by the states within which individuals reside. Moreover, such provision of public goods continues to reflect substantial 'national' differences. Indeed, even when the criteria for the provision of such goods and services have now been established at the level of the EU, their practical delivery continues to be primarily by, and through, the institutions of the member states of the EU – their social service departments and law courts in particular.

IV. CITIZENSHIP AND SOCIO-ECONOMIC GOODS

The proper role of government in the provision of a wide variety of social and economic goods for their citizens remains one of the major issues of debate and dispute within contemporary politics. However, most of the member states of the EU have conventionally identified quite a wide range of social and economic conditions as warranting public concern and, where necessary, the supply of appropriate goods and services. To define the general health of the population as a public good draws health policy into the legitimate realm of public governance within any polity; so too the definition of minimal general standards of wealth and income, education and training, or standards of public behaviour.

The processes whereby such areas of life come to be defined as matters of public concern and provision – as public goods – is, as has been suggested, definitive of the political process. An increasing range of such areas are now falling under the purview of the institutions of the EU. However, an effective polity must be able to do more than define public goods; it must also be able to provide them for the entirety of the population that it seeks to serve. It is here, however, that the EU still has a long way to go and much to do if instrumental citizenship is to be extended to its putative citizens in a manner and on a scale sufficient to attract loyalty and affection.

The measures adopted to prepare for, and then sustain, the adoption of a common currency have generated a notable level of convergence on a number of indicators of economic performance amongst the eleven, and soon to be twelve. participating members of the EU. Significant variations persist, however, with regard to a number of indicators of the economic experience of the populations of the EU's member states that are not confined to the understandable variations between EMU participants and non-participants, such as growth rates, unemployment levels, increases in earnings and consumer price rises.

Figure 8.1 Growth rates of the major EU economies (year to August 1999)

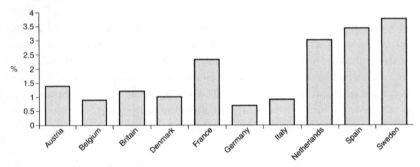

Figure 8.2 Unemployment rates in the major EU economies

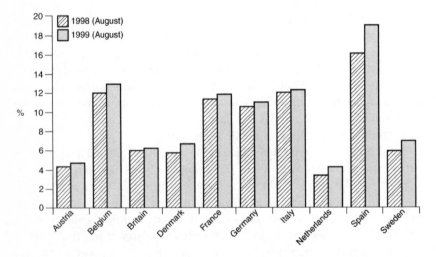

Growth rates remain significantly variable throughout the major economies of the EU, as Figure 8.1 indicates. Figure 8.2 reveals the

Figure 8.3 Wage levels in the major EU economies
(yearly increases to August 1999)

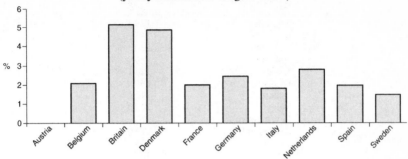

Figure 8.4 Consumer price rises in the major EU economies (year to August 1999)

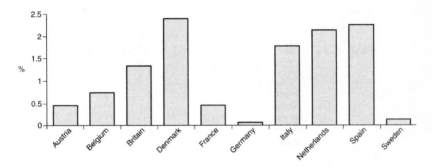

significant variations that persist in the unemployment levels experienced in the EU's major economies, whilst Figure 8.3 shows that increases the wages and earnings also vary noticeably. Finally, Figure 8.4 indicates that consumer price rises have also continued to differ, even while remaining within the Maastricht 'convergence criteria on inflation'.

Such persistent variations amongst the EU's economies occur against the background of substantial differences amongst the societies that now comprise the Union. The provision of health care has traditionally varied substantially across the countries that now constitute the EU, as Table 8.1, on health expenditure in 1996, and Table 8.2, on the provision of physicians (although the disparities apparent on this measure have to be qualified by the variations in 'national' definitions of 'physicians'), suggest. Levels of educational provision and achievement have also varied substantially, as the data on completion of secondary education in Table 8.3 indicate.

The different priorities of the member states of the EU are reflected in the varying levels of expenditure on general social protection (Table 8.4) and

Table 8.1 Total health expenditure (per head of population in pounds sterling)

EUR 15	1996
Belgium	1693
Denmark	1430
Germany	2222
Greece	748
Spain	1131
France	1978
Ireland	923
Italy	1520
Luxembourg	n.a.
Netherlands	1756
Austria	1681
Portugal	1077
Finland	1389
Sweden	1405
UK	1304

Table 8.2 Provision of physicians (per 100,000 of population)

EUR 15	1994
Belgium	365
Denmark	291
Germany	329
Greece	389
Spain	414
France	282
Ireland	200
Italy	547
Luxembourg	228
Netherlands	n.a.
Portugal	294
UK	164
Austria	339
Finland	270
Sweden	n.a.

Source: EUROSTAT – Yearbook 1997.

the levels of taxation and social contributions (Table 8.5) imposed upon their citizens in order to fund the chosen levels of social provision and protection. Unsurprisingly, there is a relatively high level of correlation (0.843) between levels of social protection, on the one hand, and levels of taxation and social contributions, on the other, as is also demonstrated by Figure 8.5.

Overall, it is the existence and persistence of significant variations in a wide range of collective provisions and collective impositions across the member states of the EU that indicates, slightly indirectly, that the citizens

Table 8.3 Percentage of the population aged 25 to 59 having completed at least upper secondary education

	Total 25–59	Total 25–29
EUR 15	58	68
Belgium	60	76
Denmark	79	84
Germany	80	84
Greece	48	70
Spain	34	55
France	62	74
Ireland	52	69
Italy	40	52
Luxembourg	47	51
Netherlands	65	74
Austria	73	81
Portugal	24	39
Finland	71	88
Sweden	76	88
UK	53	58

Figure 8.5 EU member states: social protection; taxes and social contributions (1994)

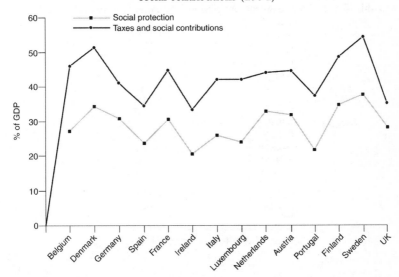

of the EU continue to be tied much more closely to their member states, and their structures and institutions of policy, than to the more remote EU and its policies and institutions on the kinds of 'bread-and-butter' issues that most attract their concern and most arouse their emotions.

Equally problematical, from the point of view of the development of any robust European citizenship, is the instrumental role of the established

Table 8.4 Total expenditure on social protection at current prices (as a % of GDP)

	1994
EUR 15	29.1
Belgium	27.0
Denmark	34.2
Germany	30.7
Greece	15.6
Spain	23.6
France	30.4
Ireland	20.4
Italy	25.8
Luxembourg	23.9
Netherlands	32.8
Austria	31.9
Portugal	21.7
Finland	34.8
Sweden	37.7
UK	28.1

Source: EUROSTAT – Yearbook 1997.

Table 8.5 Taxes and social contributions at current prices (% of GDP)

EUR 15	1994
Belgium	45.93
Denmark	51.32
Germany	41.17
Greece	n.a.
Spain	34.49
France	44.76
Ireland	33.52
Italy	42.24
Luxembourg	42.21
Netherlands	44.15
Austria	44.94
Portugal	37.42
Finland	48.66
Sweden	54.47
UK	35.26

Source: EUROSTAT – Yearbook 1997.

states in delivering many of those collective provisions that have been defined at the European level. Thus, national courts have to be used for the realization of 'European rights' in all but those relatively few cases of a reference to the European Court of Justice of appeals to the new European Ombudsman. Moreover, in the area of legal rights and referents, many human rights issues are defined by the non-EU institutions of the European

Convention on Human Rights and the European Court of Human Rights. Again, provisions under the Social Chapter and the more recent working hours directive will have to be implemented (or more probably not implemented) by state authorities.

The combined effects of the substantial corpus of state-level control of policy on a wide range of collective provisions and the practical implementation of many European-level collective previsions by state authorities are to diminish the apparent level of positive salience of the EU to the majority of its putative 'citizens' and weaken the strength of notions of an emergent multiple or dual citizenship (Monar, 1998). Worse, headline EU developments are far more likely to be such as to encourage the suspicion, if not the outright hostility, of the citizenry, as in the case of the 1999 crisis over maladministration within the Commission, or periodic rows over directives that appear to threaten the integrity of local products, practices or conventions, like the past rows over the acceptable constituents of chocolate bars or beers. The acquisition by the EU of formal powers against its member states, as with the power of the European Court of Justice to fine member states for non-compliance with EC regulations, directives or Court judgements, exemplifies the double-edged nature of many of the EC/EU's formal powers and institutions, as little is more likely to inflame 'national' opinion against the EU and its institutions than a fine imposed upon its government for an action that might have attracted widespread popular support locally.[3]

Against such a background, it is not surprising that the population of the EU continues to express apparently little relish for citizenship of the embryonic polity. The 1999 elections for the European Parliament fully exemplified this recalcitrance. The first, and most obvious, feature of the elections was the massive variation in turnout within the various members of the 'Union'. Allowing for differences of 'national' legal requirements and attitudes towards electoral responsibilities, the turnout still ranged from 90.2 per cent in Belgium down to 24 per cent in the UK (see Table 8.6 for the full range). Moreover, many of those who did bother to vote seemed to be motivated far more by local political considerations than European ones (*The Economist*, 19 June 1999, pp. 41–4), and where the European dimension figured it often did so negatively.

VI. CONCLUSIONS

The EU is one of the great constructivist enterprises of the post-World War Two era. The integrationist impulse has been sustained, time and again, by the determined efforts of committed policy-makers and political leaders. The progress of the EU is thus one of the outstanding practical experiments in

Table 8.6 Turn-out in the 1999 elections for the European Parliament
(% of electorate)

Country	% turnout
Belgium	90.2*
Luxembourg	85.8*
Italy	70.8
Greece	70.1*
Spain	64.3
Ireland	50.5
Denmark	50.4
Austria	49.0
France	47.0
Germany	45.2
Portugal	40.4
Sweden	38.3
Finland	30.1
Netherlands	29.9
UK	24.0

Note: *compulsory voting
Source: *The Economist*, 19 June 1999, pp. 42–3.

constructivist politics. The range of essays within the special issue of the *Journal of European Public Policy* (1999) on 'the social construction of Europe' attests to both the intentional efforts that have been devoted to such a constructional effort and to their many limitations. Nonetheless, such constructivist endeavours must overcome such hurdles as the clear majorities of the British, Swedes, Portuguese, Fins, Danes, Irish, Greeks, Austrians, Germans and even the Belgians who still identify themselves solely in terms of their established nationalities, and the tiny factions who see themselves as purely 'Europeans' (*The Economist*, 19 June 1999, pp. 41–4), and the considerable resistance to the formation of a single European government in the UK and Denmark (*The Economist*, 5 June 1999, p. 43).

Equally significant, however, will be the test of constructivist endeavours in terms of the locus of definition and provision of valued public goods and/ or those goods and services which might be enjoyed disproportionately by some portion of the population, but for the collective provision of which there is general support. Such provisions take citizenship beyond the mere formal and into the realms of instrumental citizenship. Without a rich, and widely appreciated, structure of instrumental citizenship at the level of the EU, it remains to be seen whether any significant levels of affective European citizenship will develop amongst the population of the EU and, thereby, give it the robustness necessary for any political institution that has to face, as it ultimately must, difficult choices and costly undertakings.

NOTES

1. Antje Wiener, however, argues that a decision was made to emphasize legal rights rather than feelings of belonging in the construction of 'European citizenship' (Wiener, 1998).
2. The argument that issues concerned with work should be considered as central to those of European citizenship is made forcefully by Harry Coenen and Peter Leisink (Coenen and Leisink, 1993).
3. As may well prove to be the case in judicial actions against the French, and possibly German, governments over continued refusal to authorize imports of British beef.

REFERENCES

Coenen, Harry and Leisink, Peter (1993) 'Work and Citizenship in the New Europe', in Harry Coenen and Peter Leisink (eds), *Work and Citizenship in the New Europe* (Aldershot: Edward Elgar Publishing), pp. 1–32.

Frohlich, N., Oppenheimer J. A. and Young, O. R. (1971) *Political Leadership and Collective Goods* (Princeton, NJ: Princeton University Press).

Gabel, M. J. (1998) *Interests and Integration: Market Liberalization, Public Opinion, and European Union* (Ann Arbor: University of Michigan Press).

Giddens, Anthony (1984) *The Constitution of Society: Outline of the Theory of Structuration* (Cambridge: Polity Press).

Hirst, P. and Thompson, G. (1996) *Globalization in Question* (Cambridge: Polity Press).

Hollis, M. and Smith, S. (1991) *Explaining and Understanding International Relations* (Oxford: Clarendon Press).

Jones, R. J. Barry (1995a), 'The United Nations and the International Political System', in D. Bourantonis and J. Wiener (eds), *The United Nations in the New World Order* (London: Macmillan), pp. 19–40, esp. pp. 22–4.

Jones, R. J. Barry (1995b) *Globalization and Interdependence in the International Political Economy* (London: Pinter).

Jones, R. J. Barry (1999) 'Globalization and Change in the International Political Economy', *International Affairs* 75: 2 (April 1999) pp. 357–67.

Jones, R. J. Barry (2000) *The World Turned Upside Down? Globalization and the Future of the State* (Manchester: Manchester University Press).

Journal of European Public Policy (1999) Special Issue on 'The Social Construction of Europe', 6: 4, edited by Thomas Christiansen, Knud Erik Jørgensen and Antje Wiener.

Keohane, R. O. (1988) 'International Institutions: Two Approaches', *International Studies Quarterly* 32, pp. 379–96.

Lippolis, Vincenzo (1998) 'European Citizenship: What it Is and What it Could Be', in M. La Torre, *European Citizenship* (The Hague: Kluwer Law International) pp. 317–25.

Marias, Epaminondas A. (1994) 'From Market Citizen to Union Citizen', in Epaminondas A. Marias, *European Citizenship* (Maastricht: European Institute of Public Administration) pp. 1–24.

Meehan, Elizabeth (1993) *Citizenship and the European Community* (London: Sage).

Monar, Jörg (1998) 'A Dual Citizenship in the Making: the Citizenship of the European Union and its Reform', in M. La Torre, *European Citizenship* (The Hague: Kluwer Law International) pp. 167–83.

O'Keefe, David and Bavasso, Antonio (1998) 'Fundamental Rights and the European Citizen', in M. La Torre (ed.), *European Citizenship* (The Hague: Kluwer Law International) pp. 251–65.

Olson, Mancur (1982) *The Logic of Collective Action: Public Goods and the Theory of Groups* (New Haven, CT: Yale University Press).

Royal Yachting Association, Information Leaflet (17 December 1992) 'Summary of EC Directive Dealing with Liability for VAT on Pleasure Boats Left Abroad in the EC'.

Ruggie, J. G. (1998) *Constructing the World Polity: Essays on International Institutionalization*, (London: Routledge).

Scotford Archer, Margaret (1988) *Culture and Agency: The Place of Culture in Social Theory* (Cambridge: Cambridge University Press).

Swan, Dennis (1983) *Competition and Industrial Policy in the European Community* (London: Methuen).

Welsh, Jennifer M. (1993) *A Peoples' Europe? European Citizenship and European Identity* (Florence: European University Institute, Working Paper ECS No. 93/2).

Wiener, Antje (1998) 'Promises and Resources – The Developing Practice of "European" Citizenship', in M. La Torre, *European Citizenship* (The Hague: Kluwer Law International) pp. 387–414.

Wouters, Jan (1994) 'European Citizenship and the Case-Law of the Court of Justice of the European Communities on the Free Movement of Persons', in Epaminondas A. Marias, *European Citizenship* (Maastricht: European Institute of Public Administration) pp. 25–61.

9

The International Protection of the EU Citizen: Problems and Prospects

STELIOS STAVRIDIS AND COLLEEN THOUEZ

I. INTRODUCTION

The question of the international protection of the EU (or European) citizen is a neglected area of study. There is very little, if any, academic work on the question, and most practitioners seem to consider the issue only when they are asked. In other words, the international protection of the EU citizen has not attracted the attention it deserves to date. Such a lack of interest in the international protection of EU citizens concerns both their protection in third countries (i.e. outside the EU) and their protection from attack by such countries. Article 20 of the post-Amsterdam Treaty on European Union provides for consular and diplomatic protection of EU citizens in third countries where their own state is not represented. However, the current situation offers only a limited system of international protection. As for the territorial integrity of the EU – when an attack on one of the member states is considered an attack upon all member states – there is still a long way to go before the EU develops an automatic defence clause, which would entail the full protection of the EU citizen by the EU itself at both the individual and the collective levels.

The concept of EU citizenship has quite a pedigree (see Warleigh, this volume) but it culminated in the Maastricht Treaty on European Union (TEU), which came into force in November 1993. The main reason for such a concept being important stems from the fact that the two main goals of the concept of EU citizenship have been, on the one hand, to bring the integration process[1] closer to the individual, and on the other, to try and contribute to the development of an EU identity. Both aspects also contain an element of democratization of the whole process of integration, which in turn is linked to the question of the role of public opinions (see Panebianco, 1996). The attempt, and remaining need, to democratize the integration process in Western Europe is clearly visible in the extension of powers for the European Parliament and the access for the newly created EU citizen to the main European institutions both directly (petitions to the European

Parliament) and indirectly (via the European Ombudsman; see Gregory and Giddings in this volume).

But when one looks at the now quite large, and still expanding, literature on 'European citizenship' (see Magnette, 1998), there is a lot that has been said about: the concept itself; the relevant Maastricht provisions; the various developments up to the Amsterdam Treaty of 1997 and its implementation in 1999; and, finally, on the current (at the time of writing) Intergovernmental Conference (IGC) which might (or might not) deal with the issue of fundamental rights (interviews, Brussels, March 2000). This literature is extremely useful and provides a background to the question under study in this chapter. However, one cannot help but think that the existing literature considers the international protection of the European citizen as a side-show. In our view, this is a pity because whether a European citizen is (or is not) properly protected in and from third countries by the EU will shape the development of a European identity. The latter question is far too vast to discuss here (see Garcia, 1993) but it is related to the topic under study in this chapter.

In addition to the 'citizenship' slant, there is at least one other way of approaching the topic of this chapter: the 'security studies' dimension. The existing international security literature is clearly split between a pre- and a post-Cold War perspective. Again, there is very little on the protection of the European citizen in/from third countries. The main emphasis is on the so-called Petersberg tasks (rescue and other humanitarian missions, peace-keeping and peace-making operations) which started under the Western European Union (WEU) in 1992 and have now been incorporated in the EU following the Amsterdam Treaty. Its provisions allow for 'humanitarian and rescue tasks, peace-keeping tasks and tasks of combat forces in crisis management, including peace-making' to be part of the Union's new prerogatives (Article 17, former Article J.7.2: Amsterdam Treaty, 1997).

Finally, there is a third dimension that we will not consider in this chapter: the international implications of cooperation in fighting drugs, crime and other areas which come under the third pillar of the Union (Justice and Home Affairs (JHA)) but where again most attention has been paid to the domestic EU dimension, whilst the crucial role of cooperation between the EU and the third countries involved has been largely ignored. This is not a criticism of the way developments in JHA have occurred. After all, it is necessary to have internal EU cohesion before exporting any policy. The most important implication of this exercise is that cooperation with third countries has been neglected, except in instances regarding applicant states and issues of illegal immigration, money laundering and so on (see Commission, 2000). This is an important point for the future as it means that the EU and its member states will have to develop their relations with third countries to make their internal policies on migration, asylum, visas, and fighting crime, drugs and other matters, more effective. However, these are considerations that fall beyond the scope of this chapter.

What follows consists of four sections. The first looks at the European citizenship concept, and how and why it has included an international dimension since its inception with the TEU. The next part considers in more detail the existing provisions for the international protection of the European citizen, which, for the time being, amount to diplomatic and consular protection. The next part examines the question under study in this chapter from the international security studies perspective. Then we deal with the vexed question of the borders of the EU in terms of the automatic defence clause issue. The conclusion is, rather ironically, that the EU citizen is currently afforded (at least in theory) more protection by the EU outside the EU than within its own territory, as there is no automatic defence clause[2] in the existing EU treaties.

II. THE PROVISIONS FOR THE INTERNATIONAL PROTECTION OF THE EUROPEAN CITIZEN: INITIAL PROBLEMS AND GENERAL CONFUSION

It is interesting to note that there was no opposition from any EU state, not even the UK, to the inclusion in the Treaty of the articles concerning diplomatic and consular protection of the European citizen in the world (Magnette, 1998: 49). In other words, within a highly politicized and ideological climate over the federal or otherwise future of the integration process, the question of how to protect the European citizen in the world did not attract too much attention. To a large extent, the uncontroversial nature of the question has helped to keep this issue out of the spotlight.

The provisions for the protection of the European citizen abroad first materialized in the TEU. Article 8c reads:

> Every citizen of the Union shall, in the territory of a third country in which the Member State of which he is a national is not represented, be entitled to protection by diplomatic or consular authorities of any Member State, on the same conditions as the nationals of that State. Before 31 December 1993, Member States shall establish the necessary rules among themselves and start the international negotiations required to secure this protection. (Maastricht, 1992)

The first important point that must be made is that this is what might best be termed a right 'by default'. In other words, it is the absence of national protection that entitles the citizen to the protection of another EU member state, and citizens are not entitled to consider their member state and its partners as equals in terms of their obligation to provide diplomatic protection. This is, nonetheless, an important new right because as the Second Commission Report on the Citizenship of the Union states: 'there are only five non-EU countries where all Member States are represented: the Russian Federation, Japan, the USA, China, and Switzerland ... there are seventeen countries where only two Member States are represented' (Commission, 1997: 11). Potentially, then, diplomatic protection is an EU citizenship right which is worth having.

The second point is that the international protection of the citizen does not fall squarely within one of the pillars of the EU. This means that sometimes it is considered as part of the first pillar, often as part of the third pillar, and occasionally as part of the second pillar. The distinction between the first and the third pillar has become somewhat blurred following the Amsterdam Treaty, which provides for most of the third pillar provisions to be integrated into the first pillar within five years of its entry into force (by May 2004), and also accounts for the integration of the Schengen Agreement into the EU (with the usual exceptions of the British, Irish and Danish opt-outs). The distinction between the European Community and the Common Foreign and Security Policy (CFSP), however, has been reinforced by Amsterdam.[3] This creates a problem of coordination. It also affects the future of European integration with regard to what type of Union will eventually be achieved: a supranational, federalistic structure, or an intergovernmental one, or, as it seems to be now, a combination of both (see Chryssochoou *et al.*, 1999). In practical terms, it means that great uncertainty surrounds which pillar is responsible for the international protection of the European citizen.

We experienced this lack of understanding and coherence at first hand when we conducted our interviews in Brussels. This was particularly true with members of the Commission who were unsure of whether such issues fell under JHA or RELEX (External Relations, an abbreviation from the French term).[4] This confusion is also noted in the first Commission Report on the Citizenship of the Union, which states that 'well before the Treaty of Maastricht came into force' work had begun in European Political Cooperation (EPC)[5] Working Group on Consular Affairs. A set of 'Guidelines for the Protection of Unrepresented EC Nationals by EC Missions in Third Countries' had been adopted in March 1993 by the Political Committee (Commission, 1993: 7). Once more we see that it is the intergovernmental cooperation of EPC which had been in charge of this aspect of citizenship. However, what is missed by the Report is that it refers to the protection given by the EC Missions in third countries, and not the embassies and consulates of other EU member states. This is an important distinction because the EC still does not possess an international legal status (see Wessel, 1997).

In the second European Commission report on European citizenship (Commission, 1997: 11), this distinction between the different pillars is reiterated with the reference to the (old number) Article J.6 of the CFSP (now Article 16). Indeed, the article states that:

> the diplomatic and consular missions of the Member States and the Commission delegations in third countries … shall step up cooperation by exchanging information, carrying out joint assessments and contributing to the implementation of the provisions referred to in Article 8c of the Treaty establishing the European Community. (Maastricht, 1992)

The question then became whether such protections could be granted by the European system itself or whether intergovernmental agreements governing the circumstances and forms of protection would prevail. Following the IGC in 1991, the European Commission and the European Parliament encouraged the establishment of a European umbrella for diplomatic and consular protections. However, as explained by Magnette (1999), a structure by which European protections would apply to EU nationals outside the Union would require a federal structure in which the EU itself would be vested with legal status and a diplomatic infrastructure. This is not the situation nowadays and there is little evidence of any move forward in that particular direction in the near future either (see Devuyst, 1998).

Instead, what was agreed upon were inter-state arrangements in which diplomatic and consular protections by one member state could extend to a national from another member state if that national's country was not able to offer such protections in the third country in question. This provision, based on the notion of 'equal treatment', is envisioned in the Vienna Convention on Diplomatic Relations (1961) and the Vienna Convention on Consular Relations (1963). The Vienna Convention on Consular Relations foresees instances in which one state will assume consular duties for nationals of a third state on the condition that the receiving state agrees. It states:

> Upon appropriate notification to the receiving State, a consular post of the sending State may, unless the receiving State objects, exercise consular functions in the receiving State on behalf of a third State. (Article 8)

Hence, there are provisions for a state's privileges and immunities extending to another state in cases, for instance, where that state would not have representation in the receiving state. The Convention goes further to state that: 'Two or more States may, with the consent of the receiving State, appoint the same person as a consular officer in that State' (Article 18). The Vienna Convention on Diplomatic Relations also states that: 'Two or more States may accredit the same person as head of mission to another State, unless objection is offered by the receiving State' (Article 6).

Article 8c of the TEU extends the same possibility for member states to protect Union nationals from a different state within a third country. The article stipulates, however, that such privileges extended by one member state to the national of another member state do not constitute a 'right' but a 'benefit' that a national may enjoy (Magnette, 1999). Extending diplomatic and consular protections constitutes a discretionary act both for nationals of the country in question and for Union nationals from different member states. An EU national, whether requesting some form of consular assistance or diplomatic protection from a member state other than his/her own, outside Union territory, may be eligible for such protections, but will not be granted them automatically nor definitively.

Thus, the notion of one state representing another and exercising protections for its nationals is not a novel one. Further, it would seem quite logical that such provisions would apply within the EU framework, where some form of a supranational structure is taking shape. However, both Conventions are silent about how these protections would be extended in functional terms. Moreover, as stipulated in the preamble of the Convention on Diplomatic Relations, such privileges and immunities are intended to 'ensure the efficient performance of the functions of diplomatic missions as representing States' and *not* 'to benefit individuals'.

Indeed, despite these documents – international conventions regarding diplomatic and consular protections, and more recent arrangements at the EU level in the TEU – the logistics have yet to be worked out. Member states, for instance, must still negotiate what exactly such protections would entail. In addition, the guidelines for such protections have not yet been formalized. Signatory states are left with the leeway to accept or reject the extension of consular protections. Furthermore, issues such as whether Union nationals will have the choice of which member state's protections they wish to solicit still have to be addressed. Thus, despite Article 16 (in Amsterdam numbering, the old J.6 in Maastricht) of the TEU that set a December 1993 deadline on the establishment of such mechanisms, such steps have yet to take place (Magnette, 1999).

Similarly, (at the time of writing) in the debate due to conclude by the end of 2000 on the Charter of Fundamental Rights, the right to protection in third countries is not currently included in the draft list of fundamental rights. If this right, which already exists in the Amsterdam Treaty, is disregarded, its exclusion from the Charter could be seen as a step backwards, even if it could be reinstated in the future. Its inclusion now is supported by certain Members of the European Parliament (MEPs).[6] The EP has pushed for the Charter to be included in the agenda for the IGC[7] and become legally binding through its incorporation in the Treaties. The absence of the issue of the right to protection in third countries from the present debate, however, also reflects the difficulties in treating diplomatic and consular protection as a legally enforceable right.

III. DIPLOMATIC AND CONSULAR PROTECTION: A DEGREE OF PROGRESS

A certain amount of headway has nonetheless been made with respect to diplomatic and consular protections afforded to EU citizens outside the Union. In the mid-1980s, the debate was initiated with talk of extending diplomatic protections to nationals of a member state outside the Union by another member state when the national in question did not have diplomatic immunity in the third country. It was hoped that the 'interchangeability' of EU nationalities, and the subsequent protections afforded to nationals by their respective member governments, would heighten the notion of a unified European identity for EU nationals and vis-à-vis third countries as well.

As for the nature of protections, some progress had been made by the end of 1993, thereby proving that the delayed entry into force of the Maastricht Treaty[8] had not had a negative effect on this aspect of European citizenship. In practical terms, it means that in cases of 'death, accident, violent attack, severe illness or arrest', unrepresented EU citizens can use the diplomatic and consular facilities of other EU member states according to the same provisions that apply for their own nationals. In addition, the first Commission report refers to an information campaign carried out by all the EU member states' foreign ministries, together with the Commission missions and delegations in the world.

The second Commission report also refers to legislative work having been done in late 1995: two Council decisions were adopted – one on the protection of citizens by diplomatic and consular representations, and the second on the implementing measures to be adopted by consular officials (Commission, 1997: 11). However, the report stressed that not all member states had implemented the necessary arrangements, and that a review of these provisions is scheduled 'after a five year implementation period'. Moreover, a new leaflet on 'Consular Protection for Citizens of the European Union' was produced in 1996 and distributed throughout embassies and delegations, as well as being included in the 'Citizens First' information initiative carried out by the European Commission. Finally, on 25 June 1996, the Council issued the rules for an 'Emergency Travel Document' (ETD). 'The ETD may be issued, for one return journey, to EU nationals who find themselves in distress whilst in a third country because, for example, their travel documents have been lost or stolen' (Commission, 1997: 11).

Based upon the above decisions recently adopted by member states, a few guidelines now determine the extent of the protections offered, the reimbursement mechanisms envisioned and the establishment of provisional '*titre de voyage*' available to all Union nationals. The nature of the protections is closely linked to the traditional duties of diplomatic and consular activities in a third country. Assistance provided ranges from help in the event of death, accident or serious disease; assistance in cases of arrest or detention, or after an aggression; and help with the repatriation of a citizen in difficulty. Pecuniary arrangements are also foreseen between the member state and the national, and between the national's member state and the member state that provided the assistance in the third country at the time that protections were sought. As Magnette (1999) suggests, the reimbursement of the member state that assumed the protections of a Union national of different nationality than its own highlights the intergovernmental nature of such arrangements. This distinguishes itself from a supranational structure in which the EU itself would be responsible for the charges incurred. What we see then is a system of inter-state assistance within the larger EU framework in which, notwithstanding its not having a superstructure or federal arrangement, the EU would assume the costs of an EU citizen.

IV. INTERNATIONAL SECURITY STUDIES

The question of the security of the European citizen in non-EU member countries (third countries) also falls within the study of the evolving institutional structure of European security. Though an expanding body of literature evaluates the various aspects surrounding the evolution of a CFSP for the EU, very little has been uncovered about the physical security of the *individual* outside the realm of Europe's security apparatus. Discussion over what countries constitute a part of Europe as defined in the post-Cold War era, and the subsequent obligations of these countries vis-à-vis each other, falls short of illuminating the protections afforded EU citizens outside the emergent regional security regime. In fact, as encapsulated by a European security scholar: 'the EU does not have any institutional policy regarding the protection of EU nationals outside the EU. This is the responsibility of the individual member-states.' He points to the example of French nationals residing in Algeria who are dependent on protections negotiated between France and Algeria, and not at the EU institutional level.[9] With so much attention focused on the nature of a

CFSP, and the new forms of threats to peace and security in the twenty-first century, are European citizens being overlooked in future security arrangements? Might the European be afforded greater protections by his/her national state rather than as an EU citizen in his/her own right? Will the European citizen be better protected within an intergovernmental framework rather than through a European system of protections? These questions are addressed in more detail below. What follows is a brief overview of the security literature.

A number of reasons point to why the contemporary literature on European security largely overlooks the issue of individual protection outside the EU. The stagnant evolution of a comprehensive security policy hampered by the incompatibility of member states' interests, and the divergence in their individual priorities (highlighted during the recent Balkan wars), monopolize the debate over the nature of the emergent regime. How then must we approach EU protections for citizens outside EU territory, when the geographical space itself is in constant amalgamation, and the common approach to the security challenges is in flux, at best, and inconsistent at worst?

Moreover, oversight concerning the individual level of analysis, as contended here, applies to other areas of EU intergovernmental and supranational cooperation. Most of the advances made with respect to a European migration regime, for example, focus on police and judicial cooperation and coordinating border controls – that is entry-based concerns for the 'masses'. Such advances, however, have faltered on integration, or citizenship, matters, which are often associated with the individual (here non-EU citizens) attempting to regularize his/her status within the EU. This is particularly true in early 2000 when the 'big push' is about whether or not to grant European citizenship to non-EU nationals provided they legally live on EU states' territory.[10] During a period of harmonization and consolidation at the EU institutional level, the international protection of the EU citizen is largely overlooked.

In part, the challenge of successfully defining the protection afforded citizens outside the EU is undermined by the subjects themselves. Indeed, the 'inside-and-outside' perception, by which 'different Europeans perceive themselves or are perceived by other Europeans' hampers a consolidated European identity (Park and Wyn Rees, 1998: 8). Without a common vision of 'Europeanhood', establishing a tangible outlet for protections extending to all EU citizens outside the Union may be difficult to achieve.

In addition to the confusion surrounding collective identity, the notion of security has also been transformed over the last decades. Brute force is often a weapon of last resort in diplomatic dealings, since its effectiveness and leveraging power have subsided (Keohane and Nye, 1992). Rather than traditional threats to security such as armed attack, contemporary challenges to security within the EU include drugs, migration and terrorism (Andreas, 1999). Predictably, the means of approaching these new security challenges are being devised through regional instruments that counter cross-border illegal activity. With the transformation in our perception of what constitutes a security threat, we might expect concurrent shifts in our attitude towards security safeguards outside the EU.

V. EU BORDERS AND THE INTERNATIONAL PROTECTION OF THE EUROPEAN CITIZEN: SAFER AT HOME OR ABROAD?

Clearly the provisions that exist for extending protections to the European citizen have yet to be formalized. To the outside world, then, the European citizen is still largely perceived and therefore treated as a national from his/ her own respective country. With the evolving notion of European citizenship, one could expect that parallel notions of rights and protections would develop. The provisions for representation by a third state in the Vienna Conventions (1961 and 1963) were intended, in part, to reconcile third parties' lack of diplomatic or consular representation in receiving states. The notion that third-party representation would apply for the EU and member states within it seems quite logical. These same issues are raised in the TEU. However, the logistical manoeuvering to establish formalized third-party representation has yet to take place. Moreover, such issues are still seen through the lenses of the representative state, and not through the lenses of protections for the individual. This is an important distinction as it reflects just how sparse are both the literature, and by extension, the degree of thought that has been developed on this subject.

The real issue here is the question of EU borders and an automatic defence clause à la Article 5 of NATO or the WEU (Western European Union). The automaticity of response in case of armed attack against one member of these organizations was not echoed in the Amsterdam Treaty. No member state of the EU must defend the territory of another EU state *qua* EU state, whatever other obligations the 15 may have. Although there is a difference between the two Articles 5 (NATO and WEU) due to the specificities of the American Constitution (the Congress, and not the President, authorizes war, so there cannot be an automatic response), in the real world of nuclear deterrence, any member state enjoys an automatic collective response in case of attack. However, this is not possible in the EU because of the refusal of pro-NATO countries (e.g. the UK, Portugal, the Netherlands) and of neutral states (Ireland, Sweden, Denmark, Finland, Austria) to develop a fully fledged European defence structure at the EU level (interviews with WEU Secretariat, Brussels, March

2000; see also Gribinski, 1996). Even the recent developments in the Helsinki European Council meeting of December 1999, with the eventual creation of a European rapid deployment force by 2003 and the current moves (at the time of writing) towards some securization of EU decision-making, do not amount to the kind of automatic defence clause that a full political union would entail. Although some progress on joint protection of the borders of the EU was made in Amsterdam (Tsatsos and Mendez de Vigo, 1997; Remacle, 1998), there is still a long way to go to replicate the commitments of the kind the automatic 'defence clause' presents in both NATO and the WEU.[11] The whole notion of collective security is being developed during the year 2000 when several of the WEU's competences are supposed to be transferred to the EU. The question of the possible transfer of Article 5 to the EU remains a moot point, all the same.[12]

There are two main consequences which follow from the recent developments which we have just described: the first concerns the continuing (or otherwise) applicability of the concept of 'civilian power' to the EU; the second, which is even more relevant to the discussion in this chapter, refers to the question of public support for a European defence capacity. Both aspects are analysed briefly in what follows.

The concept of 'civilian power' has been applied to the EC/EU since the early 1970s (Duchêne, 1973). Although it is not a consensus concept in the literature (see Bull, 1983), it has attracted much attention, both academic and journalistic (see Whitman, 1998; Zielonka, 1998),[13] especially since the end of the Cold War. Why such a debate is relevant to this chapter stems from the fact that the EU citizen might need a European military force to be protected both at home and in third countries, but the traditional 'civilian power Europe' approach favoured the use of non-military means to assert EU interests internationally. Many supporters of the European citizenship concept hope that the EU's ability to protect its own citizens will contribute to a new sense of European identity. However, the practical arrangements for a rapid deployment force and the institutional set-up of an autonomous EU defence structure might be more difficult to achieve. There is already an EU interim military and a political-military body in Brussels. However, the shadow of the Americans and NATO continues to loom over it. It is not a coincidence that the German Foreign Minister Joshka Fischer relaunched the overall integration debate regarding political union (May 2000) only after the commitment to an autonomous European military capability was made following a 'change of heart' in London. The Franco-British Saint-Malo Declaration in December 1998 led to the Cologne, Helsinki, and Feira European Council Conclusions, which have, to paraphrase Nicole Gnesotto, meant more progress in the field over the last two years than in the previous four decades. While these developments cannot be discussed at length here, we wish to highlight that these developments are taking place in a 'democratic vacuum' based on a 'disjunction' between the élites and public opinion.

This is because there is no European demos (public opinion)[14] in the fields of security and defence matters (see Everts and Sinnott, 1995; Sinnott, 1997; Zielonka, 1998; Stavridis, 2000). Member state nationals do not appear to agree on what the CFSP should comprise, even if certain surveys (e.g. Blondel, Sinott and Svensson 1998) appear to indicate popular support for a greater EU role in this policy area. This fact has important implications for the security dimension of the European citizenship concept. Of course, there are those (Seabra, 1998) who think that there is enough evidence of a common view in defence and security matters throughout the Union both at the élite and at the popular levels. But this view fails to encompass empirical evidence showing the opposite situation (see also Stavridis, 2000), especially in times of international crises. During such crises, diverging views may emerge, as was the case for instance during the Balkans conflict in the 1990s, and more specifically, during the 1999 Kosovo war. Moreover, such optimistic thinking incorrectly assumes that it is a general lack of knowledge and disinterest in defence matters which accounts for the divergence of views on these issues. In fact, often these differences about policy content reflect deep cleavages based on national policy agendas. Indeed, evidence of a fragmented demos is reflected in close analysis of Eurobarometer data from over the years, and the vast number of surveys and opinion polls on this subject. For instance, in 1994, a Eurobarometer poll showed that only 6 per cent in Greece favoured airstrikes against the Serbs whereas 57 per cent of French people did so (*Agence Europe*, 2 May 1994). Similarly, there were vast discrepancies between EU member states regarding the prospect of a common European army at the height of the NATO bombing of Kosovo (*Guardian*, 1 June 1999).[15] These kinds of differences mean that developing a common European defence policy is deeply problematic, and the protection of the EU citizen both in third countries and within the EU borders represents a more complex issue than is commonly assumed.

Thus, current attempts to achieve a consolidated approach to territorial defence and military interventions at the EU level may be premature, even if such an approach remains a desirable objective. For example, even in instances when the EU is consulted about defence matters, the member states continue to play the primary role in international protection, whether for their own nationals or for those of the other member states. In fact, in third countries where the EU citizens might theoretically be better protected by the EU than by any individual member state, in practice the national governments of the member states remain squarely in charge of emergency intervention. This can be demonstrated by two examples current at the time of writing: the ongoing crisis of hostage taking in the Philippines/Malaysia involving citizens from France, Germany and Austria (which remains unresolved at the time of writing), and the land redistribution/farm occupation crisis in Zimbabwe, in which the lead is being taken by the former colonial power, the UK, on behalf of all EU states.

However, we could draw initial conclusions that, if only in theory, the EU does more for its citizens' security abroad than within its own borders under existing arrangements for diplomatic and consular protection, which despite their shortcomings are, for the moment at least, more extensive than EU powers in justice and home affairs. Extra-EU and national arrangements still prevail in the fields of security and defence because of the absence of an equivalent to Article 5 of NATO/the WEU. Such a hypothesis is worthy of further study.

VI. CONCLUSIONS: 'PIECEMEAL ADVANCES' – JUDGING FUTURE RECOURSE

The limited advances made with respect to diplomatic and consular protections suggest that much like a number of cooperative spheres within European foreign and security policy, inter-state decision-making will prevail over supranational arrangements. Despite the assertions by some that the agreements reached will result in a more consolidated vision of European citizenship to the European as well as to the outsider, such predictions are debatable. In the first instance, the provisions mentioned above apply only in cases where the national is unable to request such protections from his/her own home country. Recourse to another member state is therefore due to the association between member states and not because of their 'inter-changeability', nor because of a concurrent European status that independently grants protections to its citizens. So, while the individual is accounted for in these provisions, the scope and conditions for protection are limited (as noted by several observers, see for instance Margue, 1996: 197). Furthermore, diplomatic and consular protections, such as those enumerated above, fail to consider the changing goals of European foreign and security policy generally. For example, they do not consider the implications of EU enlargement, and how such protections will have to extend to citizens of acceding states as well. And last, the changing threats to security must also take account of the new threats to the European outside EU territory. If we can speak of new threats to international peace and security, we must also see how these threats affect the individual.

As was noted above, there has been some progress on the issue of joint control of the territorial integrity of the EU in the Amsterdam Treaty, but there is still a very long way to go. The future of the integration process in Europe will decide this kind of question but it will be a lengthy and problematic affair. The protection of the EU citizen in the world or within the borders of the EU (as they stand now) remains a second- or third-order priority for the time being. The question of how to create an EU security structure when there is no evidence of the existence of a European-wide demos highlights the difficulties of trying to develop a sense of European citizenship from the security angle.

Finally, as stated from the outset of this chapter, this meditation on the international protections afforded the EU national outside EU territory should be regarded as a pilot study rather than the final word on this subject. Our preliminary conclusion that the European citizen is afforded better EU protection outside than within the EU deserves further investigation. Areas of research that would assist in developing this subject matter include the types of threats that European individuals may face in third countries; what recourse they may have (over and above that offered under the arrangements described above); the compatibility and logistics of inter-state efforts to provide security for Union nationals; the commitments of third states to endorse such provisions; and the prospects for future supranational protections for EU nationals outside the EU.

NOTES

1. We do not address here the concept and practice of European integration in any detail; see Chryssochoou *et al.*, 1999: 1–59.
2. See below under 'EU borders and the international protection of the EU citizen' for more details about defence clauses.
3. For details about the three pillars see Cloos, Reinesch, Vignes and Weyland (1993: 107–511, esp. pp. 107–34).
4. The Prodi Commission has been reorganized as a 'government-in-waiting'. The old numbering system of DGs (Directorate-Generals, i.e. Departments) has been abandoned. Since too many DGs worked on international affairs (DGI, DGIA and DGIB), they have now been merged into a new single DG RELEX (the French acronym for External Relations). DG RELEX is now in charge of diplomatic relations in third countries, a prerogative of DGIA in the recent past (taken from interviews in Brussels over many years).
5. EPC was the predecessor to the CFSP. For EPC see Nuttall (1992).
6. There is political debate over what issues should or should not be included in the IGC in addition to the decision-making rules that were not agreed at Amsterdam (number of Commissioners, qualified majority

figures in the Council, double or simple majority). At the time of writing, the Portuguese Presidency, which wanted an extensive interpretation of the agenda, has been thwarted by the next Presidency of France, which wants a more realistic outcome by December 2000 (Mr F. Seixas da Costa, Under-Secretary of State for European Affairs, Portuguese Government, Brussels talk, ULB, 27 March 2000).

7. See the EP Resolution on drawing up a Charter of Fundamental Rights of the European Union (A5-0064/2000).

8. This delay was mainly due to the Danes' initial rejection of Union membership in a referendum in June 1992.

9. Informal interview with Professor Ioannis Stivachtis, Schiller International University, Leysin Switzerland, 6 September 1999.

10. What the implications of such a move for the international protection of the EU citizen would be remains unclear.

11. The question of a defence clause at the EU level is also rather problematic since Article 5 of the WEU was amended *de facto* in 1995 when Greece joined the organization because of Turkey's membership in NATO.

12. Both Articles 5 refer to an automatic response by all other member states to an attack on a member state. However the WEU's Article 5 is 'more' automatic because NATO's counterpart is restricted by the US Constitutional requirement for the Congress to declare war. However, the 1973 War Powers Act has given the US President some leeway in deciding military action, and during the Cold War, the presence of nuclear weapons ensured that a rapid and overwhelming response was required (known as mutually assured destruction (MAD)).

13. For further details see Stavridis and Hutchence, 2000.

14. See Chryssochoou, 1998.

15. From a low 21% in Finland, 35% in Austria and the UK to a high 73% in France (the most Gaullist of all Gaullist countries).

REFERENCES

Andreas, P. (1999) *Old Walls, New Walls: The Shifting Function of Border Controls in the United States and Western Europe.* Paper presented at the American Political Science Association (APSA) Conference, Atlanta, GA, USA, 2–5 September.

Blondel, J., Sinott, R. and Svensson, P. (1998) *People and Parliament in the European Union – Participation, Democracy and Legitimacy* (Oxford: Clarendon Press).

Bull, H. (1983) 'Civilian Power Europe: A Contradiction in Terms?', in L. Tsoukalis (ed.), *The European Community – Past, Present and Future* (Oxford: Basil Blackwell), pp. 150–70.

Chryssochoou, D. (1998) *Democracy in the European Union* (London: Tauris).

Chryssochoou, D., Tsinisizelis, M., Stavridis, S. and Ifantis, K. (1999) *Theory and Reform in the European Union* (Manchester: Manchester University Press).

Cloos, J., Reinesch, G., Vignes, D., Weyland, J. (1993) *Le Traité de Maastricht: Génèse, Analyse, Commentaires* (Brussels: Emile Bruylant).

(European) Commission (1993) *Report from the Commission on the Citizenship of the Union*, 21 December, COM(93)702 final.

(European) Commission (1997) *Second Report from the Commission on Citizenship of the Union*, 27 May, COM(97)230 final.

(European) Commission (2000) Unpublished 'Tableau de Bord pour l'évaluation des progrès réalisés dans la création d'un espace de "liberté, sécurité et justice" dans l'union européenne' (communication de M. Vitorino), 16 March, COM (2000)167.

Devuyst, Youri (1998) 'Treaty Reform in the European Union: the Amsterdam Process', *Journal of European Public Policy* 5: 4, pp. 615–31.

Duchêne, F. (1973) 'Europe's Role in World Peace', in R. Mayne (ed.), *Europe Tomorrow* (London: RIIA), pp. 32–49.

Everts, P. and Sinott, R. (1995) 'Conclusions: European Publics and the Legitimacy of Internationalized Governance', in O. Niedermayer and R. Sinnott (eds), *Public Opinion and Internationalized Governance* (Oxford: OUP), pp. 431–57.

Garcia, S. (ed.) (1993) *European Identity and the Search for Legitimacy* (London: Pinter for RIIA).

Gribinski, J.-F. (1996) 'Autriche, Finlande, Suède: Trois Etats neutres dans l'Union Européenne', *Journal of European Integration* 19: 2–3, pp. 197–220.

Isnard, J. (2000) 'La sainte alliance de l'espionnage' (*Le Monde*, 30 March).

Keohane, R. and Nye, J. S. (1992) 'Complex Interdependence and the Role of Force', in R. Art and R. Jervis (eds), *International Politics: Enduring Concepts and Contemporary Issues* (3rd edition, New York: HarperCollins).

Magnette, P. (1998) 'European Citizenship from Maastricht to Amsterdam: the Narrow Path of Legitimation', *European Integration*, 21: 1, pp. 37–69.

Magnette, P. (1999) *La citoyenneté européenne: Droits, Politiques, Institutions* (Bruxelles: Editions de l'Universite de Bruxelles).

Margue, T.-L. (1996) 'L'Europe des citoyens: des droits économiques à la citoyenneté européenne', in A. Mattera (ed.), *La Conférence intergovernementale sur l'Union européenne: répondre aux défis du XXIè siècle* (Paris: Clement Juglar).

Nuttall, S. (1992) *European Political Cooperation* (Oxford: Clarendon Press).

Panebianco, S. (1996) *European Citizenship and European Identity: from the Treaty of Maastricht to Public Opinion Attitudes*. Jean Monnet Working Paper 03.96, December, University of Catania (as printed at 17 April 2000).

Park, W. and Wyn Rees, G. (eds) (1998) *Rethinking Security in Post-Cold War Europe* (New York: Addison Wesley).

Remacle, Eric (1998) 'La politique étrangère au-delà de la PESC', in Mario Telo and Paul Magnette (eds), *De Maastricht à Amsterdam – L'Europe et son nouveau traité* (Brussels: Edition Complexe), pp. 183–297.

Seabra, M.-J. (1998) 'L'opinion publique face aux développements de la PESC', in M.-F. Durand and A. Vasconcelos (eds), *La PESC – Ouvrir L'Europe au Monde*

(Paris: Presses de Sciences P.), pp. 175–92.

Sinott, R. (1997) *European Public Opinion and Security Policy* (Paris: WEU/ISS Chaillot Paper No. 28).

Stavridis, S. (2000) 'Confederal Consociation and Foreign Policy: The Case of the CFSP of the EU', *Journal of European Integration* 22: 4, pp. 1–28.

Stavridis, S. and Hutchence, J. (2000) 'Mediterranean Challenges to the EU's Foreign Policy', *European Foreign Affairs Review* 5: 1, pp. 35–62.

Tsatsos, D. and Mendez de Vigo, I. (1997) 'Egguytns twv synopwv [Garantor of the Borders]', *Kyriakatikn Elefterotypia* (Athens: 30 November), p. 98.

Wessel, R. (1997) 'The International Legal Status of the European Union', *European Foreign Affairs Review* 2, pp. 109–29.

Whitman, R. (1998), *From Civilian Power to Superpower? The International Identity of the European Union* (Basingstoke: Macmillan).

Zielonka, Jan (1998) *Explaining Euro-Paralysis – Why Europe is Unable to Act in International Politics* (Basingstoke: Macmillan).

10

Invisible Citizens? Long-term Resident Third-country Nationals in the EU and their Struggle for Recognition

THEODORA KOSTAKOPOULOU

I. INTRODUCTION

The establishment of Union citizenship by the Treaty on European Union (1 November 1993) has brought into question some central tenets of the theory and practice of citizenship. Citizenship has been propounded as a pillar of a non-statal form of governance which: a) does not have a demos conceived of as a complete, self-reproducing and non-contestable body; b) views boundaries as crossing points – not as barriers; and c) has to recognize that individual citizens have multiple and variable bonds with overlapping political communities.

At the same time, however, European developments challenge the resourcefulness of the concept of citizenship since the newly instituted formal bond between individuals and the supranational community is premised on the old concept of nationality, a clear and important paradox.[1] Whereas barriers to free movement and residence are increasingly removed for Union citizens, possession of member-state nationality remains a qualifying criterion for eligibility to the benefits afforded by Community rules in post-Amsterdam Europe. This has resulted in the relegation of long-term resident nationals of third countries to the periphery of the emerging European civil society,[2] despite the fact that these people are an integral part of the European community and contribute to the development and flourishing of European societies.

The non-citizen residents' demands for political inclusion and recognition have been viewed as a problem and/or a threat by the member states[3] whose very constitution relies on a 'trinity of unity', that is, a unitary territory, a unitary force and a unitary people (Diez, 1997). Citizenship remains firmly embedded in power structures and is entangled with narratives about historical communities with distinctive identities, institutions which have been handed down, founding myths, political traditions that are worth preserving and so on. In view of this, pluralizing the nation and officially accepting ethnic migrant communities as an integral part of a changing nation (Parekh, 1998) or transforming the nation-state into 'a democratic state of multiple minorities' (Connolly, 1996: 61) are not uncontroversial policy options. Similarly, national executives oppose the extension of Union citizenship to third country nationals (TCNs).

Scholars, practitioners and observers have criticized the exclusionary scope of Union citizenship (O'Keeffe, 1994; Kostakopoulou, 1996, 1998, 2001; La Torre, 1998; Staples, 1999). Scholars who subscribe to the logic of the cumulative development of European integration believe that the 'process of European integration will gradually lead to a replacement of the subjective standard of nationality by the objective standard of residence or domicile' (Nascibene, 1995: 11). Others disagree (Martiniello, 1995). Irrespective of such speculations about the future direction of citizenship policy in the EU, however, the crux of the matter is that long-term resident third-country nationals are no longer invisible (see the following section). Since the mid-1980s, both the European Commission and the European Parliament have taken issue with the inequitable status of third-country nationals, and the need to strengthen their legal position became a priority on the Commission's policy agenda in the post-Maastricht era (see the following section). But suggested proposals in this area fall short of recognizing long-term resident third-country nationals as respected and rightful participants with equal rights and opportunities in the workplace and society. Instead of embracing a participatory model of citizenship which would give third-country nationals a stake in the European polity, Community institutions offer them limited and qualified inclusion.

Admittedly, the transfer of immigration, asylum and matters pertaining to third-country nationals from the intergovernmental pillar of Justice and Home Affairs Co-operation to the Community pillar, coupled with the concomitant creeping full-blown supranationalism after the five-year transitional period following the entry into force of the Amsterdam Treaty (Article 67(1) and (2) EC) gives some room for optimism. But *Communitarization* has also opened the way for the installation of exclusive categories within the body of Community law (see below). Indeed, discouraged by the fact that neither extension of Union citizenship to third-country nationals nor possible harmonization of national citizenship laws for the purposes of free movement was on the agenda of the 1996 IGC, Peers (1998: 1271–2) has argued that the second-best option would be the creation of a system of denizenship. The latter would grant third-country nationals free movement and residence within the Union but would exclude them from political participation and diplomatic protection abroad. Although European denizenship is a fair policy option for new arrivals, it does not bring about equal membership for long-term resident third-country nationals. Because limited inclusion limits democracy itself, promoting democratic inclusiveness in the EU may well require the transcendence of the nationality model of citizenship underpinning European citizenship (Kostakopoulou, 1996; 2001). In this respect, the long-term resident third-country nationals' claims to inclusion and equality compel us to keep open discussions about alternative juridical options and the evolution of Union citizenship on the agenda.

In this chapter, I excavate the past in order to expose the complex institutional and ideological setting within which the national govern-ments' contingent decision to condition Union citizenship on state nationality is situated. By so doing, the self-evident character of the present personal scope of Union citizenship is put into question and alternative juridical options are retrieved.[4] After all, the past is not only what is bygone; it is also the repository of 'might have beens', the actualization of which has been interrupted. Secondly, I map the sources from which a normative sensibility and institutional innovation in this area might come in post-Amsterdam Europe. I argue that third-country nationals who are long-term residents in the EU are no longer 'invisible citizens', as the period in which this was the case (1968–1984) has been succeeded by one of awareness (1985–1993), and most recently a more thoroughgoing rights-based regime (1994–present). However, this advance requires qualification: third-country nationals remain subjects rather than actors in the post-Amsterdam Union, and the model of citizenship extended to them is not participatory but rather based on more limited approaches focusing on the concepts of vulnerability and intergovernmental restraint. Third-country nationals are still denied an 'ethics of participation' (Bellamy and Warleigh, 1998) by the EU.

II. WHOSE EUROPE? WHAT KIND OF CITIZENSHIP?

The weight of the past

The idea of a supranational citizenship implies the existence of a legal bond between a class of persons and a supranational entity from which rights and obligations may be derived. Following this definition, it can be argued that the Treaty of Rome established an embryonic form of European citizenship in so far as it stipulated that free movement rights can be enjoyed by classes of persons throughout the Community (Plender, 1976).[5] Whereas the constitutional significance of the free movement provisions of the Treaty has been highlighted by the literature, the manner in which national executives exploited the ambiguity of Article 48(1) EEC (Article 39(1) EC) and translated their ideological perceptions into Community law has received less attention.

Articles 48–51 EEC (39–42 EC on renumbering) refer simply to workers as the main beneficiaries of the free movement provisions without distinguishing as to whether workers should be residents in the territory of the member states, nationals of the member states irrespective of the place of their residence, both nationals and residents, or workers who are either nationals or residents (Hartley, 1976: 24–5). By enacting secondary legislation to give effect to the right to free movement, however, the Council confined the right to free movement to workers who are nationals of the member states (i.e. the early Regulations 15/61 and 38/64; Reg. 1612/68 and Dir. 360/70[6]). This discursive articulation 'fixed' the scope of economic rights in a way that had not been intended by the Treaty. This decision can hardly be explained on the basis of rational motives, for one would expect that decision-makers would have considered seriously the effects of the exclusion of an active part of Europe's labour force from free movement. After all, maintenance of visa requirements for non-national residents would impede the abolition of passport controls and thus the realization of the single market.

But such considerations were overshadowed by shared understandings and assumptions about immigration. In domestic political arenas, concerns about the 'problem' of immigration and the 'social repercussions of coloured migration' had already began to replace earlier discourses extolling the economic benefits of immigration and its contribution to postwar economic recovery and the expansion of European economies (Cohen, 1987; Collinson, 1993). In Britain, for example, the redefinition of immigration appeared quite early. The 1962 Commonwealth Immigrants Act had established a voucher system linking entry to a prior employment offer, and the 1968 Commonwealth Immigrants Act deprived East African Asians, who could not claim a close connection with the UK, of their right as British passport holders to enter the UK freely. The 1968 Act also introduced for the first time the concept of patriality: entry was confined only to those with an ancestral connection with the UK. According to Gilroy (1987: 45), this 'codified the cultural biology of race into statute law as part of a strategy for the exclusion of Black settlers'. Migrant workers who were nationals of third countries were not regarded as rightful beneficiaries of free movement.

The member states' decision to exclude them repressed other possible solutions and established an 'objectivity' which, as we will see below, will prove very difficult to undo; namely, that free movement applies to workers who are nationals of the member states. As the moment of the original contingency began to fade, the system of possible alternatives, including the conditioning of free movement on residence, became concealed. The member states' favoured interpretation became sedimented, that is, became routinized in ideas, practices and law, thereby rendering alternative options inconceivable.[7] The sedimentation was so complete that the original dimension of power through which that instituting act took place was far from visible. However, sedimentation and concealment of the alternative juridical and political options does not mean that they are cancelled out of existence. Under the right conditions, the contingent nature of the original decision can be recovered and the alternative juridical options can be reactivated.

In the period under examination, national governments not only managed to institutionalize exclusion at the heart of the European project, but they also determined unilaterally the scope of freedom of movement of workers via their definition of nationality.[8] Several categories of persons were excluded from the benefits of the Treaty on the basis of unilateral definitions of nationality, and the Community institutions accepted the states' exclusive competence in the sphere of determination of nationality, despite the fact that the scope and application of Community rules depends on that determination (O'Leary, 1992: 35). The declarations submitted by the UK on the definition of the term 'nationals' for Community law purposes are good cases in point. In the first declaration made at the time of the signature of the Treaty of Accession of 22 January 1972 the UK excluded from its definition of nationality for Community purposes UK citizens who were inhabitants of overseas dependencies or former dependencies (i.e. non-patrial Commonwealth and Colonial Citizens). This declaration has been criticized on ethical grounds, because non-patrial citizens of the UK from Gibraltar (predominantly white) were considered to be UK nationals for Community purposes whilst other non-patrial citizens of the UK and Colonies were excluded. Bohning (1973: 83–4) has also contended that it was incompatible with the Treaty of Rome and its derivative legislation to have one nationality definition for domestic purposes but to exclude from it certain sections of the population for EEC purposes. Similarly, the second declaration submitted by the UK following the enactment of the 1981 British Nationality Act excluded certain categories of persons who enjoyed the right to abode under domestic law from the benefits of the Treaty, while at the same time enabled Gibraltarians who did not possess the right of abode under UK law to benefit from the Community provisions on freedom of movement. By exercising hegemonic control over the scope and terms of membership in the emerging European community, the member states succeeded in grafting their notions about 'who the Europeans are' onto the emerging institutions.

This biased the process of the institutional formation of European citizenship by filtering out alternative postnational criteria of membership in the emerging Europolity. Neither the Paris Summit Conference (December 1974), which endorsed the idea of a civic European identity and propounded elections for the European Parliament on the basis of direct universal suffrage, nor the various initiatives concerning the grant of special rights to Community nationals, addressed the exclusion of third-country nationals (Bull. EC 12-1972, 1104). Instead, European policy-makers assumed that 'the persons entitled to the special rights were the nationals of the member states of the Community'.[9] The Adonnino Committee's reports on a 'People's Europe' reaffirmed this.[10]

The Commission was aware of the exclusion of third-country nationals from the privileges associated with free movement and equal treatment. In background reports it had stated that minority communities are today a permanent part of Western political life and it is, thus, essential that they be allowed the opportunity of free movement, enjoy equal treatment and freedom to participate fully in local elections and to assemble, publish and propagate political opinions within the confines of national law, without being subject to expulsion due to exercising these freedoms. Notwithstanding the radical tone of such pronouncements, however, the Commission's Guidelines for a *Community Migration Policy* (European Commission, 1985a) did not set out an ambitious programme for institutional reform which would welcome third-country nationals as equal participants in the political process. Instead, emphasis was put on improvements in working conditions and the standard of living for all workers in the Community, vocational training, the social and educational needs of second-generation migrants and migrant women, health education and housing standards.

In its efforts to extend Community competence in this area without challenging the member states' restrictive policies, the Commission proposed measures which treated ethnic migrants as vulnerable dependants: the most vulnerable section of the workforce, socially marginalized and the victims of increasing racism, xenophobia and violent intolerance (the vulnerability model). However protecting the vulnerable, in the sense of attending to their needs, providing educational opportunities, combating racism and promoting awareness in order to assure 'the harmonious co-existence of the indigenous and foreign population', falls short of affirming their claims for recognition and equality. After all, vulnerability essentially stems from powerlessness: it is a social construction and condition which is often used to justify (not to disturb) the immersion of migrants in power structures which set them apart from nationals or Community nationals. The vulnerability model thus reinforces the hierarchical distinction between members and non-members. It fails to recognize the migrants' claims to equal membership and protection. Nor does it encourage their active participation in multiple constituencies, along the lines of a neo-republican form of citizenship (Bellamy and Warleigh, 1998: 463). It is difficult to say whether the Commission adopted the vulnerability model because it lacked a daring vision about community-building in the EU or knew that more radical proposals at that stage could not possibly secure the Council's approval.

Interestingly, when the Commission (1985b) used its powers under the then Article 118 EEC to establish a prior communication and consultation procedure on migration policies in relation to third-country migrant workers, several member states filed complaints with the European Court of Justice (ECJ), arguing that the Commission had exceeded its competence and thus impinged on the member states' sovereign power in the field of immigration rules. The ECJ ruled that the Commission had exceeded its procedural powers to the extent that its consultation procedure aimed at securing conformity between national measures and Community policies and actions (*Germany and Others v Commission* (1987)). But on the question of whether migration policies fall within the social issues for which Article 118 EEC provided for cooperation among the member states, the ECJ decided positively on the grounds that the employment situation, and more generally the improvement of living and working conditions in the Community, is affected by the member states' policies towards third-country nationals. The ECJ also ruled that the Commission had exceeded its powers with respect to the part of its decision on the cultural integration of non-EC nationals.

A more coherent normative vision concerning the legal status of long-term resident third-country nationals began to emerge after the entry into force of the Single European Act (1 July 1987).[11] The European Parliament recommended that freedom of movement should apply to all resident workers irrespective of nationality, and that non-EC migrants should have the same rights of family unification as EC national workers.[12] It also suggested that non-EC migrants should enjoy protection from discrimination on the same footing as EC nationals, and that they should be granted local electoral rights.[13] The Commission maintained the view that the abolition of internal border controls applied to third-country nationals too, but this view was not shared by the Council. Indeed, driven by the prospect of the abolition of intra-Community border controls, the member states stepped up the process of informal intergovernmental cooperation in migration-related matters, and introduced a new regime of stringent outer controls and extensive internal immigration controls directed against members of ethnic migrant communities (the intergovernmental restraint model). This happened at a time when the completion of the Single Market required the Community to approach issues such as free movement, citizenship and immigration from a new angle.

Via a series of Resolutions the European Parliament sought to outline an alternative path and called for the extension of the right of residence to third-country nationals as well as for their gradual inclusion in the political process.[14] The Commission also suggested a Directive granting citizens of non-EC member states who have been legally resident for five years in the Community the same rights of free movement of persons and rights of establishment as Community citizens, in the context of its Programme Relating to the Implementation of the Community Charter of Fundamental Social Rights for Workers – Priorities for 1991/1992.[15] The European Economic and Social Committee (1991) too, stressed the need to give legally resident immigrants a stake in the 'People's Europe'. It proceeded to furnish the foundations for a 'Community statute for migrant workers from third countries' which would a) harmonize legislative provisions, regulations, instruments and measures for the social integration of migrants in the member states; and b) define the conditions for implementing freedom of movement for migrants from third countries under equal conditions to those of Community citizens'. In the Committee's opinion,

> failure to pursue these two aims would not only foster discrimination (with all the moral implications of a Community based on injustice, restricting the rights of some of those contributing to its development), and hinder the proper working of the single market, but would betray the very ideals underpinning it. The aim of a single Community employment market, alongside a single market in goods, services and capital, would effectively be abandoned: national labour markets would be kept separate due to the divergence in the treatment of third country workers. (1991: 3.4)

Ignoring these liberal recommendations and the renewed attention to the position of long-term resident third-country nationals, the member states continued to pursue their law enforcement approach to migration-related issues within the context of the TEU's intergovernmental pillar, 'Justice and Home-Affairs Co-operation'. Justice and Home Affairs Co-operation made measures concerning the rights of nationals of third countries a matter of common concern, but the intergovernmental method ensured the continuity of the previous migration regime.

The Treaty on European Union also established the institution of Union citizenship, but membership of the emerging European polity was confined to nationals of the member states.[16] The project of the construction of an artificial community beyond the nation-state which would transform aliens into associates in a collective venture became reducible to codes of nationality. The juridical option of making domicile a criterion of membership in the EU was filtered out by the past orthodoxy. As a result, third-country nationals continued to be subject to national administrative laws and to be deprived of equal standing and protection at the Community level. The only citizenship rights they enjoy on the same footing as Community nationals are the right to petition the European Parliament and to complain to the European Ombudsman. This differentiation is difficult to justify given that the principal determinant for citizenship capacity in the EU is whether a person has actually left his/her state of origin and entered the territory of another member state – and not the social fact of his/her attachment. True, it may be objected here that one does not become a citizen by simply inhabiting a place (Miller, 1994, 1998; Schnapper, 1997), but it is equally true that a community of citizens does not arise through people having feelings for one another. It arises, instead, through their being in mutual relations with one another, and through their engagement in reflexive forms of community cooperation (Kostako-poulou, 1996; Honneth, 1998).

A rare opportunity was missed for subjecting the member states' definition of 'who makes up the European people' to a normative test and for building an inclusive democratic polity which respects the Other and gives all its residents a stake in the success of the project of its 'postnational' democracy.[17] Instead of designing a pluralistic and heterogeneous political community which would then prompt national constituencies to redefine themselves in a pluralistic way, European citizenship made national citizenship more valuable.[18] The implications of this for the values underpinning the EU and its legitimacy were not considered.

Post-Maastricht (re)visions of exclusion

The intergovernmental and law enforcement approach to migration-related issues increased the vulnerability of third-country nationals vis-à-vis the EU. At the same time, however, it highlighted the contradiction between the Community's commitment to equality of treatment on the one hand and exclusion and inequality on the other. In its *Resolution on European Immigration Policy*, the European Parliament (1992) stressed the need for a fully fledged Community policy on immigration which would ensure that nationals of third countries are protected by Community law. But protection was conceived in terms of affirming a set of civil and social rights, such as the right to reunion, independent rights of residence for non-EC spouses of EC nationals on separation or divorce,[19] and extension of Directive 90/366 (replaced with Directive 93/96, OJ 1993 L 317/59) concerning the students' right of residence for non-EC nationals. Instead of recommending full citizenship, the European Parliament called for a form of denizenship, that is, the extension of freedom of movement, freedom of establishment and access to the labour market to third-country nationals, and for a policy of integration of second and third generations in the fields of education and training.

Strengthening the legal position of long-term resident third-country nationals became a priority on the Commission's policy agenda in the post-Maastricht era. In its Communication on a comprehensive migration policy, the Commission (1994) set out a policy framework based on three key priorities: reduction of the migratory pressure, control of migratory flows and strengthening of the integration of third-country nationals. According to the Commission, the status of third-country nationals would improve if they enjoyed rights of entry (the right to free circulation on presentation of a residence permit for short-stay periods) and residence (i.e. security of permanent residence status via the creation of a permanent residence entitlement; independent rights of residence for family members of third-country nationals after a qualifying period). As far as admission to another member state for the purpose of employment is concerned, the Commission stated that third-country nationals could enjoy certain rights concerning access to the labour market, but priority would be given to them if job vacancies could not be filled by workers who are Union citizens or third-country nationals legally resident in that member state.

These proposals fell short of recognizing long-term resident third-country nationals as respected and rightful participants with equal rights and opportunities in the workplace and society. The Commission's framework for a future European migration policy reflected the member states' view that integration can only succeed if external immigration is controlled and reduced. In addition, it perpetuated the socially constructed representations of migrants as a drain on the economy and a threat to the indigenous labour force. Basing a restrictive immigration policy on perceptions about immigration and its consequences tends to undercut the more liberal domestic aspects of it, which presuppose a positive view of cultural and ethnic diversity. But the tension between policies of immigration control, on the one hand, and the improvement of the position of third-country nationals and/or seeking to define membership in a multinational, multiethnic and multicultural Europe in more inclusionary terms, on the other, has been overlooked by European policy-makers.

Following the commencement of legal proceedings by the European Parliament under Article 175 EC (Article 232 EC on renumbering) for failing to present the necessary proposals for legislation as required by Article 7a EC (Article 14 EC) (*European Parliament v Commission* (1994)), the Commission adopted three proposals with a view to attaining the objective set out in Article 7a EC (Article 14 EC)[20] in July 1995. One of these concerned the right of third-country nationals who are lawfully in the territory of a member state to travel in the Community.[21] The rationale for this initiative was growing concern about the effective operation of an internal market without internal frontiers – not the need to provide equality of treatment in one of the fundamental areas of application of Community law. In any case, granting third-country nationals the right to intra-EU travel was not a novel idea: Article 21 of the 1990 Schengen Implementing Convention provided for a right to free circulation. Following this provision, the draft Directive conferred on third-country nationals who are lawfully resident in the territory of a member state the right to intra-EU travel for short stays not exceeding three months. Longer stays and access to employment or self-employment[22] were excluded from the scope of the Directive. The exercise of the right to intra-EU travel depended on the possession of a valid residence permit and travel document, and of sufficient means of subsistence both to cover the period of the intended stay or transit and his/her return to the member state of departure or a third state. Notably, the requirement of self-sufficiency is rather excessive given that economically non-active EU citizens are required to show that they have sufficient means of subsistence in order to exercise their right of residence, not their right to travel.[23] The Directive did not secure the member states' approval, but nevertheless provided an important resource for the insertion of Article 62(3) EC in the Amsterdam Treaty.

The Council's *Resolution on the Status of Third-country Nationals who Reside on a Long-term Basis in the Territory of the Member States* (European Council, 1996) furnished some non-binding principles which could guide the member states in devising policies for the integration of migrant communities in the host society. The resolution reveals the kind of integration policy national executives have in mind and their adherence to a narrow conception of community membership which does not embrace the principles of pluralism and equality. Integration is desirable because it 'contributes to greater security and stability, both in daily life and in work, and to social peace in the various Member States' (European Council, 1996: 2). The resolution provided that third-country nationals (refugees under the Geneva Convention are excluded) should be recognized as long-term residents if they have lawful and uninterrupted residence of ten years in the territory of the member state concerned, and apply for residence authorization. National authorities should grant, subject to public policy or public security considerations, either a residence authorization for at least ten years or an unlimited one. Notably, the ten-year residence requirement is quite restrictive, since most member states grant unlimited residence after a five-year-period (or less) of residence or of regular employment. In considering an application for residence authorization, national authorities can take into account 'the level and stability of the means of existence which the applicant demonstrates, in particular whether he has health insurance, and the conditions for exercising an occupation' (Title IV(2)). This gives national authorities discretion to refuse residence authorization to those with an interrupted employment record, without examining whether interruptions have been voluntary or involuntary. Member states may refuse to renew the residence authorization on the grounds of prolonged absence (which should be no less than six consecutive months), expulsion or fraudulent possession of the residence authorization. The provisions concerning cancellation or non-renewal of residence authorizations resemble the provisions entailed by Council Directive 64/221 *on the Co-ordination of Special Measures concerning the Movement and Residence of Foreign Nationals which are Justified on the Grounds of Public Policy, Public Security or Public Health.*[24] But no reference is made to procedural rights and safeguards, such as those afforded to Community nationals under Articles 6, 7, 8, and 9 of Directive 64/221.

The material scope of the resolution partly reflects Council Regulation 1612/68 on *Freedom of Movement of Workers* and the Council Directive 68/360 on *the Abolition of Restrictions on Movement and Residence within the Community for Workers of the Member States and their Families.* Unlike these instruments, however, the resolution conferred on third-country nationals limited rights: long-term residents would enjoy both unlimited travel in the territory of that member state and the same rights as nationals of the host state with regard to working conditions, trade union membership, housing, social security, emergency health care and compulsory schooling. It 'should also be possible' for them to receive contributory benefits. Long-term residents 'should be able to obtain authorisation to engage in gainful activities'; they do not have unfettered access to all occupations, bar those to exceptions under Community law. In addition, third-country nationals do not enjoy free movement rights and have no protection against discrimination as regards access to employment, enjoyment of the same social and tax advantages as national workers, and access to training in vocational schools and retraining centres. Their spouses do not have employment rights and their children are not guaranteed access to that state's general educational, apprenticeship and vocational training courses under the same conditions as its nationals. In sum, the integration resolution treats long-term resident third-country nationals as a subject class, that is, as objects of governmental policy. Hence, the model of integration underpinning it is one of qualified membership in the civil society and of hierarchization. This is ultimately sustained as an instrument of state sovereignty.

III. THE NEW TITLE IV EC: THE END OF AN ERA?

The *Communitarization* of matters pertaining to resident third-country nationals by the Amsterdam Treaty will yield measures which are legally binding on the member states. The new Immigration Title IV sets out a five-year transitional period from the entry of the Amsterdam Treaty into force, during which the Council will take decisions by unanimity and the Commission will share the right of initiative with the member states, before a possible decision at the end of that period to move to qualified majority voting and codecision with the European Parliament (Article 67 EC).

The Amsterdam Treaty ended the uncertainty as to whether the requirement of the abolition of border controls (Article 14 EC) applies to third-country nationals too. Article 62(1) EC imposes a clear obligation on the Council to adopt within a five-year period the necessary measures for the removal of 'any controls on persons be they citizens of the Union or nationals of third countries, when crossing internal borders'. This covers both long-term residents and newly admitted persons. Within the same period, the Council shall adopt measures setting out the conditions under which nationals of third countries shall have the right of intra-EU movement for short stays (Article 62(3) EC). It remains to be seen, however, whether long-term resident third-country nationals will be given the right to move and reside within the Community as freely as EC nationals and European Economic Area nationals for long stays.[25] Within a period of five years from the entry into force of the Treaty, the Council has to adopt measures concerning the conditions of entry and residence, and standards on procedures for the issue by member states of long-term visas and residence permits, including those for the family reunion (Article 63(3)(a)). Measures defining the rights and conditions under which long-term resident third-country nationals may reside in other member states will be adopted by the Council acting unanimously on a proposal from the Commission or on the initiative of a member state (Article 63(4) EC). Although the Treaty itself does not require the adoption of implementing measures within a specified time period, thereby precluding the possibility for the European Parliament to bring actions for failure to act before the ECJ, the European Council and European Commission (1998) intend to adopt implementing measures within the five-year transitional period.

The creation of a Community law competence (albeit not exclusive) in matters relating to third-country nationals is a welcome development (the Community previously had competence over the conditions of employment of legally resident third-country nationals (Article 137(3) EC)). For many, this Title signals the beginning of a more liberal and accountable migration policy which entails more favourable terms for long-term resident third-country nationals. But such claims should be handled with caution. The new system shares many of the intergovernmental features of the old system during the transitional period (unanimity, the Commission shares the right of initiative). National executives have also circumscribed the role of the ECJ by restricting requests for preliminary reference rulings to courts of the last instance (Article 68(1) EC). In addition, requests for reference by national courts of last instance are discretionary – not mandatory. Moreover, the ECJ has no jurisdiction to review operations relating to the maintenance of law and order and the safeguarding of internal security (Article 68(2) EC), but it will have jurisdiction to define what measures or decisions fall within the ambit of law and order and the safeguarding of national security. All this raises doubts as to whether the new arrangements will change the restrictive focus of the European migration policy and lead to the articulation of a principled migration policy which pushes forward the logic of membership-citizenship.

In the Tampere European Council (1999), the member states reiterated their intention to develop the Union as an area of freedom, security and justice. This implies the design of common policies on asylum and immigration and a common approach to ensure the integration of long-term resident TCNs. According to the Tampere Presidency Conclusions, 'a more vigorous approach should aim at granting them rights and obligations comparable to those of EU citizens. It should also enhance non-discrimination in economic, social and cultural life and develop measures against racism and xenophobia' (1999, p. 5). Approximation of the legal status of long-term resident TCNs to that of EC nationals would entail the grant of 'a set of uniform rights which are as near as possible to those enjoyed by EU citizens; e.g., the right to reside, receive education and work as an employee or self-employed person as well as the principle of non-discrimination vis-à-vis the citizens of the state of residence' (European Council, 1999: para. 21, at p. 5). Although the emergent rights-based approach to issues concerning long-term resident TCNs is a positive step, it falls short of granting them either denizenship (the right to free movement) or citizenship.

The Commission, for its part, has taken some important initiatives. In February 1999, the Commission (1999a and b) proposed two Directives *on Extending the Freedom to Provide Cross-border Services to Third Country Nationals established within the Community* under Article 59(2) EC (49 EC on renumbering) – an extension provided for by the EC Treaty since 1957 – and *on the Posting of Workers who are Third Country Nationals for the Provision of Cross-border Services* respectively. On the production of a document known as an 'EC service provision card' the service provider or posted worker will be able to enter freely and reside in a member state in order to provide services or engage in paid employment. The Commission (1998) has also proposed a Council Regulation amending Regulation 1408/71 (EEC), thereby extending Community coordination of social security schemes to employed and self-employed persons who are insured in a member state and who are not Community nationals.

The most comprehensive initiative in this area, however, was taken on 30 July 1997 when the Commission proposed a Decision on establishing a Convention regulating the first admission of third-country nationals to the member states of the Union for long stays (i.e. for periods exceeding three months) and improving the rights of long-term resident third-country nationals in the EU, under Articles K1(3)(a) and (b) and K3(2)(C) TEU. In the explanatory memorandum, the Commission stated that the integration of long-term resident third-country nationals is an imperative dictated by the democratic and humanitarian tradition of the member states and constitutes a fundamental aspect of immigration policy: 'the integration of immigrants is essential to safeguard equilibrium in our societies'. To achieve this, long-term resident status should be granted to those third-country nationals (including refugees under the Geneva Convention) who have lived legally in a member state for at least five years and hold a residence authorization which guarantees rights of residence for a total period of at least ten years from the first admission (Article 30). Recognition of long-term resident status shall be endorsed on the residence permit and long-term residents will have the right to free movement in the member state of residence and increased protection against expulsion. They will also be authorized to reside there for all purposes set out in Titles VI and VII and engage in all economic activities covered by the Convention. In addition, they enjoy the same treatment as Union citizens with regard to access to employment or self-employment, training, trade union rights, the right of association, access to housing and schooling (Article 32). They could apply for employment in another member state in response to a vacancy, and assuming that the post cannot be filled by EC nationals or legally resident third-country nationals who are part of the labour market of that member state and they obtain a work contract, they will be entitled to move there. The host state is obliged to admit them on production of a valid work contract or an enrolment certificate and to issue the necessary authorizations. After two years of residence there, third-country nationals will be recognized as long-term residents in that state and cease to be long-term residents of the previous state. Possible loss of resident status in the original state of residence where third-country nationals have family ties and property, however, will discourage their movement to another member state. This provision shows the big gap that exists between the rhetoric of equity and the real persistence of inequality and subjecthood. Resident migrants continue to be the 'property' of the original state of residence or the host member state. And by being offered conditioned and limited movement in the EU, they are denied full membership and equal participation in the European polity.

More favourable terms for third-country nationals were contained in Title VII of the Convention dealing with family reunification.[26] The provisions of the Title made no differentiation between long-term resident third-country nationals and first admissions: third-country nationals who are legally resident in a member state at least for a year and have a right of residence for at least one year on the date when their application for family reunion is submitted, have the right to family reunion (Article 23). Family members of Union citizens who have or have not exercised the right to free movement, will be entitled to be joined by their spouse, children and dependent relatives in the ascending and descending line of any nationality under Article 10 of Council Regulation 1612/68. This solves the problem of 'purely internal situations', that is, of the state of affairs where Community nationals who have not exercised their free movement rights cannot invoke the more favourable Community provisions on family reunion against their state of origin.[27] Notwithstanding the favourable terms, however, the draft convention's provisions on family reunion do not institutionalize equity between Union citizens and third-country nationals: the requirements for admission of family members entitled to be reunited are more restrictive and the category of family members refers to spouses and children below the age of majority (Article 24); spouses and children are to be excluded if it is (subjectively) assessed that the sole purpose of the marriage or adoption is entry to the state; and family members will not be permitted to engage in economic activities for the first six months of residence.

Drawing on the Convention's provisions and following the Council and the Commission's Action Plan (1998) and the Tampere Presidency Conclusions (1999), the Commission took the first initiative in the field of migration since the entry into force of the Treaty of Amsterdam by proposing a Directive on family reunification (1999c). In so doing, it confirmed Hailbronner's (1995: 199) observation that achieving consensus on certain common standards on family reunion seems to be easier than reaching agreement on other aspects of migration and asylum policy. The legal basis of the Directive is Article 63(3)(a) EC. Ireland and the UK do not participate in the adoption of the Directive and for Denmark the permanent exception applies. The proposed Directive does not differentiate among the categories of third-country nationals; it establishes a right to family reunification for third country-nationals – including refugees under the Geneva Convention of 1951, who reside lawfully in a member state and hold a residence permit for at least a year for the purposes of employment, self-employment, activity and study. It also covers Union citizens who have not exercised their right to free movement whose situation has hitherto been subject solely to national rules (Articles 1 and 3). The family members who are eligible for family reunification are the applicant's spouse or cohabitee (who may be of the same sex[28]), their children and the children of just one of the spouses or partners under her/his actual custody and responsibility, and relatives on the ascending line and children of full age who have no family support in the country of origin and are dependent on the applicant (Article 5). The right to family reunification is subject to public policy, domestic security and public health considerations, the availability of adequate accommodation, sickness insurance and resources. The member states may also set a qualifying period before the applicant exercises the right to family reunification. All family members will enjoy access to education, and spouses and children have access to employment, self-employed activity and to all forms of vocational training (Article 12). An autonomous right of residence is given to members of the nuclear family after four years' residence, but there is the possibility of an early application on separation, divorce or death. After one year's residence, if the applicant is in a particularly difficult situation, the member states are obliged to issue an autonomous residence permit. For other family members dependent on the applicant, the member states retain the possibility of granting autonomous status.

All this suggests that the time is ripe for the formulation and adoption of instruments addressing the position of long-term resident third-country nationals with a view to promoting integration. It has taken almost 30 years for European policy-makers to realize that the objective of creating a fairer, prosperous and principled community for citizens and residents alike requires settlement of the position of long-term resident third-country nationals.

IV. CONCLUSION

Long-term resident third-country nationals in the EU are no longer invisible. The period of invisibility (1968–1984) has been succeeded by a period of awareness (1985–1993) and, more recently, by a rights-based approach to matters concerning third-country nationals resident in the EU (1994–). Although these developments are a source of modest optimism, it is important to remember that the shift from subjecthood to actorhood has yet to be achieved. As the foregoing discussion has shown, settlement of the position of long-term resident third-country nationals in post-Amsterdam Europe is likely to be achieved though a combination of the vulnerability model and the intergovernmental restraint model, and not by embracing a participatory model of EU citizenship which affirms their claims to equal membership and participation.

True, a domicile-based paradigm of European citizenship would free the emerging European demos from the grip of state nationality and ensure the formal inclusion of long-term resident third-country nationals in the European political process. But the political will for such a model is absent at the moment. And although the discussion here has focused on the third-country nationals' struggle for formal inclusion in the personal scope of Union citizenship, it is important to bear in mind that maintaining inclusiveness in the practice of citizenship would require further-reaching reforms designed to tackle multifaceted exclusion and to promote the equal incorporation of minority constituencies in the European polity. Put in another way, it would require a politics of positive appreciation of diversity coupled with an ethics of participation: that is, with policies designed to promote full and active participation in political and socio-economic life (Bellamy and Warleigh, 1998).

In this respect, it is doubtful whether the adoption of a European Union Charter of Fundamental Rights, pursuant to the Conclusions of the Cologne and Tampere European Councils in June and October 1999 respectively, would remedy the civic inclusiveness deficit in both the scope and practice of European citizenship. Although the rationale behind this initiative is to strengthen the EU's social legitimacy by consolidating existing rights and 'making their overriding importance and relevance more visible to the Union's citizens' (Draft Charter, 1999), and although crucial issues such as the status of the Charter (i.e. whether it will be a legally binding instrument or declaratory), its enforceability and the jurisdiction of the Court are yet to be resolved, the Charter is bound to raise expectations and bring issues such as the relationship of the Union and its institutions to the ECHR (see the opinion of the Court 2/94 [1996] ECR I-1759) back on the agenda.

The Charter is expected to contain the fundamental rights and freedoms as well as basic procedural rights guaranteed by the European Convention on Human Rights; rights derived from the constitutional traditions of the member states; rights which are protected as general principles of Community law, rights that pertain only to the Union citizens under the Treaties; and economic and social rights contained in the European Social Charter and the Community Charter of the Fundamental Social Rights of Workers. The inclusion of socio-economic rights may prove contentious even though it is deemed that their inclusion will not enlarge the Community competence by the back door (Article 46 of the Charter). Another crucial issue is the extent to which the rights enunciated in the Charter will apply to non-EU citizens. The draft Charter recognizes the right

to asylum for nationals of third countries (Article 21), the right to vote and
stand as a candidate in EP elections for all residents (Article 25) and the
right of migrant workers to equal treatment in the member states (Article
40), but it also reaffirms the existing confinement of a core of civic and
political rights to Union nationals (*The Times*, 1 June 2000, p. 4). If this
position is endorsed by the Nice European Council, then the Charter will be
yet another missed opportunity for the fashioning of a democratic and
inclusive European public sphere and for promoting equal opportunities
and an anti-discrimination culture in the EU.

Arguably, the realization of the latter requires a further-reaching and a
greater commitment than enhancing the structural visibility of fundamental
rights. What is needed is a more holistic approach under which
considerations of issues concerning democratic participation, rights protection and the treatment of citizens, residents and others are subsumed under
an overall understanding and broader debate over the constitutional
identity of the EU: a debate which not only recognizes the linkage between
European identity, citizenship and immigration, but also provides a plausible
alternative vision to territorial populism, civic exclusiveness and bounded
allegiances. After all, the real test of the European integrative project is
neither the establishment of 'an area of freedom, security and justice', nor
the acceptance of the abstract legitimacy of political values. Rather, it is the
determination to build a democratic, inclusive and heterogeneous European
polity which gives these values explicit political as well as legal status. In
this respect, unless serious efforts are made to incorporate long-term
resident third-country nationals politically and give them a stake in the
polity, the project of European citizenship will remain unfinished.

NOTES

The discussion in this chapter states the law as of 1 June 2000.
1. According to Article 17(1) EC, 'Every person holding the nationality of
   a member state shall be a citizen of the Union. Citizenship of the Union
   shall complement and not replace national citizenship'. See also the
   Declaration *on Nationality of a Member State* which was annexed to the
   Final Act of the Treaty on European Union.
2. See Castles (1995); Castles and Miller (1998[1993]); Safran (1997).
3. The discussion focuses on the process of political incorporation of long-
   term non-citizen residents who do not derive rights from Community
   law. The chapter does not address the position of third-country
   nationals who enjoy Community law rights as family members of
   Union citizens, employees of undertakings providing services in another
   member state, or beneficiaries of the association and cooperation

agreements signed by the Community and third countries. For a discussion on the latter, see A. Willy 'Free Movement of Non-EC Nationals: A Review of the Case-Law of the Court of Justice', *European Journal of International Law* 3, pp. 53–64 (1992); A. Evans 'Third Country Nationals and the Treaty on European Union', *European Journal of International Law* 5, pp. 199–219 (1994); Peers (1996); and E. Guild (ed.), *The Legal Framework and Social Consequences of Free Movement of Persons in the European Union* (The Hague: Kluwer, 1999).

4. According to Pierre Schlag, exclusion and marginalization of certain perspectives, conceptions and ideas has always been part of the character of traditional legal discourse, despite the fact that the latter has always denied that such exclusion has ever taken place. Postmodern critiques of modern legal thought have set out to retrieve these dangerous 'supplements' of the Enlightenment tradition and show that these excluded elements are, in fact, an integral part of the law: see 'Le Hors De Texte, C'est Moi: The Politics of Form and the Domestication of Deconstruction', *Cardozo Law Review*, 11:5–6, pp. 1631–74 (1990).

5. See Bull. EC, 1:11 (1968), pp. 5–6.

6. See Regulation (EEC) 1612/68 of the Council of 15 October 1968 on *Freedom of Movement for Workers within the Community* (OJ 1968 L 257/ 2), as amended by Regulations 312/76 and 2434/92 (OJ 1992 L 245/ 1); Council Directive No. 68/360/EEC of 15 October 1968 on *the Abolition of Restrictions of Movement and Residence within the Community for Workers of the Member States and their Families* (OJ 1968 L 257/13; OJ Special Edition 1968–69 485). This legislation confined the personal scope of the free movement provisions to workers who are nationals of the member states.

7. The discussion here draws on literature on historical institutionalism; see Pierson (1996); P. Pierson (1997), 'Increasing Returns, Path Dependence and the Study of Politics', *Jean Monnet Chair Papers*, 44; P. Hall and R. Taylor, 'Political Science and the Three New Institutionalisms', *Political Studies*, 44:4, pp. 936–57 (1996). Compare also Armstrong and Bulmer (1998).

8. In *Michelletti*, the ECJ confirmed that determination of nationality falls within the exclusive competence of the member states, but it went on to add that this competence must be exercised with due regard to the requirements of Community law: Case C-369/90 *M. V. Michelletti and Others v Delegacion del Gobierno en Catanbria* [1992] ECR I-4329. D'Oliveira thought that the ECJ may be finally prepared to assert a degree of Community competence in this area: see his note on *Michelletti*, 30 *Common Market Law Review* (1993), pp. 623–37.

9. See the Commission's Report on *Granting of Special Rights* which was presented to the Council on 3 July 1975; Bull. EC, Suppl. 7, 26 (1975). The Report states that special rights include the right to vote, to stand for election and to become a public official at local, regional and national level – political rights which 'have been traditionally withheld from foreigners'. Although the implementation of special rights could be achieved by the relaxation of naturalization procedures, so that nationals of other member states would acquire the nationality of the host member state, preference was given to the option of creating an additional tier of rights to already existing rights in the host state, since this precluded the loss of the former nationality. Another important matter of concern was that simple exchange of nationality would end up giving prominence to the nationality principle.

10. This was set up by the Fontainebleau European Council meeting in 1984. For a detailed discussion of the 'developing practice of European citizenship', see Wiener (1998).

11. The Single European Act's preamblic references to democracy, fundamental rights, the Convention for the protection of Human rights and Fundamental Freedoms and the European Social Charter gave impetus to calls for inclusion. Notably, the preamble does not carry formal legal weight, but it serves as both an interpretational device and a constitutional ground for proposals for further institutional reforms.

12. EP Resolution on the *Joint Declaration Against Racism and Xenophobia and an Action Programme by the Council of Ministers* A2-261/88, OJ C 69/42, 1989, Art. 5 (1), (2); EP Resolution *on Freedom of Movement for Non-EEC Nationals*, A3 175/90, OJ C 175, 16.7.90.

13. EP Resolution on *the Rights of Migrant Women* OJ C 46/42, 17/1/1984; Resolution A2-133/87 *On discrimination against Immigrant Women and Female Workers in Legislation and Regulations in the Community* OJ C 305/70, 16.11. 87, Art. 48. Doc. A2-261/88, OJ No. C 69/42, Art. 9.

14. EP Resolution on *the Free Movement of Persons* A3 0199/91, 91/C 159/05, OJ C 159/12-15, 17.6.91; on *Union Citizenship* A3-0300/91, OJ C 183, 15.7.91; on *Immigration Policy* A3-0280/92 OJ C 337/94, 21.12. 92, Art. 30.

15. See A 3-175/90, OJ 260 15.10.90, 173. The Commission was hesitant in this domain. For an explication of the Commission's approach as well as the reasons behind this, see the Joint Answer to Written Question 673/89 by Mrs Winifred Ewing (ARC) and 732/89 (732/89) given by Mr Bangemann on behalf of the Commission, OJ No. C 97/12.

16. For a detailed discussion, see Closa (1994); O'Leary (1996); Shaw (1998).

17. Dahl (1989: 129) regards inclusiveness as a *sine qua non* element of a

democratic polity: 'experience has shown that any group of adults excluded from the demos – for example, women, artisans and labourers, the unpropertied, racial minorities – will be lethally weakened in defending its own interests'.

18. Connolly (1996: 57) asks: 'Is it possible to imagine a multicultural pluralism where the centre itself is more pluralised? To imagine, for instance, multicultural differences and interdependencies across several overlapping dimensions, where no single source of morality inspires everyone and yet where the possibility of significant democratic collaboration across multiple lines is very much alive?'

19. In its proposal for a European Parliament and Council Regulation amending Council Regulation No. 1612/68, the Commission has broadened the definition of spouse so as to include cohabitees which are recognized as spouses under the legislation of the host member state. Additionally, in the event of dissolution of marriage with a Community national, family members who are TCNs would not lose their right of residence in the host member state provided that they have lived there for three consecutive years; COM (1998) 394 final – 98/0229 (COD) OJ 1998, C 344/9.

20. Proposal for an EP and Council Directive *amending Directive 68/360/ EEC and Directive 73/148/EEC on the Abolition of Restrictions on Movement and Residence within the Community for Community Workers and for Professionals and Service Providers Respectively* COM(95) 0348-C4-0357/95-95/0202(COD); Proposal for a Council directive on *the Elimination of Controls on Persons Crossing Internal Frontiers* COM(95)0347-C4-0468/95-95/0201(CNS); and Proposal for a Council Directive on *the Right of Third Country Nationals to Travel in the Community* COM(95) 0346-C4-04420/95-95/0199(CNS), the amended proposal of which was adopted by the Commission on 17 March 1997 OJ C 139, 6.5.97; COM(97) 106.

21. In *Wijsenbeek*, the ECJ ruled that Article 14 EC (formerly 7a EC) does not create a directly effective right not to be subject to border checks which is enforceable before national courts; Judgement of the Court of 21 September 1999. The Court of Appeal has also ruled that Article 14 EC does not impose a clear and precise obligation on the member states and is contingent upon discretionary measures to be adopted by the institutions and dependent upon the agreement of the Member States; *R. v. Secretary of State for the Home Department, ex parte Donald Walter Flynn* [1997] 3 CMLR 888.

22. Compare, however, Article 49 EC, which stated that the Council could extend the provisions of the Chapter to nationals of a third country who provide services and who are established within the Community.

23. Council Directives 90/364 (OJ 1990 L 180/26), 90/365 (OJ 1990 L 180/30), 93/96 (OJ 1993 L 317/59).
24. In line with Articles 2, 3(1) of Directive 64/221, Title VI of the Resolution stated that the expulsion measure shall be based exclusively on the personal conduct of the individual concerned. This means that previous criminal convictions shall not in themselves constitute grounds for the taking of such measures, and that the applicant's criminal behaviour or activities must be sufficiently harmful in order to pose a genuine and sufficiently serious threat to the requirements of public policy affecting one of the fundamental interests of society (Case 30/77 *R v. Bouchereau* [1977] ECR 1999; C-350/96 *Clean Car* [1998] ECR I-2521). In any case, the requirement of personal conduct can never justify deportation as a general preventive measure (Case 67/74 *Bonsignore v. Oberstadtdirector der Stadt Koln* [1975] ECR 297).
25. According to the Action Plan of the Council and the Commission (1998: 8), developments on this front would have to take into account the impact of extending free movement on the social equilibrium and the labour market.
26. Earlier initiatives include the 1993 Resolution *on the Harmonisation of National Policies on Family Reunification*: SN 282/1/93 WGI 1497 REV 1; and the 1997 Resolution *on Measures to Combat Marriages of Convenience*; OJ C 382, 16/12/1997, p. 1.
27. See Cases 35/82 and 36/82 *Morson and Jhanjan v. The Netherlands* [1982] ECR 3723, [1983] 2 CMLR 221; Joined Cases C 64-65/96 *Uecker and Jacquet* [1997] 3 CMLR 963; Case C-370/90 *R v. Immigration Appeal Tribunal and Surinder Singh (ex parte Secretary for the Home Department)* [1992] ECR I-4265, [1992] 3 CMLR 358.
28. Concerns have been expressed about the right to family reunification of unmarried partners including same sex partners; European Council Meeting, Justice and Home Affairs, 22229th Meeting, Brussels, 2 December 1999, 13461/99 (Presse 386).

CASES

Bonsignore v. Oberstadtdirector der Stadt Koln (Case 67/74) [1975] ECR 297; [1980] 1 CMLR 472.
Clean Car (Case C-350/96) [1998] ECR I-2521.
European Parliament v. Commission (Case 445/93) [1994] OJ C1/24.
Germany and Others v. Commission (Joined Cases 281/85, 283-5/5, 287/85) [1987] ECR 3203.
M. V. Micheletti and Others v. Delegacion del Gobierno en Catanbria [1992] ECR I-4329.

Morson and Jhanjan v. The Netherlands (Cases 35 & 36/82) [1982] ECR 3723, [1983] 2 CMLR 221.

R v. Bouchereau (Case 30/77) [1977] ECR 1999; [1977] 2 CMLR 800.

R v. Immigration Appeal Tribunal and Surinder Singh (ex parte Secretary of State for the Home Department) (Case C-370/90) [1992] ECR I-4265; [1992] 3 CMLR 358.

R v. Secretary of State for the Home Department, ex parte Donald Walter Flynn [1997] 3 CMLR 888.

Uecker and Jacquet v. Land Nordrhein-Westfalen (Cases C-64 and 65/96) [1997] ECR I-317; [1997] 3 CMLR 963.

Wijsenbeek (Case C-378/97) [1999] Judgement of 21 September 1999.

REFERENCES

Armstrong, K. and Bulmer, S. (1997) *The Governance of the Single European Market* (Manchester: Manchester University Press).

Bellamy, R. and Warleigh, A. (1998) 'From an Ethics of Integration to an Ethics of Participation: Citizenship and the Future of the European Union', *Millennium* 27: 3, pp. 447–70.

Bohning, W. R. (1973) 'The Scope of the EEC System of Free Movement of Workers: A Rejoinder', *Common Market Law Review* 10, pp. 83–4.

Castles, S. (1995) 'How nation-states respond to immigration and ethnic diversity' (*New Community* 21: 3, pp. 293–308).

Castles, S. and Miller, M. (1998 [1993]) *The Age of Migration: International Population Movements in the Modern World* (Basingstoke and London: Macmillan).

Closa, C. (1994) 'Citizenship of the Union and Nationality of Member States', in O'Keeffe, D. and Twomey, P. (eds), *Legal Issues of the Maastricht Treaty* (London: Wiley).

Cohen, R. (1987) *The New Helots: Migrants in the International Division of Labour* (Farnborough: Avebury).

Collinson, S. (1993) *Beyond Borders: West European Migration Policy towards the 21st Century* (London: RIIA).

Connolly, W. (1996) 'Pluralism, Muticulturalism and the Nation-state: Rethinking the Connections', *Journal of Political Ideologies* 1: 1, pp. 53–73.

Dahl, R. (1989) *Democracy and its Critics* (New Haven: Yale University Press).

Diez, T. (1997) 'International Ethics and European Integration' (*Alternatives* 22: 3, pp. 287–312).

Draft Charter of Fundamental Rights of the EU (1999) http://db.consilium.eu.int/DF/intro.asp?lang=en

European Commission (1985a) *Guidelines for a Community Migration Policy* COM(85)48 final.

European Commission (1985b) *Decision 85/381*, OJ L 217/25.

European Commission (1994) *Communication on Immigration and Asylum Policy* COM(94) 23 final, 23.02.94.

European Commission (1997) *Proposal for a Decision on Establishing a Convention on Rules for the Admission of Third Country Nationals to the Member States of the European Union* COM (97) 387, 30 July 1997, Bull. EU 7/8, 111–12.

European Commission (1998) *Proposal for a Council Regulation amending Regulation 1408/71* OJ C 6, 10.1.98.

European Commission (1999a) *Proposal for a Council Directive Extending the Freedom to Provide Cross-border Services to Third-country Nationals established within the Community* COM (1999) 3 final – 1999/0013(CNS).

European Commission (1999b) *Proposal for a Directive of the European Parliament and of the Council on the Posting of Workers who are Third-country Nationals for the Provision of Cross-border Services* COM (1999) 3 final – 1999/0012 (COD).

European Commission (1999c) *Proposal for a Council Directive on the Right to Family Reunification* COM (1999) 638 final of 1.12.99.

European Council (1996) *Resolution on the Status of Third Country Nationals who Reside on a Long-term Basis in the Territory of the Member States* 96/C 80/01 OJ C 80, vol. 39.

European Council (1998) *Strategy Paper on Immigration and Asylum Policy* 9809/98, Brussels, 1 July 1998.

European Council (1999) *Presidency Conclusions Tampere 15 and 16 October 1999* SN 200/99, Brussels, 16 October 1999.

European Council and European Commission (1998) *Action Plan on How Best to Implement the Provisions of the Treaty of Amsterdam Establishing an Area of Freedom, Security and Justice*, 12/7/98 (http://ue.eu.int/jai/article.asp?lang=en&-id=39813844).

European Economic and Social Committee (1991) *Opinion on the Status of Migrant Workers from Third Countries* 91/C 159/05, OJ C 159/12, 17.6.91.

European Parliament (1992) *Resolution on European Immigration Policy* A3-0280/92 OJ 337/94 21.12.92.

Gilroy, P. (1987) *There Ain't No Black in the Union Jack: The Cultural Politics of the Race and the Nation* (London: Hutchinson).

Hailbronner, K. (1995) 'Third Country Nationals and EC Law', in A. Rosas and E. Anatola (eds), *A Citizens' Europe. In Search of New Order* (London: Sage).

Hartley, T. C. (1976) 'The International Scope of the Community Provisions concerning the Free Movement of Workers', in F. Jacobs (ed.), *European Law and the Individual* (Amsterdam: North Holland).

Honneth, A. (1994) *The Struggle for Recognition* (Oxford: Polity Press).

Honneth, A. (1998) 'Democracy as Reflexive Cooperation: John Dewey and the Theory of Democracy Today', *Political Theory* 26: 6, pp. 763–83.

Kostakopoulou, T. (1996) 'Towards a Theory of Constructive Citizenship in Europe', *Journal of Political Philosophy* 4: 4, pp. 337–58.

Kostakopoulou, T. (1998) 'European Citizenship and Immigration After Amsterdam: Silences, Openings, Paradoxes', *Journal of Ethnic and Migration Studies* 24: 4, pp. 639–56.

Kostakopoulou, T. (2001) *Citizenship, Identity and Immigration in the European Union: Between Past and Future* (Manchester: Manchester University Press).

La Torre, M. (ed.) (1998) *European Citizenship – An Institutional Challenge* (The Hague: Kluwer).

Martiniello, M. (1995) 'European Citizenship, European Identity and Migrants: Towards the Postnational State?', in R. Miles and D. Thränhardt (eds), *Migration and European Integration: The Politics of Inclusion and Exclusion in Europe* (London: Pinter) pp. 37–52.

Miller, D. (1994) 'The Nation-state: a Modest Defence', in C. Brown (ed.), *Political Restructuring in Europe* (London: Routledge).

Miller, D. (1998) 'The Left, the Nation-state, and European Citizenship', *Dissent*, pp. 47–51.

Nascibene, B. (ed.) (1995) *Nationality Laws in the European Union* (London: Butterworths).

O'Keeffe, D. (1994) 'Union Citizenship', in D. O'Keeffe and P. Twomey (eds), *Legal Issues of the Maastricht Treaty* (London: Wiley).

O'Leary, S. (1992) 'Nationality Law and Community Citizenship: A Tale of Two Uneasy Bedfellows', *Yearbook of European Law* 12, pp. 17–32.

O'Leary, S. (1996) *The Evolving Concept of Community Citizenship* (The Hague: Kluwer).

Parekh, B. (1998) 'Integrating Minorities in a Multicultural Society', in U. Preuss and F. Requezo (eds), *European Citizenship, Multiculturalism, and the State* (Baden-Baden: Nomos).

Peers, S. (1996) 'Towards Equality: Actual and Potential Rights of Third Country Nationals in the European Union', *Common Market Law Review* 33, pp. 7–50.

Peers, S. (1998) 'Building Fortress Europe: The Development of EU Migration Law', *Common Market Law Review* 35, pp. 1235–72.

Pierson, P. (1996) 'The Path to European Integration: A Historical Institutionalist Analysis', *Comparative Political Studies* 29: 2, pp. 123–63.

Plender, R. (1976) 'An Incipient Form of European Citizenship', in F. Jacobs (ed.), *European Law and the Individual* (Amsterdam: North Holland).

Safran, W. (1997) 'Citizenship and Nationality in Democratic Systems: Approaches to Defining and Acquiring Membership in the Political Community', *International Political Science Review* 18: 3, pp. 313–35.

Schnapper, D. (1997) 'The European Debate on Citizenship', *Daedalus* 126: 3, pp. 199–222.

Shaw, J. (1998) 'The Interpretation of European Union Citizenship', *Modern Law Review* 61: 3, pp. 293–317.

Staples, H. (1999) *The Legal Status of Third Country Nationals Resident in the European Union* (The Hague: Kluwer).

Tully, J. (1995) *Strange Multiplicity: Constitutionalism in an Age of Diversity* (Cambridge: Cambridge University Press).

Wiener, A. (1998) *Citizenship Practice: Building Institutions of a Non-state* (Oxford: Westview).

Young, I. M. (1990) *Justice and the Politics of Difference* (Princeton: Princeton University Press).

Appendix: Treaty Provisions on European Citizenship (Post-Treaty of Amsterdam)

Article 17 (ex Article 8)

1. Citizenship of the Union is hereby established. Every person holding the nationality of a Member State shall be a citizen of the Union. Citizenship of the Union shall complement and not replace national citizenship.

2. Citizens of the Union shall enjoy the rights conferred by this Treaty and shall be subject to the duties imposed thereby.

Article 18 (ex Article 8a)

1. Every citizen of the Union shall have the right to move and reside freely within the territory of the Member States, subject to the limitations and conditions laid down in this Treaty and by the measures adopted to give it effect.

2. The Council may adopt provisions with a view to facilitating the exercise of the rights referred to in paragraph 1; save as otherwise provided in this Treaty, the Council shall act in accordance with the procedure referred to in Article 251. The Council shall act unanimously throughout this procedure.

Article 19 (ex Article 8b)

1. Every citizen of the Union residing in a Member State of which he is not a national shall have the right to vote and to stand as a candidate at municipal elections in the Member State in which he resides, under the same conditions as nationals of that State. This right shall be exercised subject to detailed arrangements adopted by the Council, acting unanimously on a proposal from the Commission and after consulting the European Parliament, these arrangements may provide for derogations where warranted by problems specific to a Member State.

2. Without prejudice to Article 190(4) and to the provisions adopted for its implementation, every citizen of the Union residing in a Member State of which he is not a national shall have the right to vote and to stand as a candidate in elections to the European Parliament in the Member State in which he resides, under the same conditions as nationals of that State. This right shall be exercised subject to detailed arrangements adopted by the Council, acting unanimously on a proposal from the Commission and after consulting the European Parliament; these arrangements may provide for derogations where warranted by problems specific to a Member State.

Article 20 (ex Article 8c)

Every citizen of the Union shall, in the territory of a third country in which the Member State of which he is a national is not represented, be entitled to protection by the diplomatic or consular authorities of any Member State, on the same conditions as the nationals of that State. Member States shall establish the necessary rules among themselves and start the international negotiations required to secure this protection.

Article 21 (ex Article 8d)

Every citizen of the Union shall have the right to petition the European Parliament in accordance with Article 194. Every citizen of the Union may apply to the Ombudsman established in accordance with Article 195. Every citizen of the Union may write to any of the institutions or bodies referred to in this Article or in Article 7 in one of the languages mentioned in Article 314 and have an answer in the same language.

Article 22 (ex Article 8e)

The Commission shall report to the European Parliament, to the Council and to the Economic and Social Committee every three years on the application of the provisions of this Part. This report shall take account of the development of the Union.

On this basis, and without prejudice to the other provisions of this Treaty, the Council, acting unanimously on a proposal from the Commission and after consulting the European Parliament, may adopt provisions to strengthen or to add to the rights laid down in this Part, which it shall recommend to the Member States for adoption in accordance with their respective constitutional requirements.

Index